BREAKING BOUNDARIES:
POLITICS AND PLAY IN THE DRAMA
OF SHAKESPEARE
AND HIS CONTEMPORARIES

For Duane and Kit

Breaking Boundaries: politics and play in the drama of Shakespeare and his contemporaries

Molly Smith

Ashgate

Aldershot • Brookfield USA • Singapore • Sydney

Published by
Ashgate Publishing Limited
Gower House
Croft Road
Aldershot
Hants GU11 3HR
England

Ashgate Publishing Company
Old Post Road
Brookfield
Vermont 05036–9704
USA

British Library Cataloguing-in-Publication data.

Smith, Molly
Breaking boundaries: Politics and play in the drama of
Shakespeare and his contemporaries
1. Politics and literature – England – History   2. English
drama – Early modern and Elizabethan, 1500–1600 – History
and criticism
I. Title
822.3

Library of Congress Catalog Card Number
97–077874

ISBN 1 85928 395 0

Printed on acid-free paper

Phototypeset in Sabon by Intype London Ltd
and printed in Great Britain by Biddles Limited, Guildford

Contents

Acknowledgements

Work on this project began in late 1989 and my institutional debts are many: the American Council of Learned Societies for a summer grant, the Cornell University Humanities Centre for a summer fellowship, the NEH for a grant which enabled me to participate in a summer seminar at Berkeley, St Louis University for a series of Mellon stipends, the Institute for Humanities at the University of Edinburgh for a fellowship, the John Rylands library in Manchester for a research grant and the University of Aberdeen where during the last year I have been allowed to arrange my teaching schedule to maximize my research time.

My personal debts are even more numerous but I would like to mention in particular Stephen Greenblatt to whom I owe an immeasurable intellectual debt, Kiernan Ryan whose kindness and encouragement have been invaluable, the reader or readers at *Studies in English Literature* who read sections on *The Spanish Tragedy* and *Titus Andronicus*, the reader at *Papers on Language and Literature* who read the section on *The Woman's Prize*, and the reader at Ashgate Publishing whose suggestions improved my arguments considerably. I would also like to thank Graeme Roberts and George Watson for their encouragement during the last two years and my colleagues in the department of English at Aberdeen, especially Flora Alexander, Jeannette King and Maureen Wilkie, whose congeniality and camaraderie provided an atmosphere conducive to research and productivity. Words cannot express my gratitude to Duane Smith who read and commented on every version of my manuscript and whose friendship above all else remains beyond quantification.

I should also like to thank my in-house reader at Ashgate, Rachel Lynch, and my editor, Ellen Keeling, for the careful attention they paid to my work through its passage from manuscript to print. Any errors that remain result from my own failings.

I am grateful to the editors of *Studies in English Literature* for permission to reprint versions of my essays on *The Spanish Tragedy* and *Titus Andronicus* and to the editors of *Papers on Language and Literature* for permission to reprint a version of an essay on *The Woman's Prize*.

Acknowledgements

1

Breaking boundaries: politics and play on the Renaissance stage

Until recently Renaissance drama was seen as reaching its height in the era of Shakespeare's great tragedies and then falling off into increasing decadence until the wars of the mid-century forced the closing of the theatres in 1642. M. C. Bradbrook, for example, espoused this view and located the inauguration of this decadence in the plays of Beaumont and Fletcher. In their works she saw 'a taste for the more extraordinary sexual themes (rape, impotence, incest) combined with the blurring of the aesthetic difference between tragedy and comedy and the moral distinction between right and wrong' (Bradbrook 1935 p.243). To Bradbrook this blurring of boundaries between categories that should have remained discrete is naturally linked to moral decrepitude and lack of value. Bradbrook's location of decadence in Beaumont and Fletcher points to generic hierarchies that inform her criticism, for Fletcher developed and defined the tragicomic mode and, as Gordon McMullen and Jonathan Hope point out, remained highly influential in the development of this so-called 'mongrel' genre during the seventeenth century (McMullen and Hope 1992 p.2). McMullen and Hope's convincing call for a revaluation of this genre as energetic and innovative rather than decadent indicates a change of direction in recent attitudes towards Renaissance drama, but not all new work in the Renaissance can be regarded as dispelling the implicit hierarchies that informed earlier criticism such as Bradbrook's.

Influential new historicists such as Leonard Tennenhouse, for example, gesture towards radical revisionist criticism in their vocabulary and tone while reinvesting in earlier demarcations. Tennenhouse insists on a clearly drawn boundary between the drama prior to 1604 and that which followed: 'Around the year 1604, dramatists of all sorts suddenly felt it appropriate to torture and murder aristocratic female characters in a shocking and ritualistic manner. This assault was quite unlike anything seen on the Elizabethan stage – even at its most Senecan' (Tennenhouse 1989 p.77). He attributes this dramatic imperative – to stage violent assaults on female aristocratic bodies – to the refiguring of the body politic as male that followed James's arrival in England and the new monarch's explicit invocation of patriarchal ideals. Tennenhouse thus reinstates the boundaries formulated by Bradbrook, though he does so in a new vocabulary and with a greater emphasis on the political locus of texts. Explicit moral condemnation may be absent in this political reading of the Renaissance, but Tennenhouse's theory about increasing violence against females and the emergence of an entirely new conception of the body politic as male does not radically alter the picture presented by Bradbrook. A similar stance informs Lorraine Helms's study of androgyny which also sees a dramatic change of direction in the course that theatre took in the year 1603: 'When James succeeded to the throne in 1603, a new politics of androgyny emerged. The martial-spirited virgin prince ceded her authority to a misogynistic pacifist. . . . In the court of King James, androgyny became a male prerogative; the image of the Amazonian queen regnant soon dwindled into wife' (Helms 1989 pp.60–61). Even the tone of condemnation that informed Bradbrook's choice of the word 'decadent' manifests itself in Tennenhouse's focus on gendered violence and Helms's charge of misogyny. These influential recent studies of the Renaissance have perhaps been less radically revisionist than might first appear.

My work in the following pages offers a response to both Bradbrook and Tennenhouse, to earlier and recent attempts to erect stark boundaries between Elizabethan and early Stuart drama. Like Bradbrook I regard Renaissance drama as increasingly concerned with breaking boundaries; unlike her and like most new-historicist critics, I refrain from equating this experimenting in boundaries with moral decadence. Indeed some recent readings of the Renaissance have reversed the moral attitude of critics such as Bradbrook, suggesting that texts become especially important when they question and re-examine social and political norms rather than reiterate them.[1] Renaissance plays are most interesting when they threaten to dissolve social, generic and moral boundaries; the chapters that follow focus on dramatic experimentation with boundaries as marks of the intense innovation that characterizes this period. Unlike critics such as Tennenhouse, I insist that the beginnings of this intense experimentation emerge clearly in the work of Elizabethan dramatists, in the tragedies of Kyd and the early plays of Shakespeare. In other words, the relationship between Elizabethan and early Stuart drama remains a matter of degree rather than of radical and stark difference that manifests itself suddenly in 1604.

Among those who have influenced my attitudes towards Renaissance drama, four theorists/critics require particular mention, for they also express interest in the concept of boundaries and their violation, though their perceptions of this violation remain quite different: Mikhail Bakhtin, Stephen Greenblatt, Michel de Certeau and Gregory Bateson. Some of these writers also share an interest in tracing interrelationships among literary, social and cultural texts, an impulse which, however inadequately realized, also motivates the following study.

Bakhtin was among the first to insist that the most intense intellectual and political reconceptualizations of a society occur at the boundaries of cultural discourses rather than at the centres. His call for a rereading of cultural discourses along entirely different lines than had been typical of literary criticism may be especially appropriate to Renaissance contexts; he insists that

> literary scholarship should establish links with the history of culture. . . . we have
> ignored questions of the interconnection and interdependence of various areas of
> culture; we have frequently forgotten that the boundaries of these areas are not

absolute, that in various epochs they have been drawn in various ways; and we have not taken into account that the most intense and productive life of culture takes place on the boundaries of its individual areas and not in places where these areas have become enclosed in their own specificity.

(Bakhtin 1986 p.2)

The argument seems valid for the early modern age in general when demarcations among various cultural practices were particularly fragile and movement between cultural zones occurred frequently. Theatre, itself an activity located at the boundaries of society on the outskirts of the city amid whore houses, ale houses and bear-baiting arenas, as Steven Mullaney has so carefully documented, provides an especially fruitful avenue of research for students of Renaissance culture and society (Mullaney 1988). The importance of activity at the boundaries of cultural space is also emphasized by the Bakhtinian critic Yuri Lotman who suggests that

at the centre of the cultural space, sections of the semiosphere . . . become rigidly organized and self-regulating. But at the same time they lose dynamism and having once exhausted their reserve of indeterminacy they become flexible and incapable of further development. On the periphery – and the further one goes from the centre, the more noticeable this becomes – the relationship between semiotic practice and the norms imposed on it become ever more strained. . . . This is the area of semiotic dynamism. This is the field of tension where new languages come into being.

(Lotman 1990 p.134)

The theatrical space in early modern England may be regarded as just such a 'field of tension' where new languages came into being. The dynamic nature of these fields of tension and the consequent formation of new vocabularies provide the focus for this study.

Like Bakhtin, Greenblatt stresses the importance of movement among cultural activities and his own criticism of the Renaissance invariably seeks to expose the exotic, quixotic and marvellous as they emerge at the boundaries of social and cultural texts. He insists that traces of transference and appropriation are evident throughout the early modern period; 'the textual traces that have survived from the Renaissance,' he writes, 'are products of extended borrowings. They were made by moving certain things – principally ordinary language, but also metaphors, ceremonies, dances, emblems, items of clothing, well-worn stories, and so forth – from one culturally demarcated zone to another.' He argues that 'we need to understand not only the construction of these zones but also the process of movement across the shifting boundaries between them' (Greenblatt 1988 p.7). Greenblatt's term 'borrowing' to describe the movement between cultural activities suggests a benign and natural process evident in texts that have survived from the Renaissance. His interest in 'shifting boundaries' reiterates Bakhtin's conviction that areas of cultural activity rarely remain discrete and whole. In recognizing the constant reformulation of cultural activities as they borrowed from each other, Greenblatt seems to concur with Douglas Bruster's point about the location of Renaissance theatres; Bruster argues that while theatre may have developed on the boundaries of the city of London, we should not make the mistake of seeing theatrical activity as an outside factor separated from the city and its culture, for by their very existence theatres ultimately contributed to the expansion of the city and a reformulation of its boundaries (Greenblatt 1988 pp.9–10; Bruster 1992 pp.9–10). In Lotman's terms 'the notion of boundary is an ambivalent one' for 'it both separates and unifies' and cultural space inevitably produces constant shifts between centre and periphery (Lotman 1990 pp.136–137). Indeed the relationship between theatre and society in the Renaissance confirms this notion of boundaries and cultural space as inevitably subject to shifts and rearticulations.

Like Greenblatt, de Certeau in his arguments concerning the practice of daily living focuses on infinite borrowings among sociocultural practices, the 'tactics' of consumption and appropriation that 'lend a political dimension to the practice of everyday life' (de Certeau 1984 p.xvii). 'Everyday life,' he insists, 'invents itself by poaching in countless ways on the property of others' (de Certeau 1984 p.xii). The same might be said about the dramatic mode in particular in early modern England as it poached on other cultural practices to market and create itself. Like Greenblatt and Bakhtin, de Certeau regards cultural activity as a fluid process of constant formation and reformation; but his choice of a more decisive term, 'poaching', to describe this movement suggests a transgressive and intrusive rather than benign process of assimilation between zones. His term 'tactics' further suggests a conscious rather than natural process and he insists that such poaching invariably carries political implications. De Certeau's theory, which provides an useful gloss on the notion of boundaries, may be particularly relevant to Renaissance drama, a cultural form that established itself in the late sixteenth century as an alternative to other long-established cultural practices. Dramatists frequently engaged in active assimilation of other cultural practices as they marketed their products for popular consumption.

As Bakhtin, Greenblatt and de Certeau argue, the work of cultural history mandates scrutiny of breaking and shifting boundaries between sociocultural activities. Renaissance texts remain most interesting where they threaten to dissolve social and generic boundaries rather than when they reiterate the enclosed specificity of these areas. In many cases this collapse results from the manner in which playwrights poached on other equally popular cultural practices such as public punishments, carnival-like activities and devotional writing to market their products. Theatre's violation of boundaries thus results quite naturally from the cultural institutions on which it draws to market itself as a viable alternative to long-established sports and customs. The most interesting instances of such poaching occur where dramatists exploit the marketability of the spectacles central to these other popular activities and at the same time challenge the function of these activities as non-threatening reiterations of social, religious and political norms. As Julia Gasper argues, 'The theatre's active involvement in religious-political affairs was of course illegal, but it was also characteristic of the age. Censorship does not seem to have dampened the creativity of the Elizabethan dramatists' (Gasper 1990 p.10). Active involvement in social, religious and political affairs is especially intense in those works which insistently call attention to their violation of boundaries. In this sense the process I describe remains closest in conception to the movement described by de Certeau. My study insists that theatre's sense of rivalry and appropriation remains crucial to understanding the movement between cultural zones in the Renaissance and, like many of the cultural activities on which it draws, theatre increasingly provided an occasion for seriousness and play simultaneously.

Bateson's argument about the seriousness embedded within the structures of certain forms of play provides an useful addendum to the theories regarding cultural activities and zones outlined above. Bateson argues that in metacommunicative statements such as 'This is play', 'the subject of discourse is the relationship between speakers' and participants recognize the paradox generated by the statement which is 'a negative statement containing an implicit negative metastatement'. As he insists, 'Expanded, the statement . . . looks something like this: "These actions in which we now engage do not denote what those actions *for which they stand* would denote" ' (Bateson 1985 p.133). The idea holds also for specific forms of play such as theatre, a cultural form which calls attention to its artificiality. The communication 'This is play', in which participants recognize the metacommunicative implications of the statement, involves a complex set of rules and 'language bears to the objects which it denotes a relationship comparable to that which a map bears to territory' (Bateson 1985 p.134). But as Bateson insists, 'the discrimination between map and territory is always liable to break down' and we frequently encounter situations which involve a more complex form of play where the game is constructed 'not upon the premise "This is play" but rather around the question "Is this play?" ' (Bateson 1985 p.135). As I demonstrate, we encounter this complex form of play in many Renaissance plays which conclude by posing the question 'Is this play?' Dramatists who invoke this complex form of play also reveal a greater degree of engagement with the sociopolitical contexts of Renaissance England.

Of course engagement with sociopolitical contexts has dominated Renaissance literary criticism in the last decade; Stanley Stewart in a review of the year's work for *Studies in English Literature* in 1991 attributed this continuing interest in history to the persistent appeal of the new historicism: 'Among more than one hundred volumes of this year's studies in the Renaissance,' he noted, 'history was the big winner, not history in the old-fashioned sense of "historiography" as distinct from "literary criticism". That boundary, which has for some time become increasingly hard to defend, seemed to disappear completely, as representations by some recent "historicists" and even the term "history" itself came into question' (Stewart 1991 p.179). More recently James Shapiro, reviewing the year's work for 1996 in the same journal, points to the new historicism's continuing appeal though, as he points out, it is 'gradually becoming subsumed under the category of cultural criticism' (Shapiro 1996 pp.516–517).[2] The following study, which draws its impulse from new historicist revaluations of Renaissance culture, sees this methodology as particularly suited to the Renaissance, sharing as it does the cultural sensibility that informed Renaissance interest in history and historiography; it is a sensibility evident for example in a representative Renaissance history such as Hayward's *Annals of Queen Elizabeth* (1612).

Contemporary accounts of the development of historiography do not always acknowledge the complexity of this genre in pre-modern times. John Kronik, for example, introduces a *Publications of the Modern Language Association* volume on 'The Theory of Literary History' thus:

> Once upon a time, *history* was an innocent word in an innocent world. In that time, long ago, professors and people lived happily. They didn't know there was an old history and a new one. They had never heard of intrahistory or metahistory. They suffered no confusion between history and historicity. They went about their daily labors in the simple belief that history was facts, occurrences, story, unsuspecting that it was, instead, discourse and narrative. . . .
>
> Times have changed. History, whether national or literary, isn't what it used to be. Stripped of its luster, history, when not berated or ignored, is now the site of anxiety and wrangling. But we are, come to think of it, the richer for our loss of innocence, as the essays in this issue – and some recent definitions – prove.
>
> (Kronik 1992 p.9)

Even the simplest of Renaissance histories resists such reduction to 'facts, occurrences, story' and in their resistance to reduction Renaissance histories share an implicit theoretical affiliation with movements such as the new historicism and the new cultural history.[3] It may be no accident therefore that the last decade's renewed interest in history, at least in the field of literary studies, developed first among scholars of Renaissance literature.

That Renaissance histories resist reduction to 'facts and figures' becomes readily apparent in a text such as Hayward's *Annals*, written initially for Prince Henry whose untimely death led the author to rededicate his work before publication to the less enthusiastic Prince Charles. Hayward was not a newcomer to writing histories and his unfortunate experiences subsequent to writing a history of *Henry IV* in 1599 provide remarkable insight into his career as a historian under James and testify to the essentially precarious nature of history writing in the Renaissance. Hayward dedicated his history to the Earl of Essex in highly eulogistical terms that, in light of subsequent political events, including the attempt by some followers of Essex to stage a production of *Richard II* to incite audiences and Elizabeth's insistent analogy between herself and Richard, proved most unfortunate. Hayward's text, though it condemns the usurpation by the House of Lancaster and argues for succession by divine right, nevertheless provoked Elizabeth's anger against the author; the history even figured as evidence against Essex in the Star Chamber proceedings against him and Hayward was shortly after committed to prison.[4] He apparently escaped the more dire fate determined for him by the Queen through the intervention of Lord Bacon, who saw the author's transgressions with regard to plagiarism as considerably more serious than any attempt at political subversion (Bruce 1840 p.xiv). Nevertheless Hayward seems to have remained in prison until the ascension of James I who later made him (along with Camden) a historiographer for the Royal College at

Chelsea, in which position Hayward composed his *Annals*. The circumstances surrounding Hayward's imprisonment point to the controversial nature of history writing in the Renaissance.

Hayward's description of the process of historiography, especially with regard to the *Annals*, proves remarkably interesting in light of his disastrous experiences under Elizabeth. Prince Henry had decried the dearth of English histories narrating English achievements for posterity. Hayward's shrewd response to this may be regarded as commentary on the very art of historicizing: 'I answered, . . . that men may safely write of others in manner of a tale, but in manner of a history safely they could not: because . . . some aliue, finding themselues foule in those vices which they see . . . condemned in others, their guiltinesse maketh them apt to conceiue, that whatsoeuer the words are, the finger pointeth onely at them' (Bruce 1840 pp. xviii–xix). Hayward thus insists on the precarious nature of history writing, perhaps alluding to his unfortunate experiences under Elizabeth. However his remarks also highlight his awareness that history could become a process of contemporary social commentary under the guise of impartial narrative about the past. Indeed he admitted as much when, in response to Henry's query about whether he had written any English histories, he noted that 'I had wrote of certaine of our English Kings, by way of a briefe description of their liues: but for historie, I did principally bend and binde myselfe to the times wherein I shoulde liue; in which my owne obseruations might somewhat direct me' (Bruce 1840 p.xx), an implicit acknowledgement perhaps of the contemporaneity of his earlier history of Henry IV. *The Annals*, then, despite its choice of Elizabeth as subject may be regarded as a document as much about the Jacobean period as the Elizabethan. Hayward appears to have been acutely aware that 'history' constituted not an impartial account of the past but an individualized narrative revealing an author's observations about the present.[5] In this sense Renaissance historians such as Hayward illustrate an ideal set forth more recently by Peter Erickson for new historicists in particular and historicists in general:

> Historicism, when fully historicized, implies historical consciousness of our immediate context as well of the Renaissance; the latter does not reduce the former, but the two are inextricable. This means that the present cannot be treated as a nuisance or irrelevance . . . but must be accorded the same intellectual sophistication and emotional investment as our assertions about the past.
>
> (Erickson 1987 p.336)

Hayward's comments about the dangers of history writing also share an affinity with new historicist convictions that texts can simultaneously reflect and subvert ideologies, a dichotomy manifested critically in contemporary concerns with the issues of 'subversion' and 'containment'. In light of Hayward's awareness of history as a site for subversion and criticism, one might even argue that contrary to John Bruce's claim that the *Annals* presents a 'highly favourable picture of Queen Elizabeth, – whose memory Hayward had certainly no personal cause to revere, and dispraise of whom would not have been unacceptable in the court of her successor', the text remains cautious in its portraiture of the Queen, representing her as a politically shrewd and successful strategist.[6] Hayward's very choice of subject under a king acutely conscious of the previous monarch's popularity may be seen as remarkably similar to his earlier dangerous choice of Henry IV under Elizabeth. In this sense, Greenblatt's claim about the political dimensions of Renaissance drama applies equally to histories of the period, whether composed for the stage as Shakespeare's *Richard II* (1592) was or for royal consumption as Hayward's *Annals* was: 'Shakespeare's plays,' Greenblatt contends, 'are centrally, repeatedly concerned with the production and containment of subversion and disorder' (Greenblatt 1988 p.40).

Other aspects of Hayward's history also illustrate his concerns with issues that have become central in modern theorizings about history. Narrative accounts of momentous events such as the re-establishment of the Church of England and the war against the French intermix with anecdotes about topical catastrophes and happenings around London. In this intermingling of 'high' and 'low' narratives, Hayward's history anticipates modern attempts at writing history from below as well as from above. His account of preparations for war against France includes a description of the whipping of William Geffry, a heretic who claimed that a friend of his was Jesus Christ. Descriptions of the change in religion intermix with a seemingly casual anecdote about violent tempests in London when a number of churches were struck by lightning: 'The spire of Allhallow church . . . being then of stone, was smitten aboute ten foote beneath the topp, from which place a stone was strucke that slew a dogg and overthrew a man with whom the dogg played' (Bruce 1840 p.29). An account of monetary devaluations concludes with the description of a local disaster: 'In the monthe of Julie, certeyne gunpowder was fired in Crooked Lane by crooked and carelesse dischargeinge of a piece, with the violence wherof, fower howses were torne and cast up, and diverse other sore shaken; nine persons were slayne outright, and manie more greivouslie hurt' (Hayward 1840 p.74). In its close attention to daily events and reactions of the populace to these events, the *Annals* thus combines the 'high' history of Elizabeth's ascension to the throne with the 'low' history of Elizabethan London and its environs.

Hayward's simultaneous tendency to assert and subvert existing systems, his interest in 'high' and 'low' culture, his acknowledgement of historicizing as artistic recreation rather than an unproblematic enumeration of facts and figures and his stylistic indulgence in personalized narrative that is clearly fictitious even while it mimics the tone of a documentary, make the *Annals* a typical example of history writing in the Renaissance.[7] Renaissance dramatic histories such as Shakespeare's *Richard II* and *Henry VIII* (1613) and Jonson's *Sejanus* (1603) also propound a similar vision of history, radically different from Kronik's edenic world of simple facts and figures.

Henry VIII, written in the same period as Hayward's history, illustrates a precarious balance between writing about the past and the present; excessive praise of the infant Elizabeth which concludes the play is rendered inoffensive to the current monarch James, known for his jealousy regarding her reign, by equally exuberant praise of James himself. As Kim Noling argues, the play may even be read as an authorization of patriarchy at the expense of Elizabeth's virginity:

> the image of asexual procreation found in the 'maiden phoenix' should have appealed . . . to the dynastic patriarch to whom the compliment of the prophecy is paid. . . . In loading upon the animate stage-representation of the princess not only Queen Elizabeth's but also King James's glory, Shakespeare momentarily turns female absence into male presence. This is the play's final subversion of queens into no more than the means by which kings are produced.'
>
> (Noling 1988 pp.305–306)

Both princes, Elizabeth and James, are also hailed as preservers of religion in the manner of Henry VIII himself; however, such praise appears undercut by the play's insistence on the purely selfish motives that governed Henry's shift from Catholicism to Anglicanism. Hayward likewise presents Elizabeth's choice of religion as a result of practicality and necessity:

> So it was a marveilous motive for Queen Mary to embrace and advance the authority of the Bishop of Rome, for that the validity of King Henryes marryage with Queene Katherine her mother, was thereupon grounded: . . . But on the other side, because yf the Bishop of Rome had power to dispense in the first marryage of King Henry the eyght, then was the subsequent marryage with Anne Boleyn voyde; besides the command of conscience, it was also an inducement in reasone for Queene Elizabeth to reject his authority.
>
> (Hayward 1840 p.5)

Hayward's *Annals* and Shakespeare's last play maintain a precarious balance between praise of the ruling monarch and his forbears and covert commentary on the arbitrary nature of seemingly momentous policy changes in religion and social practices.

A similar tension characterizes Jonson's Roman tragedy which even presents an interesting counterpart to Hayward's *Annals*. *Sejanus* was written during Jonson's retirement from the theatre after his legal troubles over satiric portrayals in *Poetaster*. Quite naturally the first fruit of his retirement obsesses over the issue of what constitutes treason. The most interesting figure caught in the debate over this issue is the court poet Cordus, who may be an analogue for Jonson himself; after all, Jonson seems to have envisioned himself as poet laureate in the 'Apologetical Dialogue' that concludes *Poetaster*: 'I, that spend half my nights, and all my days, / Here in a cell, to get a dark, pale face, / To come forth worth the ivy, or the bays, / And in this age can hope no other grace' (Jonson 1979 pp.223–26). Cordus may also have been modelled on Hayward, for his experiences parallel Hayward's after his history of Henry IV was published.[8] Cordus is introduced to us by Latiaris as an eminent poet, 'one that has writ / Annals of late, they say, and very well' (I, i, ll.75–76). The discussion that follows emphasizes the dangers of writing history, especially a history of Caesar and Brutus; Natta points out that 'Those times are somewhat queasy to be touched' (I, i, l.83). The play that follows demonstrates the validity of Natta's caution, for Cordus is seen by Sejanus as a threat to Tiberius. Sejanus in fact presents Cordus as a traitor conveniently masquerading as historian:

> Then, there is one Cremutius
> Cordus, a writing fellow, they have got
> To gather notes of the precedent times,
> And make them into annals; a most tart
> And bitter spirit (I hear) who, under colour
> Of praising those, doth tax the present state,
> Censures the men, the actions, leaves no trick,
> No practice unexamined, parallels
> The times, the governments, a professed champion,
> For the old liberty –

(II, ii, ll.303–312)

The unfortunate Cordus is soon summoned by Tiberius for treason and, like Hayward under Elizabeth, sent off to languish in prison while Tiberius decides his fate. His trial presents an interesting parallel to Hayward's experiences under Elizabeth and Jonson's own narrow escape from a similar fate over his writings. Accused by Satrius of praising the past in order to condemn the present, Cordus's meagre defense consists of the recitation of a long tradition of praise for Brutus and Cassius, from Titus Livius to Catullus, to which he subscribes. He concludes with a charged speech that both emphasizes the innocence of his writings and reiterates the superiority of poetry and tradition over Princes' whims:

> But, in my work,
> What could be aimed more free, or farther off
> From the time's scandal, than to write of those,
> Whom death from grace, or hatred had exempted?
> Did I, with Brutus, and with Cassius,
> Armed, and possessed of the Philippi fields,
> Incense the people in the civil cause,
> With dangerous speeches? or do they, being slain
> Seventy years since, as by their images
> (Which not the conqueror hath defaced) appears,
> Retain that guilty memory with writers?
> Nor shall there want, though I condemned am,
> That will not only Cassius well approve,
> And of great Brutus' honour mindful be,
> But that will, also, mention make of me.

(III, i, ll.445–460)

Unconvinced by this invocation of tradition, Tiberius orders that Cordus's books be gathered and burnt by the hangman. The play's final view seems to sanction the poet's claim about the power of tradition and poetry over the petty whims of monarchs. Arruntius condemns the court's decision as small-minded and worthless: 'Let 'em be burnt! O, how ridiculous / Appears the Senate's brainless diligence, / Who think they can, with present power, extinguish / The memory of all succeeding times!' (III, i, ll.471–474), and Sabinus points out that Tiberius might even have contributed to Cordus's subsequent popularity by his adverse sentence: "Tis true, when (contrary) the punishment / Of wit, doth make th' authority increase. / Nor do they aught, that use this cruelty / Of interdiction, and this rage of burning; / But purchase to themselves rebuke, and shame, / And to the writers an eternal name' (III, i, ll.475–480). This optimistic view needs to be supplemented by our historical awareness that most of Cordus's books were burnt and only a few fragments saved by his daughter survived.

In their expression of history as complex and subject to varied interpretations, writers such as Hayward and Jonson articulate a vision not unlike that expressed by recent historians such as Hayden White who emphasize the narrativist nature and creative function of all history writing (H. White 1978). Writing in the wake of White's revaluations of history, Lloyd S. Kramer recently defined the new cultural history thus: 'the one truly distinguishing feature of the new cultural approach to history is the pervasive influence of recent literary criticism, which has taught historians to recognize the active role of language, texts, and narrative structures in the creation and description of historical reality' (Kramer 1989 pp.97–98). Hayward makes a similar point when he warns about the dangers of speech, though his comment on the malleability of words extends equally to written discourses such as the *Annals* 'in disputatione by words, besides confusiones, besides digressiones, which are often occasioned, the truth many tymes, eyther by boldnesse of spirit, or by nimblenesse of wit, or by strength, or by readinesse, or smoothnesse of speech . . . is eyther altogether overborne or much obscured. Hereupon the Apostle sayeth, to contend with words is profitable to nothing but onely to the subversione of the hearers' (Hayward 1840 p.20). *Sejanus* presents a similar disclaimer about the unreliability of words, even written ones. In a remarkable scene that captures the post-modern conviction about the inadequacy of language to communicate meaning, Terentius, Laco and Lepidus ponder the issue of authorial intention as they peruse Tiberius's letters. Terentius at first sees praise for Sejanus in Tiberius's reference to him as the partner of his cares but Laco points out that there must be insult intended in the Emperor's calling Sejanus by his first name without reference to his titles. Every argument in favor of Sejanus suggests a counter-argument that indicates Tiberius's disgruntlement. Finally, unable to decide whether Tiberius intends to reward Sejanus or condemn him, the readers conclude that the contents of the letters are 'puzzles' intended to baffle rather than explicate the author's intentions. This comic, almost post-modern, interlude about the undecipherability of authorial intention remains close in conception to new historicist interest in the contradictory and multiple meanings embedded in texts, both literary and cultural.

Renaissance histories such as Hayward's *Annals* and Jonson's *Sejanus* thus incorporate a vision of the intimate relations between history writing and verbal fictionalizing.[9] History in the Renaissance was neither innocent nor simple. Renaissance prose and dramatic histories demonstrate an attitude towards history and historicizing that have been recovered in new historicist re-readings of the English Renaissance and the pages that follow as they re-examine the drama of Shakespeare and his contemporaries. The quintessential value of the new historicism, a literary methodology which continues to influence my work, seems to me embodied in its conviction that literary texts simultaneously reflect, question and influence the ideological concerns of a society, a sensibility that seems to have been shared by Renaissance authors of history and drama.

Chapter 2 begins my analysis of breaking boundaries between cultural practices by reading theatre's invocation of public punishment, its simultaneous exploitation and undermining of the audience's reliance on spectacles of death for entertainment. The blurring of boundaries between punitive practices and theatrical spectacles of death and dying is vividly demonstrated in popular tragedies such as Kyd's *The Spanish Tragedy* (c. 1587), Shakespeare's *Macbeth* (c. 1605), Webster's *The Duchess of Malfi* (1614) and Massinger's *The Virgin Martyr* (c. 1622). The last two plays present especially interesting demonstrations of female punishment and martyrdom.

Chapter 3 compares Roman plays in their invocation of the Self–Other dichotomy, polarities which continually merge and deconstruct during the course of these tragedies. In Shakespeare's *Titus*, Jonson's *Sejanus* and Fletcher's *The Virgin Martyr* (c. 1622), the playwrights' reliance on violence for theatrical effect accompanies an interest in demarcating boundaries between the civilized Self and barbaric Others; the inevitable collapse of the Self–Other dichotomy in these plays typifies Renaissance theatre's continuous preoccupation with exploring alterity through the location of its central actions in foreign lands such as Spain or Italy.

Theatre's sense of rivalry and appropriation are also evident in comedies such as *Twelfth Night* (1600) which may be read as a discourse on the comparative values of theatre and bear-baiting as forms of public entertainment and *The Taming of the Shrew* (1592) which blatantly appropriates the format of the skimmington.[10] Chapter 4 focuses on theatre's appropriation of carnival festivity; the first half of the chapter examines a specific aspect of this appropriation, gender reversals and transgressions. I begin by analysing comedies which appropriate carnivalesque gender inversion to more radical purposes than either of the above Shakespearean comedies: Fletcher's *The Woman's Prize or the Tamer Tamed* (1612) and Middleton's *The Family of Love* (1608). In tragedies carnivalesque gender inversions frequently accompany social transgressions such as adultery and patricide; I relate these transgressions in *The Maid's Tragedy* (1611) and *The Duchess of Malfi* to the sociopolitical contexts of early Stuart England. The second half of this chapter focuses on carnivalesque debasement in three plays of the late Jacobean years: *The Changeling* (1621), *Women Beware Women* (1622) and *The Bloody Banquet* (c. 1622). The last of these concentrates on the crowning and decrowning of kings, a central carnival activity.

Chapter 5 concentrates on theatre's appropriation of religious vocabulary to depict the most serious of social transgressions, incest. I examine theatrical depictions of incest as a threat to sociocultural boundary formation in plays such as *The Revenger's Tragedy*, *The Duchess of Malfi* and *Women Beware Women*; Ford's disturbing tragedy, '*Tis Pity She's a Whore* (1633), provides the most vivid example of a text which relies on breaking boundaries for its theatrical effect. Ford's lovers appropriate the vocabulary of conventional devotional literature to define their love; the play thus deconstructs the sanctioned and traditional tropes of devotional literature by recontextualizing the relationship between adorer/lover and God/Father/Son/Spouse within the secular world of private intrigues. Through the voice of his male protagonist, Ford in fact suggests that the incentive for worldly incest actually springs from accepted modes of devotional praise. Ford's dramatic departure from his predecessors thus lies in his almost complete deconstruction of the boundaries that separated the sacred from the secular. In many of the above plays, as Bradbrook has recognized, dramatic violation of social boundaries through the depiction of adultery, incest, or patricide also involves transgressing formal or generic norms. A section of the sixth chapter focuses, therefore, on blurring boundaries between tragedy and comedy evident in plays such as Tourneur's *The Revenger's Tragedy* and Middleton's *The Changeling*, but most vividly apparent in another disturbing play that treats the subject of incest, Massinger's *The Unnatural Combat* (c. 1620).

The last chapter studies the collapse of theatre, carnival topsy-turviness and religious fervour in the public drama of the mid-century, namely, the execution of King Charles I on 31 January 1649, after a public trial. It may be no accident that this social drama which concluded the Renaissance, a theatrical spectacle staged before a bewildered crowd, involved a similar appropriation and redefinition of established cultural practices such as theatre and festivity. For the first time in English history a lawfully appointed king mounted a scaffold after being tried *as king* by his own people and the event, I argue, marketed itself by implicitly invoking the traditions of theatre and festivity. I conclude with an analysis of this cultural text, a fascinating moment of coalescence between politics and theatre, between seeming communal desire and quintessential public spectacle. Ultimately Charles I's trial and execution validate most emphatically Barry Reay's insistence that 'our own neat division between religion, politics, and society would have made little sense to the majority of women and men of the seventeenth century, and it is better to think in terms of overlap or interaction' (Reay 1984 p.3). This event blurred the boundaries that separated theatre, festivity and public punishment even as it relied on an invocation of the sense of play central to our recognition of theatre and festivity as framed and temporary activities. This final blurring of boundaries in a spectacular public drama that captured the attention of a large audience may be understood as the culmination of intensifying experimentations with boundaries throughout the late sixteenth and early seventeenth centuries. Ironically it would appear that the appropriation of theatrical power by political authorities may have been made possible by the reflexive metatheatrics of Renaissance drama itself, a drama sanctioned and appreciated most by the monarchs earlier. In this sense *all* Renaissance drama rather than merely 'all early Stuart drama' remains 'prerevolutionary' 'in the strong sense' as Walter Cohen argues (W. Cohen 1992 p.123).

Mid-seventeenth-century politics thus provides a vivid instance of what Greenblatt describes as the refiguration of cultural boundaries, in this case between theatre and the scaffold and between theatre and festivity. The reconstitution of these shifts, what he calls a 'poetics of culture' which studies 'the collective making of distinct cultural practices' and inquires both into the construction of these zones and also 'the process of movement across the shifting boundaries between them' remains the fundamental purpose behind the following enterprise (Greenblatt 1988 p.7). My study explores interrelationships between social and literary dramas of the Renaissance, traces 'the circulation of social energy' from the scaffold and festivity to theatre in the late sixteenth and early seventeenth centuries in playwrights such as Kyd, Shakespeare, Beaumont and Fletcher, Tourneur, Massinger, Webster, Middleton and Ford and from the theatre to the scaffold in the mid-seventeenth century in the political and social drama that concluded the Renaissance.

Most importantly, while some critics perceive a contrast between earlier drama's concern with moral norms and maintaining social and generic boundaries and later drama's decisive violation of these social and literary codes from the year 1604, and new historicists see the emergence of a consciously political theatre in the early Stuart period, I argue only for varying degrees of experimentation in the work of Elizabethan and early Stuart dramatists. P. N. Medvedev argues that

> the literary work is an immediate part of the literary environment . . . But the literary environment itself is only a dependent and therefore actually inseparable element of the general ideological environment of a given epoch and a given sociological unit. . . . We thus have a complex set of interconnections and mutual influences. . . . The work of the literary historian should therefore proceed in unbroken interaction with the history of other ideologies and with unbroken socioeconomic history.'
>
> (Medvedev and Bakhtin 1978 pp.27–28)

The pages to follow provide a glimpse of these interactions, mutual influences and interconnections between society and theatre as they emerge in theatrical texts of the Renaissance. My readings draw their inspiration from contemporary revisionist attitudes towards culture, literature and society, attitudes that dominate current revaluations of Renaissance drama, but I focus specifically on breaking boundaries between literary and cultural zones. Ultimately I hope to show that, on closer scrutiny, the artificial boundary between Elizabethan 'high drama' and early Stuart 'decadence' invoked and reiterated by generations of Renaissance scholars and given greater credence by scholars such as Tennenhouse and Helms, collapses entirely.

Notes

1. For example, see studies by Steven Mullaney (1988) and Douglas Bruster (1992).
2. This is not to imply that criticism of the new historicism (or cultural studies in general) has been muted. Edward Pechter, who was among the first to raise a dissenting voice, has recently collected his essays in a volume that 'offers a lively

critique of the excitement and anxieties generated a decade ago by Stephen Greenblatt and other historicist and materialist critics on both sides of the Atlantic'
(Shapiro 1996 p.517). A sustained argument against many contemporary critical
practices has been mounted by Brian Vickers who has nothing new to add to the
criticisms levelled during the last decade in various journals and other publications,
though he summarizes and elaborates on some of these criticisms, bringing them
together in a single and conveniently organized volume (Vickers 1993). Vickers in
fact champions traditional humanism against all critical modes that have emerged
in recent years. With calculated disingenuity, he presents himself as a critic free from
any bias or ideological commitment, a marked contrast, he would have us recognize,
to the various squabbling schools of critics now dominating Shakespeare studies.
'Shakespeare's plays,' he insists, 'for so long the primary focus of the critic's and
scholar's attention, are now secondary, subordinated to the imperialism and self-
advancement of the particular group' (Vickers 1993 p.xii). His edenic vision of the
past ignores such turf wars as those between the New Critics and the Chicago critics
in the 1960s ('a family quarrel' Wilbur Scott called it in his introduction to critical
approaches [Scott 1962]); in Vickers's fairy-tale history of critical theory 'Once upon
a time the student of Shakespeare could read a wide range of books and articles
devoted primarily to interpreting the plays in a modern critical-analytical way, with
varying emphases on their historical context.' (Vickers 1993 p.x). Of course all that
has changed and Vickers sets out to tell us why criticism should retrace its steps to
the days of its pristine glory when gentlemanly goodwill reigned supreme; he concludes with a naive call for a return to the text: 'the play cannot resist; we can'
(Vickers 1993 p.416).

   My point here is simply that continuing critical engagement with the practice of
cultural studies and the new historicism, whether laudatory or critical, points to
their continuing appeal among Renaissance scholars.

3. I use the term 'new historicism', despite the departure from it by critics such as
    Greenblatt, to denote recent developments in literary studies marked by their
    emphasis on interrelationships between culture and literature; I use the term 'the
    new cultural history', taken from a collection of essays under that title edited by
    Lynn Hunt, to denote a similar movement in historical circles (Hunt 1989).

4. For a discussion of the political dimensions of the Richard II story, especially
    Shakespeare's play, see David Bergeron (1991 pp.33–34).

5. Elizabeth herself seems to have been increasingly insecure about the proliferation of
    satire under the veil of history; thus a 1599 order forbade satire and tightened
    control over history writing (Hamilton 1992 p.87).

6. My reading of Hayward's history differs from that of scholars such as D. R. Woolf
    who sees the very concept of history as undergoing a transformation in the mid-
    seventeenth century; Woolf argues that 'all Tudor and early Stuart historical
    writing ... reflects a conservative ideology of obedience, duty, and deference to
    social and political hierarchy. ... It would take the civil war to shatter what by the
    1630s had become a relatively monochromatic, and almost universally shared, image
    of the national past' (Woolf 1990 p.xiii). My point is that 'controversy, dispute, and
    debate' which Woolf sees in post civil war history is apparent even in Jacobean
    histories such as Hayward's.

7. Similar claims might be made about Samuel Daniel's history of England or John
    Bale's politically astute history of women in England attached to Elizabeth's *Glass
    of the Sinful Soul.*

8. Instances of the precarious nature of history writing abound in the Renaissance:
    Samuel Daniel's play, *Philotus*, which foregrounded a rebellion against Alexander
    the Great, was seen as showing sympathy for the executed Essex and Daniel appeared
    before the Privy Council to defend the charges against him (Gasper 1990 p.48).
    Even Romance could invoke suspicion as veiled political allegory: James VI (later

James I of England) took offence at the Una–Duessa episodes in *The Faerie Queene* as a defamatory attack on his mother and sought to bring Spenser to trial for it (Gasper 1990 p.9).

9. Jonson's history play has traditionally been seen as scholarly and accurate in its depiction of Rome but Philip Ayres's argument that Jonson is less of an historiographer and more of a poet 'who turns the materials of history into poetry' particularizes my own argument about history writing as a literary and creative project during the Renaissance (Ayres 1987 p.222).

10. For *Twelfth Night*'s invocation of the spectacle of bear-baiting, see Stephen Dickey's essay (1991); for a comprehensive analysis of the relationship between *The Taming* and taming rituals such as skimmingtons, see Linda Boose (1991).

2

Theatre and punishment: spectacles of death and dying on the stage

The famous Triple Tree, the first permanent structure for public hangings, was erected at Tyburn in 1571 during the same decade which saw the construction of the first permanent structure for the performance of plays. At Tyburn seats were available for those who could pay and rooms could be hired in houses overlooking the scene; the majority of spectators stood in a semicircle around the event while hawkers sold fruits and pies and ballads and pamphlets detailing the various crimes committed by the man being hanged. Other kinds of peripheral entertainment also occurred simultaneously. In short, hangings functioned as spectacles not unlike tragedies staged in the public theatres. The organization of spectators in these two arenas and the official localization of these entertainments, despite their long and hitherto divergent histories, through the erection of permanent structures during Elizabeth's reign suggests the close alliance between these communal worlds in early modern England.[1] Evidence also suggests that theatre and public punishment provided entertainment to upper and lower classes and that both events were generally well attended. Contemporary letters abound in accounts of executions and hangings, details of which are interspersed amid court gossip and descriptions of Parliament sessions. In a letter to Dudley Carleton, for example, John Chamberlain describes the hanging of four priests on Whitsun eve in 1612, noting with mild surprise the large number of people, among them 'divers ladies and gentlemen' who had gathered to witness the event which took place early in the morning between six and seven (Birch 1849 Vol.1 p.173).

I am not alone in suggesting links between these modes of popular public spectacle.[2] Greenblatt argues for the implicit presence of the scaffold in certain kinds of theatre when he writes

> the ratio between the theater and the world even at its most stable and unchallenged moments, was never *perfectly* taken for granted, that is, experienced as something wholly natural and self-evident. . . . similarly, the playwrights themselves frequently called attention in the midst of their plays to alternate theatrical practices. Thus, for example, the denouement of Massinger's *Roman Actor* (like that in *The Spanish Tragedy*) turns upon the staging as a mode of theater in which princes and nobles take part in plays in which the killing turns out to be real. It required no major act of imagination for a Renaissance audience to conceive of either of these alternatives to the conventions of the public playhouse: both were fully operative in the period itself,

in the form of masques and courtly entertainments, on the one hand, and public maimings and executions on the other.

(Greenblatt 1988 p.15)

Presumably the relationship between theatre and the scaffold worked both ways: if dramatic deaths could suggest public maimings and executions, the latter could as easily and as vividly evoke their theatrical counterparts.

Indeed contemporary narratives about public hangings and executions, whether fictional or documentary, frequently insist on the analogy. I would like to consider two such narratives, Dudley Carleton's documentary letter to John Chamberlain describing the near hangings of Cobham, Markham and Grey in 1604 and Thomas Nashe's fictional narrative about the execution of Cutwolf witnessed by Jack Wilton.

Carleton details in vividly theatrical terms the trial, hangings and near executions of several conspirators, including two priests, implicated in a plot to harm King James I shortly after his ascension to the throne in 1603. The letter moves from a casual narrative to a concentrated exposition of the drama as it unfolded. Carleton begins his account with the hangings of two papist priests: 'The two priests that led the way to the execution were very bloodily handled; for they were cut down alive; and Clark to whom more favour was intended, had the worse luck; for he both strove to help himself, and spake after he was cut down. . . . Their quarters were set on Winchester gates, and their heads on the first tower of the castle.' This was followed by the execution of George Brooke whose death, Carleton points out, was 'witnessed by no greater an assembly than at ordinary executions', the only men of quality present being the Lord of Arundel and Lord Somerset. Three others, Markham, Grey and Cobham, were scheduled to be executed on Friday; Carleton narrates the sequence of events as they occurred retaining information about their narrow escape from the gallows until the very end:

> A fouler day could hardly have been picked out, or fitter for such a tragedy. Markham being brought to the scaffold, was much dismayed, and complained much of his hard hap, to be deluded with hopes, and brought to that place unprepared. . . . The sheriff in the mean time was secretly withdrawn by one John Gill, Scotch groom of the bedchamber . . . The sheriff, at his return, told him [Markham] that since he was so ill prepared, he should have two hours respite, so led him from the scaffold, without giving him any more comfort . . .

(Birch 1849 Vol.1 p.29)

Lord Grey's turn followed and he spent considerable time repenting for his crimes and praying to be forgiven, all of which, Carleton wryly remarks, 'held us in the rain more than half an hour'. As in the case of Markham, the execution was halted, the prisoner being told only that the sequence of executions had been altered by express orders from the King and that Cobham would die before him. Grey was also led to Prince Arthur's Hall and asked to await his turn with Markham. Lord Cobham then arrived on the scaffold but unlike the other two, came 'with good assurance and contempt of death'. The sheriff halted this execution as well, telling Cobham only that he had to first face a few other prisoners. Carleton then describes the arrival of Grey and Markham and the bewildered looks on the three prisoners who 'nothing acquainted with what had passed, no more than the lookers on with what should follow looked strange one upon another, like men beheaded, and met again in the other world'. 'Now' Carleton continues, 'all the actors being together on the stage, as use is at the end of the play', the sheriff announced that the King had pardoned all three. The last-minute pardon, always a possibility in executions, arrive in time to save at least three of the conspirators. Carleton concludes his account by noting that this happy play had very nearly been marred 'for the letter was closed, and delivered him unsigned; which the King remembered, and called for him back again. And at Winchester there was another cross adventure: for John Gill could not go so near the scaffold that he could speak to the sheriff, . . . but was fain to call out to Sir James Hayes, or else Markham might have lost his neck' (Birch 1849 Vol.1 pp.31–32).

The initial hangings of the priests and George Brooke and the last-minute pardons to Cobham, Markham and Grey are invoked by the sheriff as examples of the 'justice and mercy' of the monarch. But Carleton's narrative, despite its support of this view, hints at the possibility of reading the King's final sentence as indecision rather than a calculated balancing of justice and mercy. The King resolved this issue 'without man's help, and no man can rob him of the praise of yesterday's action', Carleton tells us, but goes on to explain that

> . . . the Lords knew no other but that execution was to go forward, till the very hour it should be performed: and then calling them before him, he [the King] told them how much he had been troubled to resolve in this business; for to execute Grey, who was a noble, young, spirited fellow, and save Cobham, who was as base and unworthy, were a manner o injustice. To save Grey, who was of a proud, insolent nature, and execute Cobham, who had shown great tokens of humility and repentance, were as great a solecism; and so went on with Plutarch's comparisons in the rest, till travelling in contrarieties, but holding the conclusion in so indifferent balance that the lords knew not what to look for till the end came out, 'and therefore I have saved them all.'
> (Birch 1849 Vol.1 pp.31–32)

Strikingly absent from the King's reasoning is any consideration of Markham, who we remember 'almost lost his neck' and who we have been told earlier was expressly ordered to go first to his death by the King. Did the manner of the last-minute pardon deliberately arrange for the possibility that if any hanging took place, Markham, who seemed in the king's disfavour, would be the only one to lose his neck? Remarkably Carleton himself mimics the power of abeyance in his method of narration, retaining the surprise of the outcome until the very end and keeping his reader confused even as the court had been.

The extended theatrical metaphor used by Carleton emerges also in Thomas Nashe's *The Unfortunate Traveller, or the Life of Jack Wilton* (1987) which concludes with Jack Wilton's narration of his experiences in Bologna where he witnesses the execution of Cutwolf, a notorious murderer. The promised account of Cutwolf's wrack upon the wheel proves to be tortuous and we are led to it through yet another narrative, this time by Cutwolf himself who, before he dies, provides an 'authentic' account of the villainy that has led him to the wheel. Jack reproduces Cutwolf's 'insulting narration' as he terms it because of its punitive value:

> Prepare your ears and your tears, for never, till this thrust I any tragical matter upon you. Strange and wonderful are God's judgements; here shine they in their glory. . . . Murder is wide-mouthed, and will not let God rest till he grant revenge. . . . Guiltless souls that live every hour subject to violence, and with your despairing fears do much impair God's providence, fasten your eyes on this spectacle that will add to your faith.
>
> (Nashe 1987 p.302)

Several points in this exhortation are worth noting. Not by accident, this dramatic narrative has been reserved for the conclusion of the work. Jack here invites the reader to witness the spectacle of the execution, and as we shall see, the reader's role, initially analogous to Jack's, gradually merges with that of the crowd; that is, his role as witness gradually transforms into a more ambiguous one, somewhere between spectator of and participant in the torture. The incident, we are told, exemplifies God's glory and though we know that Jack refers here to the idea of divine retribution, the words suggest that he might be referring also to the nature of the execution itself as it dwells on torture rather than quick death. Jack insists that 'guiltless souls' who have not yet experienced violence but who live in constant fear of it can hope to strengthen their faith in the Almighty from this vision. In other words, this spectacle of torture should produce effects such as might follow a divine vision. Most importantly, the event on which we are expected to 'fasten' our eyes provides, according to Jack, a supreme example of the enactment of divine revenge. Like Carleton's narrative which purported to illustrate monarchical power even while it exposed its arbitrariness, Jack's account, despite its claim about illustrating divine authority, emphasizes instead its precarious similarity to mortal vengeance.

Cutwolf follows this dense exhortation with a long-winded narrative of the murder of Esdras of Granado. He prefaces his story with a strange assertion of his dignity: 'My body is little but my mind is as great as a giant's. The soul which is in me is the very soul of Julius Caesar by reversion. My name is Cutwolf, neither better nor worse by occupation than a poor cobbler of Verona – cobblers are men, and kings are no more' (Nashe 1987 pp.302–303). The analogies between body and mind and body and soul seek to offset the ugliness of the speaker, 'a wearish, dwarfish, writhen-fac'd cobbler' as Jack describes him. But while they serve to dignify the speaker, they work in reverse as well: Cutwolf's insistence on the manhood of kings and his reminder about the public death of Julius Caesar suggest not a fantastic and unreal substitution of important figures for common villains, but a very *possible* replacement, whose reality would have been apparent to the spectators and to contemporary readers of this narrative (indeed, only some years earlier in 1587, Mary Queen of Scots had been beheaded on English soil). And as visitors to London such as Thomas Platter note, the heads of several traitors from noble families graced London Bridge and provided a constant source of tourist attraction (Platter 1937 p.103). The thirty to thirty-five heads on display at any given time intended to provide a grim warning to those entering the city but descendants of the 'traitors' frequently regarded the heads of their forbears as trophies of past glories. The thin line that divided royalty from traitors who nearly managed to seize the throne was evident daily to travellers and residents in the city and Cutwolf's highly suggestive substitution of royal bodies for criminal ones was, as I hope to show, implicit in all executions, especially narrated or dramatized ones like that being described here by Nashe.

Cutwolf's mesmerizing narrative follows this bold preface detailing similarities between his death and that of royal traitors. Cutwolf tells the crowd that to revenge the murder of his elder brother he had hunted Esdras for twenty months across Europe. He describes his joy at finally chancing upon him on the streets of Bologna: 'O, so I was tickled in the spleen with that word; my heart hopped and danced, my elbows itched, my fingers frisked, I wist not what should become of my feet nor knew what I did for joy' (Nashe 1987 p.303). His emotions parallel the mirth of the crowds who have also 'made holiday' to view Cutwolf's torture. Cutwolf then describes how he visited Esdras at his lodgings the next morning and confronted him with the murder of his brother. Faced with Cutwolf's determination to bury a bullet in his breast, Esdras eloquently tries several arguments to stay Cutwolf's revenge. He first promises money, then eternal service, and proceeds to request that his arms and legs be cut off and he himself left to live a year in prayer and repentance. When this fails, he requests that he might be tortured: 'To dispatch me presently is no revenge; it will soon be forgotten. Let me die a lingering death – it will be remembered a great deal longer' (Nashe 1987 p.304). Is the narrator, himself to be tortured and allowed to die slowly, perhaps taunting his spectators into revising their sentence on him through this ambiguous request spoken by a similar murderer? Or is he suggesting his inevitable power as a lingering example for the future, as one who through this double narration will remain forever in memory and in print? After all, pamphlets and ballads enumerating various atrocities committed by criminals circulated during such executions and popularized the figures thus condemned. The ambiguous nature of the condemned man, both powerful and powerless, both mesmerizing the crowds and used by them as part of their festivity, seems to have been an inherent element of execution rituals. A similar ambivalence becomes a central ingredient also in Charles's execution performed more than half a century later, an event treated in detail in Chapter 6.

Esdras continues to reason with Cutwolf, alternating between promises and pleas, but his murderer remains undeterred. Cutwolf relishes the moment to the fullest and seems to be offering Esdras what he asked for earlier, a lingering mental torture. He even presents himself as a divine avenger:

> There is no heaven but revenge. . . . Divine revenge, of which (as of the joys above) there is no fullness or satiety! Look how my feet are blistered with following thee from place to place. I have riven my throat with overstraining it to curse thee. I have

ground my teeth to powder with grating and grinding them together for anger when any hath named thee. My tongue with vain threats is bollen and waxen too big for my mouth. My eyes have broken their strings with staring and looking ghastly as I stood devising how to frame or set my countenance when I met thee. I have near spent my strength in imaginary acting on stone walls what I determined to execute on thee.

(Nashe 1987 pp.305–306)

Cutwolf thus presents himself as the frightening figure of death himself, one who has rehearsed the drama of this encounter again and again. Esdras continues to plead for time, claiming that bodily torture would delay his death and provide him with an opportunity to save his soul. His assailant, however, determines to extend his power beyond the grave: 'My thoughts travel'd in quest of some notable new Italianism whose murderous platform might not only extend on his body, but his soul also' (Nashe 1987 p.306). In a spectacular *coup de theatre* he asks Esdras to renounce God and swear allegiance to the devil. The reader thus perceives a seemingly bewildering set of relationships: Esdras has requested that he be tortured rather than killed in order that he might have time to save his soul; Cutwolf, as if in response to this request, orders Esdras to give his soul to the devil and forswear all hope of salvation; and Esdras, in direct opposition to his earlier request and hoping to be saved from death, seizes the opportunity and gives Cutwolf more than he had hoped for by renouncing God and salvation completely. Does Cutwolf's request function as a test of the victim's authenticity in professing a desire to save his soul? At any rate Esdras's response actually takes Cutwolf by surprise:

Scarce had I propounded these articles unto him but he was beginning his blasphemous abjurations. I wonder the earth opened not and swallowed us both, hearing the bold terms he blasted forth in contempt of Christianity. . . . My joints trembled and quaked with attending them; my hair stood upright, and my heart was turned wholly to fire. . . . The vein in his left hand that is derived from the heart, with no faint blow he pierced, and with the full blood that flowed from it writ a full obligation of his soul to the Devil.

(Nashe 1987 p.307)

Having thus forsworn salvation, Esdras expects to be spared. Thus when his assailant asks him to open his mouth and gape wide, he does so without demur. The entire event, described by Cutwolf as the enactment of a ceremony, parodies Catholic communion rites and Esdras seems to regard Cutwolf's request as another stage in this enactment. Cutwolf's description of what follows, Edsdras's murder, is significant in its choice of words: 'therewith made I no more ado, but shot him full into the throat with my pistol. No more spake he, *so did I shoot him that he might never speak after*, or repent him' (Nashe 1987 p.307, emphasis added). The revenge directs itself specifically against the spoken word for it alone, as the narrative strives to show throughout, retains the supreme power to create reality. To Cutwolf at least, not Esdras's actions but his sworn allegiance to the devil, which he has no time to retract, damns him to hell. His murderer in a final paean to revenge allies himself clearly with God and heaven:

'Revenge is whatsoever we call law or justice. The farther we wade in revenge the nearer come we to the throne of the Almighty. To His scepter it is properly ascribed, His scepter he lends unto man when He lets one man scourge another' (Nashe 1987 pp.307–308). This appropriation of godly powers incenses the crowd who apparently reserve the honour for themselves: 'Herewith, all the people (outrageously incensed) with one conjoined outcry yelled mainly: "Away with him, away with him! Executioner, torture him, tear him, or we will tear thee in pieces if thou spare him" ' (Nashe 1987 p.308). Their desire to torture Cutwolf parallels Cutwolf's earlier treatment of Esdras and both actions mimic the Almighty's ever-vigilant vengeance invoked throughout this narrative.

We arrive thus to the centrepiece of Jack's story, the torture of Cutwolf, a festive communal celebration which both fascinates and unsettles Jack; presumably the reader too would find the culinary metaphors used to describe the occasion both fascinating and horrifying. I quote the passage in full:

> At the first chop with his wood-knife would he fish for a man's heart and fetch it out as easily as a plum from the bottom of a porridge pot. He would crack necks as fast as a cook cracks eggs. A fiddler cannot turn his pin so soon as he would turn a man off the ladder. Bravely did he drum on this Cutwolf's bones, not breaking them outright but, like a saddler knocking in of tacks, jarring on them quaveringly with his hammer a great while together. No joint about him but with a hatchet he had for the bones he disjointed half, and then with boiling lead soldered up the wounds from bleeding. His tongue he pulled out, lest he should blaspheme in his torment. Venomous stinging worms he thrust into his ears to keep his head ravingly occupied. With cankers scruzed to pieces he rubbed his mouth and his gums. No limb of his but was lingeringly splinter'd in shivers.
>
> (Nashe 1987 p.308)

The analogies comparing the executioner to a fisherman, a cook, a fiddler, a drummer and a saddler present Jack's fascination with the scene, shared also by the crowd who have instigated the tortures. 'This truculent tragedy of Cutwolf and Esdras' produces its desired effect on Jack who, sobered by the scene, marries his courtesan and leaves 'the Sodom of Italy' to live an honest life thereafter in England.

Contrary to being a sharp contrast to England, the Italy of Jack's narrative provides an exaggerated version of events such as public executions witnessed around London. This 'truculent tragedy' might easily provide a narrative of staged public punishments in England, and the reaction of the crowds, though it disgusts Jack, differs hardly at all from similar reactions by English crowds to the deaths of personalities such as the Earl of Strafford and Archbishop Laud in the seventeenth century.[3] Jack's disgust does, nevertheless, underscore the stance of many literary figures as they both exploit and criticize London's fascination with the spectacle of death. The author's ambivalent stance combining horror and fascination may be treated as typical of many Elizabethan depictions of punishment whether in popular narratives of travel or on the public stage. These accounts of public punishment exploit the reader's fascination with the spectacle of death but, by evoking horror and revulsion, they mock his reliance on spectacles of torment for entertainment. As Jonathan Bate describes it, the 'structure of the [Nashe's] story leaves the reader with more than a sneaking sympathy for what has been said on the scaffold, especially as the act of execution has a clinical cruelty which makes it in effect no different from the act for which it is a punishment. The narrative has made us discover the Italian within all of us' (Bate 1996 p.70).

A series of questions may be raised about these documents, especially Nashe's detailed narrative. Is Cutwolf the devil's emissary who deceives Esdras into damning himself or a divine agent avenging an unjust murder? Is the executioner a victim of the people's desire to see some sport or an agent of vengeance? Does the text negate or authorize the power of the word? Do the events constitute 'a truculent tragedy' as Jack claims or do they enact a festive communal ritual? Some of these ambiguities and paradoxes, especially the ambivalent positions of the victim, the crowd and the executioner, so clearly dramatized in Nashe's fictional account, were inherent to the ritual of execution itself and occurred also at actual executions in the Elizabethan and Stuart periods.

Nashe's account also provides a prose analogy to numerous tragedies of revenge enacted on the Elizabethan and early Stuart stage; it incorporates many ingredients that have been identified with this dramatic genre: obsessive revenge pursued by a melancholy revenger who physically and mentally degenerates through his pursuit of the victim, inordinate delay characteristic of this pursuit, the ambivalent tension between revenge and justice that remains unresolved, the viciously circular nature of revenge that destroys many in its course, and the public death of the revenger himself often performed in the midst of communal celebration and festivity. Nashe's theatrical account incorporates all the major ingredients of the Elizabethan revenge tragedy.[4]

This alliance between theatre and public punishment evident in Carleton's and Nashe's narratives and throughout the early modern period could be extended even farther: the masked and hooded dramatist, both present and absent from his production, invites comparison with the hangman. Like the hangman, the dramatist created spectacles and functioned as an entertainer whose efficiency was subject to the strictest scrutiny and criticism. Even his precarious position, as servant both to the Crown which sanctioned his activity and the populace who viewed his spectacle, compares with the hangman's. The hangman functioned as the most important instrument of the law; dramatists also repeatedly envisaged themselves as holding an analogous position. Thomas Heywood, for example, in *The Apology for Actors* (1612) insists on the moral efficacy of stage plays which could incite confessions from villains by the mere spectacle of horror and villainy. He cites three instances where spectators, moved by the dramatic events they witnessed, confessed to previous crimes and were thus brought to justice (Heywood 1941 pp.G–G2). One of his examples, a woman who at the end of a performance confessed to having poisoned her husband seven years earlier, also provides a remarkable instance of what Hamlet seems to expect from Claudius (and less directly from Gertrude) after the staging of *The Murder of Gonzago* when he tells us

> I have heard
> That guilty creatures sitting at a play
> Have, by the very cunning of the scene,
> Been struck so to the soul that presently
> They have proclaimed their malefactions.
> For murder, though it have no tongue, will speak
> With most miraculous organ.
>
> (Act II, ii, ll.584–590)

The power of theatre to provoke transformation had become commonplace in the period and receives ironic treatment in a later tragedy, *The Roman Actor*, where Caesar tries to cure avarice in Philargus by staging a play. The comic resolution of the staged play in which a miser repents of his earlier folly finds little satisfaction in Philargus who would prefer a tragedy: 'had he died / As I resolue to doe, not to be alter'd, / It had gone off twanging' (II, i, l.407–409). Philargus thus resolves to guard himself against the possibility of transformation, only to contend with the frustration of Caesar who demands that he 'make good vse of what was now presented? / And imitate in thy suddaine change of life, / The miserable rich man, that expres'd / What thou art to the life? (II, i, ll.431–434); when thwarted in this desire to see Philargus transformed by theatre, Caesar orders that he be hanged instead. Renaissance familiarity with the concept that theatre could provoke transformation may be gauged by the recurrence of this idea on the stage, whether it is invoked seriously as in *Hamlet* or treated ironically as in *The Roman Actor*.

Depictions of evil and tragedy on the stage, as Heywood argues, performed both punitive and psychological functions. And like tragedies in general, public executions and hangings served both as a negative example and a reminder that past villainies would not remain undiscovered or unpunished forever. The sentiment expressed by Samuel Johnson in the late eighteenth century, that there was no point in hanging a man if it was not going to be done in public, certainly prevailed in the earlier period and provided philosophical justification for the staging of both real and spectacle dismemberment, actual and theatrical tragedy, in early modern England. 'Cruelty,' Colin Burrow argues, 'is part of Shakespeare's world, and it generates a high proportion of the energy of his drama' (Burrow 1994 p.9); the attitude applies to Renaissance drama in general and perhaps even to the public execution of Charles I by Parliament in 1649, a theatrical spectacle which historically demarcates a boundary for this period.

I do not intend to collapse these modes of spectacle completely but to suggest that the close connection between these forms of popular public entertainment may be worth exploring in detail. The theatre and the scaffold provided occasions for communal festivities whose format and ends emerge as remarkably similar. More specifically, I would like to use the erection of the Triple Tree and the public execution of Charles I as events which frame a period remarkable for its vibrant, intense and highly competitive dramatic creativity. Both forms of festivity underwent radical scrutiny in later years, though the removal of hangings and executions from the public arena occurred only considerably later. Despite their divergent histories in later years, theatre and the scaffold merged in January 1649 to provide an unique and unprecedented spectacle of public tragedy and apparent political liberation. I trace the influence of the scaffold on the development of theatre in the late sixteenth century and the contribution of theatre to the staged political drama of the mid-seventeenth century.

The close alliance between these popular entertainments emerges most vividly in plays of the late sixteenth century such as Kyd's *The Spanish Tragedy* and Shakespeare's *Titus Andronicus*. But even plays such as Shakespeare's *Macbeth* and *King Lear*, Jonson's *Sejanus* and Webster's *The Duchess of Malfi* which do not stage hangings and executions invoke the format of public punishments, frequently to undermine the state's efficacy in staging deaths as a deterrent to further crimes and sometimes to mock the audience's reliance on the value of death as entertainment. Kyd's tragedy, which simultaneously invokes the spectacle of death and threatens to destroy the frame that separates theatre from the scaffold, more than any other early play insists on the precarious distance that separates staged dramas of death from public punitive events such as hangings.

Traditional criticism regards Kyd's *Spanish Tragedy* as important primarily for its historical position at the head of the revenge tradition. Its violence has frequently been attributed to Senecan models and its dramatic deaths, including the spectacular *coup de theatre* in the closing scene, analysed primarily for their influence on Shakespeare's dramaturgy. And yet, though the Senecan influence has been well documented, critics have only recently drawn attention to contemporary cultural practices such as public hangings at Tyburn to explain the play's particular fascination with the hanged man and the mutilated and dismembered corpse (Shapiro 1991). No other play of the Renaissance stage dwells on the spectacle of hanging as Kyd's does and the Senecan influence will not in itself account for the spectacular on-stage hangings and near-hangings in the play.

During Elizabeth's reign 6160 victims were hanged at Tyburn and though this represents a somewhat smaller figure than those hanged during Henry VIII's reign, Elizabethans were certainly quite familiar with the spectacle of the hanged body and the disembowelled and quartered corpse. In Kyd's treatment of the body as spectacle, we witness most vividly the earliest coalescence of the theatrical and punitive modes in Elizabethan England. Kyd also heightens the ambivalence inherent in the public hanging as spectacle and deliberately weakens the frames that separated spectators from the spectacle.

Despite my collapse of the theatrical and punitive modes, however, the important distinction drawn earlier between the festivity of theatre and the spectacle of the scaffold needs to be emphasized. Theatre establishes distance between spectacle and spectators and festivity implicitly or explicitly invokes the frame to separate itself from everyday living. Indeed, distance in the theatre and framing in festivity perform similar functions. However, the authenticity in the enactment of public punishment makes its distance considerably more nebulous. In fact participants in public executions and hangings remained acutely aware of their profound relevance both to the authorities who orchestrated the performance and to the spectators who viewed it. Such awareness sometimes resulted in conscious attempts by victims to manipulate and modify the distance that separated criminals from onlookers. In such circumstances the formal efficacy of the execution diminished considerably and events could easily transform into celebration of the condemned victim's role as a defier of repressive authority. As Michel Foucault illustrates,

> the public execution allowed the luxury of these momentary saturnalia, when nothing remained to prohibit or punish. Under the protection of imminent death, the criminal could say everything and the crowd cheered. . . . In these executions, which ought to show only the terrorizing power of the prince, there was the whole aspect of the carnival, in which the rules were inverted, authority mocked and criminals transformed into heroes.
>
> (Foucault 1979 p.61)

Executions where the margins remained tenuously defined and where festivity merged so fully with the enactment of terror may be especially important to an understanding of the drama of death on the Renaissance stage. In early plays such as Kyd's, in the concluding representation of theatre within theatre, for example, we witness a conscious manipulation of distance and framing, dramatic exposition of the precarious nature of public spectacle itself as an illustration of royal and state power. The inner play's exposition of the shallowness of state authority gains added potency from the composition of its audience, the royal houses of Spain and Portugal. Hieronimo, the author of the inner play, even taunts his audience's reliance on the framed nature of theatrical tragedy:

> Haply, you think, but bootless are your thoughts,
> That this is fabulously counterfeit,
> And that we do as all tragedians do:
> To die today, for fashioning our scene,
> The death of Ajax or some Roman peer,
> And in a minute starting up again,
> Revive to please to-morrow's audience.
>
> (IV, iv, ll.76–82)

At this, its most clearly self-reflexive moment, Kyd's tragedy simultaneously indulges and exposes its reliance on the drama of terror and, through the mixed reactions of its stage audience who first applaud the tragedy for its realistic enactment and then condemn it for its gory authenticity, invites a revaluation of the spectacle of terror itself.[5]

The close relationship between punitive practices and theatre as forms of entertainment perhaps accounts for the hangings, murders and near deaths which abound in the play. Lorenzo and Balthazar hang Horatio in the arbour in a spectacularly gruesome scene, Pedringano's death by hanging occurs on-stage, Alexandro narrowly escapes being burnt at the stake, Villuppo exits the play presumably to be tortured and hanged and Hieronimo tries unsuccessfully to hang himself in the last scene, though he duplicates the effects of a hanging by biting his tongue out. Of all these, Horatio's gruesome murder in the arbour remains the centrepiece; we come back to it again and again through Hieronimo's recounting of it and, as if to reiterate its centrality, the playwright exploits the value of the mutilated body as spectacle by holding Horatio's body up to view either literally or metaphorically several times in the course of the play.

Kyd thus exploits thoroughly the audience's voyeuristic interest in the hanged and mutilated corpse but he prepares us for his centrepiece, Horatio's murder in the arbour, even from the opening scene through promises of torture, mutilation and death. Repeated promises of more blood and gore, in fact, distinguish Kyd's version of the revenge play from Shakespeare's later rendering in *Hamlet*. While in the later play, Hamlet Senior insists that the torments of the netherworld are too horrible to be recounted (he is also forbidden to reveal its secrets), in the opening scene of Kyd's tragedy, Don Andrea's ghost provides with relish a vivid and detailed account of his sojourn through the underworld:

> Through dreadful shades of ever-glooming night,
> I saw more sights than a thousand tongues can tell,
> Or pens can write, or mortal hearts can think.
> Three ways there were: . . .
> The left-hand path, declining fearfully,
> Was ready downfall to the deepest hell,
> Where bloody Furies shake their whips of steel,
> And poor Ixion turns an endless wheel;
> Where usurers are choked with melting gold,
> And wantons are embraced with ugly snakes,
> And murderers groan with never killing wounds,
> And perjured wights scalded in boiling lead,
> And all foul sins with torments overwhelmed.

(I, i, ll.56–71)

The underworld, not constrained by economic considerations, retains ancient methods of public deaths such as boiling and drowning, punishments long abandoned in England as too costly and troublesome; indeed at the end of the play, Don Andrea's ghost envisions similar elaborate deaths for his murdered enemies in the afterworld. The opening and concluding accounts of the underworld which frame the play emphasize the tragedy's links with the spectacle of public punishment, the primary purpose of which was to replicate torments awaiting the victim after death. The opening scene concludes with Revenge promising us better entertainment than that detailed by Don Andrea, more blood and gore through the murder of the princely Balthazar by Don Andrea's 'sweet' Belimperia.

The very next scene provides more elaborate fare; the King's request for a 'brief discourse' concerning the battle between Spain and Portugal elicits from his general a detailed description complete with similes and accounts of mutilated and dismembered bodies:

On every side drop captains to the ground,
And soldiers, some ill maimed, some slain outright:
Here falls a body sundered from his head,
There legs and arms lie bleeding on the grass,
Mingled with weapons and unbowelled steeds,
That scattering overspread the purple plain.

(I, ii, ll.56–62)

The King's satisfied response to this narrative, which ultimately details Spain's success in battle, captures the value of death as entertainment, an idea emphasized throughout the play in a variety of ways.

The audience hears four different versions of the battle in succession in these opening scenes – by Don Andrea, the Spanish general, Horatio and Villuppo in the Portuguese court – and each account either elicits pleasure from the listener as in the scene just described or reveals the delight and ingenuity of the speaker.[6] The latter seems true of Villuppo's account of Balthazar's death to the Viceroy in the scene which follows. Jealous of Alexandro's success at court, Villuppo fabricates a tale about Balthazar's treacherous betrayal by Alexandro in the midst of battle. The temperamental and fickle Viceroy responds to the tale of his son's death with 'Ay, ay, my nightly dreams have told me this' (I, iii, l.76) and immediately has Alexandro imprisoned. Villuppo closes this scene with an aside in which he revels in the ingenuity of his 'forged tale'. However, Villuppo's fantastic narrative must remind the audience of the uncanny way in which art mirrors life, for we have already been promised Balthazar's death by Revenge; when his murder occurs later in the play, its sequence mimics Villuppo's account, for the unsuspecting Balthazar is killed by his supposed wife-to-be, Bel-imperia, at what appears to be the height of his success. Even the Viceroy's claim about his prophetic dreams gains ironic accuracy as the scene provides a narrative account of events yet to occur.

We arrive thus, via numerous accounts of death and mutilation, to the scene in the arbour where Bel-imperia and Horatio meet. Already aware of Pedringano's betrayal, however, the audience would view the images of war and love in the opening section of this scene as ominous. Interestingly Pedringano, like the hangman who sometimes remained masked and hooded, conducts the ceremony of the hanging in disguise with the aid of his assistant Serebrine while Lorenzo gives orders and joins in the stabbing after Horatio has been hanged. Though stage directions remain unclear, we can assume that Balthazar and Bel-imperia witness the stabbing, for Bel-imperia responds immediately to the horrible crime. Their function as spectators parallels our own and underscores Kyd's exploitation of the event as public spectacle. Foucault's argument that in early modern Europe 'in the ceremonies of the public execution, the main character was the people, whose real presence was required for the performance' (Foucault 1979 p.57) proves especially appropriate to this hanging performed on a raised stage for an audience whose arrangement in 'the pit' and the balconies above recalls the scaffold, and which certainly indulges the spectators' voyeuristic interest in death as spectacle. The double framing of this event – the audience as spectators watching an already framed event – also anticipates the play within the play in Act V which more explicitly raises questions about the value of death as entertainment.

A few scenes later we are treated to a review of this event and later to another hanging (Pedringano's) whose format remains remarkably different from the one we have just witnessed. Before turning to the later hanging, I would like to consider briefly the play's uncanny reliance hereafter on the spectacle of Horatio's mutilated body.

We are never allowed to forget this spectacle and characters keep reminding us of this event in various ways. In fact after the staging of this gory death, the earlier revenge plot associated with Don Andrea is all but forgotten; Horatio's murder and the collusive revenge orchestrated by Bel-imperia and Hieronimo on his behalf take centre stage. Horatio's body, hanged and mutilated before a full house, thus takes precedence over Don Andrea whose death has been narrated rather than witnessed. Don Andrea's funeral rites were conducted by Horatio in a private ceremony and all that remains of him is a bloody scarf; it might even be argued that the complete obliteration of Don Andrea's corpse and the repeated emphasis on Horatio's symbolically reiterates the precedence of the second revenge plot over the first. Even Don Andrea's bloody scarf is duplicated through the rest of the play by Horatio's handkerchief which Hieronimo dips in his son's blood and presents on-stage several times as a reminder of his unavenged death. This token of death recalls a conventional practice at hangings and executions; onlookers sometimes dipped their handkerchiefs in the blood of the victim which was believed to carry curative and divine powers (Linebaugh 1967 pp.109–110).

Unlike in *Hamlet* where murdered corpses remain hidden behind curtains or stuffed under the stairwell, Kyd's play presents death in vivid detail and follows this up with an elaborate scene of discovery in which both Hieronimo and Isabella identify Horatio's corpse. The Ghost, perhaps echoing the audience's reaction to these events, expresses dismay at witnessing Horatio's murder rather than Balthazar's as promised but Revenge, relishing the gory detour, insists on the relevance of these events as preambles to more cunning deaths yet to occur: 'Thou talkest of harvest when the corn is green: / The end is crown of every work well done; / The sickle comes not till the corn be ripe' (II, vi, ll.7–9).

After this murder, the focus of the play shifts to the psychological dilemma faced by Hieronimo as he plans revenge. The most interesting aspect of his character hereafter becomes his mental fascination with duplicating the murder that occurred. At first he tries to duplicate bodies by re-enacting the event with himself as victim; in a vividly dramatic scene which takes place at court, he enters with a poniard in one hand and a rope in the other and debates his route to death: 'Turn down this path, thou shalt be with him [Horatio] straight; / Or this, and then thou need'st not take thy breath. / This way or that way?' (III, xii, ll.14–16). Tormented by his inability to accomplish revenge, he spends most of his time wandering in the arbour looking for his son; here, near the very tree on which Horatio was hanged, the painter Bazulto, seeking justice for his own son's murder, visits him. In a psychologically revealing moment explored in one of the 'Additions' to the text, Hieronimo requests Bazulto to paint the scene of Horatio's murder complete with the victim's doleful cry and his own emotional frenzy at discovering his son's body. In language he tries to recreate the event for us yet again: 'Well sir, paint me a youth run through and through with villains' swords, hanging on this tree'; and later, describing his discovery of the body, he wishes to 'behold a man hanging: and tottering, and tottering as you know the wind will weave a man' (Additions between III, xii and xiii, ll. 128–129 and ll.148–149). His desire to recreate events through painting contrasts sharply with Isabella's desire a few scenes later to destroy the arbour and the tree on which her son was murdered. Both scenes serve to keep the gruesome murder firmly in our minds.

Of course Hieronimo's repeated attempts to recreate the original event invariably end in failure. His dissatisfaction with painting as an art form because it only partially emulates life results in his beating Bazulto. His frustration stems in part from his recognition that the painter can capture the scene but not his or Horatio's pain; 'Cans't paint me a cry?' he asks, to which Bazulto can only give a partially satisfying reply, 'Seemingly, Sir'. In this scene as in various others, Kyd dramatizes the inadequacy of language for the expression of pain. *The Spanish Tragedy* thus provides a vivid illustration of Elaine Scarry's point about the primacy of pain: 'Physical pain does not simply resist language but actively destroys it, bringing about an immediate reversion to a state anterior to language, to the sounds and cries a human being makes before language is learned' (Scarry 1985 p.4). Hieronimo makes a similar point by staging his final theatrical spectacle in sundry tongues as if to reiterate that words and language remain unnecessary for the intimation of pain. In this final re-enactment of the original crime, through the form of theatre rather than painting, Hieronimo at least achieves partial success.

The play even provides a semi-comic version of Horatio's murder in another hanging a few scenes later. Pedringano's hanging also takes place on-stage and provides a semi-comic and officially authorized spectacle, a direct contrast to Horatio's base and treacherous murder committed in secret and under cover of night. Through the attitudes of Pedringano who reaches his death with a merry jest and the Clown who cannot resist the event despite his sympathy for the deluded victim, the scene simultaneously exploits and satirizes the value of the public hanging as a reiteration of justice.

Commenting on the propensity for travesty inherent in the format of the public execution, Foucault illustrates that because the ritual of torture was sustained 'by a policy of terror' which made everyone aware 'through the body of the criminal of the unrestrained presence of the sovereign', it was especially susceptible to manipulation by its participants (Foucault 1979 p.49). The public execution's social relevance depended so fully on its proper enactment through the collusion of all participants, including the hangman as an instrument of the law, the criminal as a defier of divine and sovereign authority and spectators as witnesses to the efficacy of royal power and justice, that the slightest deviation could lead to redefinitions and reinterpretations of power relations between subjects and the sovereign. This happened frequently enough to cause some concern to the authorities.[7] The speech delivered on the scaffold by the victim provided an especially suitable opportunity for such manipulation; intended to reinforce the power of justice, it frequently questioned rather than emphasized legal efficacy. Chamberlain, for example, bemoans the custom of allowing the condemned to address the audience and cautions about the inherent danger of this practice; describing the bravely rendered speech by a priest who hanged at Tyburn, he notes that 'the matter is not well handled in mine opinion, to suffer them [condemned prisoners] to brave and talk so liberally at their execution' (Birch 1849 p.215).

Pedringano's attitude when faced with death, like Cutwolf's in Nashe's narrative, reiterates the carnivalesque possibilities of the public execution. Duped by Lorenzo into thinking that he will be pardoned, Pedringano insists on mocking the authorities who sentence him. Even the hangman expresses shock at his callous indifference to death: 'Well, thou art even the merriest piece of man's flesh that e'er groaned at my office door' (III, vi, ll.81–82). It might even be argued that despite his role as victim, Pedringano has the final say on this travesty of justice, for he exposes Lorenzo's crimes in a letter and thus forces Hieronimo to confront the inadequacy of the judicial system. In his mockery from beyond the grave, Pedringano becomes a version of the grinning skeleton in the *danse macabre* as he exposes the futility of human endeavour. The Clown's attitude also reiterates the inherent irony of this grotesque enactment of state justice. Having opened the empty box which supposedly contains a pardon sent by Lorenzo, the Clown reacts to the trick with infinite glee; his reaction parodies similar responses towards death voiced throughout the play by many characters, among them Balthazar, Lorenzo, Villuppo and Pedringano himself:

> I cannot choose but smile to think how the villain will flout the gallows, scorn the audience, and descant on the hangman, and all presuming of his pardon from hence. Will't not be an odd jest, for me to stand and grace every jest he makes, pointing my finger at this box, as who would say, 'Mock on; here's thy warrant.' Is't not a scurvy jest that a man should jest himself to death?
>
> (III, v, ll.10–19)

He relishes the spectacle so much that he expedites Pedringano's death by playing his part to perfection.

In effect the Clown's attitude parallels the court's applause for the 'Tragedy of Soliman and Perseda' staged as part of Bel-imperia's nuptial ceremony. After the tragedy Hieronimo holds up his son's body to the bewildered court as justification for the multiple deaths that have occurred: 'See here my show; look on this spectacle' (IV, iv, l.89). The court's reaction as the truth unfolds changes from applause to anger and condemnation. Implicitly Kyd invites the audience to re-evaluate its response to the tragedy of evil so cunningly staged, for Hieronimo's theatrical production necessarily draws attention to the nebulous nature of the boundary that separates spectators from the spectacle.

Kyd's conscious exposition of this fragile distance may be best understood perhaps through Gregory Bateson's theory about frames in 'play' and 'fantasy' activities referred to earlier. By organizing his tragedy as a series of frames within frames and through Hieronimo's final mockery of the inner audience for its reliance on death for entertainment, Kyd ultimately implicates the outer audience as well in this charge. *The Spanish Tragedy* thus concludes by posing the question 'Is this play?' Indeed in problematizing boundaries, Kyd's tragedy imitates the scaffold most vividly; it also begins a trend in theatrical experimentation with framing that culminates in radical realignments considerably later in the tragedies of Middleton, Ford and Shirley.

Kyd's tragedy closes by reminding us of yet another frame, that provided by Don Andrea and the Ghost who have witnessed events with the theatrical audience and whose pleased reactions underscore the value of death as entertainment. The Ghost catalogues the list of deaths with obvious relish:

> Aye, now my hopes have end in their effects,
> When blood and sorrow finish my desires:
> Horatio murdered in his father's bower,
> Vild Serebrine by Pedringano slain,
> False Pedringano hanged by quaint device,
> Fair Isabella by herself misdone,
> Prince Balthazar by Bel-imperia stabbed,
> The Duke of Castile and his wicked son
> Both done to death by old Hieronimo,
> My Bel-imperia fall'n as Dido fell,
> And good Hieronimo slain by himself.
> Ay, these were spectacles to please my soul.
>
> (IV, v, ll.1–12)

His response reminds us of several such reactions to death in the course of the play: the court witnessing the 'Tragedy of Soliman and Perseda' had commended the actors; Villuppo had revelled in anticipation as he plotted the death of Alexandro; the Clown had marvelled at the plot to send Pedringano to his 'merry' death. Revenge even concludes the play with promises of further torments for the villains in the underworld. Thus the play blatantly presents its multiple deaths as dramatic entertainment but, through Hieronimo's taunting condemnation of his audience's expectations, also raises questions about theatre's status as a framed event and about the value of death as entertainment.

The spectacular success of Kyd's play might be attributed in part to the author's ingenious transference of the spectacle of public execution with all its ambiguities from the sociopolitical to the cultural worlds. The play, to use de Certeau's terms, 'poaches' on the spectacle of public punishment to market itself as a genre. The same might be said about the dramatic mode in particular in early modern England and Shakespeare's early Roman tragedy *Titus Andronicus* but, because I treat this play in detail in the next chapter within the context of Renaissance notions of alterity, I will proceed here to a discussion of Shakespeare's obsession with the issues of treason and punitive practice in *Macbeth*.

Macbeth provides an extended discourse on the issue of public punishment as an extension of monarchical authority. Critics have long recognized that *Macbeth* presents a strong case for being considered the bloodiest in the Shakespeare canon; as Francis Barker describes it, '*Macbeth* is, throughout, a play of hurt and violence. It begins and ends in violent insurrection and invasion; coupled at the beginning, merged at the end. And of the high tragedies, *Macbeth* is without doubt the most bloody, both in terms of the violence of its events and of the symbolization of the blood that has fascinated so many commentators' (Barker 1993 p.58). The play centres on the issue of treason and its consequences. It starts with open acts of treason by two separate Scottish factions and with the monarch's agent of justice, Macbeth, seeking to punish their transgression. After a determined and successful search for Macdonwald through the battlefield, Macbeth enacts on his body the violence reserved for traitors. The general narrates the scene with vivid detail that immediately exposes the brutality of Macbeth's punishment, though he acts here under the sanction of monarchical authority:

> For brave Macbeth (well he deserves that name),
> Disdaining Fortune, with his brandish'd steel,
> Which smok'd with bloody execution,
> Like Valour's minion, carv'd out his passage,
> Till he fac'd the slave;
> Which ne'er shook hands, nor bade farewell to him,
> Till he unseam'd him from the nave to th' chops,
> And fix'd his head upon our battlements.
>
> (I, ii, ll.16–23)

Macdonwald's head, painted and set aloft for all to mock, a conventional Renaissance outcome for traitors, presumably exhibits the power of the monarch and the State's extensive invisible power that seeks out and punishes those who threaten its stability. Ironically, however, the head actually glorifies the power of military leaders such as Macbeth on whom, as Alan Sinfield points out, Duncan's authority seems to rest rather precariously (Sinfield 1992 p.97). A few scenes later we are given yet another account of the state's display of power as the Thane of Cawdor is executed for treason. Cawdor, as Malcolm describes it, goes to his death a model prisoner, repentant for his misdeeds and reconciled to the enormity of his crime. His 'deep repentance' and self-fashioning moments on the scaffold evoke admiration even from Malcolm: 'Nothing in his life / Became him like the leaving of it: he died / As one that had been studied in his death, / To throw away the dearest thing he ow'd, / As 'twere a careless trifle' (I, iv, ll.7–11). The narrative even draws pity from the monarch who ruefully notes that 'There's no art / To find the mind's construction in the face' (I, iv, ll.12–13). But these swiftly resolved conflicts that open the play nevertheless reveal the tenuous nature of Duncan's power over his kingdom. As Sinfield argues, 'the manifest dependency of Duncan's state upon its best fighter sets up a dangerous instability' (Sinfield 1992 p.97).

And if these lessons in cruelty are intended to act as deterrents to others who might contemplate similar actions, their point is missed even by those who play primary roles in the orchestration of these punishments. Macbeth, in fact, re-enacts the crimes of his compatriots with greater success, using their failure as an educational process to ensure better results. Shakespeare here dramatizes the ineffectiveness of public displays of monarchical and state authority. The play's cyclical pattern further undermines the efficacy of state authority. In fact, as Sinfield and others recognize, the last scene closely resembles the opening scene, with Macduff now playing Macbeth's part and Malcolm, Duncan's. As Macduff, the general who recovers the kingdom for Malcolm, holds Macbeth's head aloft, we are reminded of Macbeth's similar treatment of Macdonwald. Macduff even promises to treat Macbeth in similar fashion: 'Then yield thee, coward, / And live to be the show and gaze o' th' time: / We'll have thee, as our rarer monsters are, / Painted upon a pole, and underwrit, / 'Here may you see the tyrant' (V, viii, ll.23–27). We might recall in this context that Shakespeare had already explored the capabilities of a man who had been untimely born, Richard III; Macduff's similar status thus disturbs the seeming calm of the concluding scene. And if Macduff 'at the end stands in the same relation to Malcolm as Macbeth did to Duncan in the beginning' (Sinfield 1992 p.102), we might also remember that this sequence remains renewable beyond the actions of the play until Fleance's line usurps power. After all, a major prophecy spoken by the witches at the very beginning of the play remains yet to be fulfilled – Fleance's heirs, we can presume, will wrest the throne from Macduff's line. *Macbeth*, in other words, ends on the promise of more than the one sequel that Sinfield acknowledges; of course, these sequels do not require dramatic elucidation, so closely will their actions parallel the parent play. Even more importantly, the play promises that the treasonous acts in each sequel to come will be proportionately more successful (and perhaps more violent) than acts just completed; Macbeth's usurpation goes a step farther than Macdonwald's as Macduff's will surely surpass Macbeth's. This brutal progress of history will presumably halt only when the most successful usurper, having learnt from the past most fully, will ensure the throne for his line. Shakespeare thus posits a cyclical vision of history not unlike that described by Hayward in his *Annals*, but at the core of Shakespeare's vision lies a picture of the monarch as a self-appointed and self-anointed individual whose right to power has been bought dearly by the successful treasons of past generations. Burrow argues that *Macbeth* is a profoundly disturbing tragedy which registers 'undertones of unease with the new king: a play concerned with a murderous Scottish ruler must have had some courtiers squirming in their seats in the early years of the reign of the first Scottish king of England' (Burrow 1994 p.10); the unease that this history play registers springs from much more than its Scottish contexts.

The blurring of the boundaries that separate state authority from treacherous acts of violence is vividly enacted in the scene on the heath as the witches present Macbeth with visions of crowned and bloody heads. These images, symbols of Macbeth's imminent defeat at the hands of Macduff, mimic the state's reliance on severed heads for the reiteration of its authority; ironically, the witches' roles at this point coincide fully with the authority of Malcolm and Macduff against the unfortunate Macbeth. The lines that separate good and evil, authority and treason, legitimacy and usurpation, king and devil have collapsed.

Macbeth thus extends a metaphor Shakespeare had already explored in *Titus* more than a decade earlier; *Titus*, as we shall see, presents opening images of a headless body as symbol for a kingless state and concludes with a bodiless head, perhaps denoting Lucius's role as emperor without subjects. At the end of the play the balance of power shifts to Rome's former enemies, the Goths, who make Lucius emperor. *Macbeth* more emphatically envisions a monarchy with no subjects by presenting us with numerous bodiless heads through the course of the play. The play's concluding vision is equally ambivalent, for Malcolm's role as king is compromised by the presence of powerful kingmakers in his country, the English soldiers who have fought on his behalf and the English monarch who from afar monitors the transfer of authority in Scotland. The image of Macbeth's armed head brought on-stage for the public display of Malcolm's authority as king projects a tone of intrusive mockery on the proceedings of the final scene. Joad Raymond notes that 'An image of a head' presents 'a dramatic violent moment which has both an incommunicable personal dimension, and a politically charged meaning' (Raymond 1993 p.298), but in *Macbeth* the nature of that meaning remains elusive and contradictory.

Indeed tragedies of state such as *The Spanish Tragedy* and *Macbeth* and, as I will demonstrate, *Titus Andronicus* and *Sejanus* debate the fate of the body politic through vivid enactments of punitive violence that nevertheless convey a sense of the ambivalent relationship between these subjects in early modern England. Burrow points out that 'Shakespeare was trained at school to argue on both sides of a question' and that 'this habit of mind makes Shakespeare's drama, and Renaissance drama generally, rootedly dialectical' (Burrow 1994 p.9). This very trait, he insists, makes Shakespeare's plays disturbing; on the contrary, the plays' disturbing effects result from their resistance to dialectical resolution. *The Spanish Tragedy* and *Macbeth* demonstrate that the disturbing aspects of Renaissance drama are most vividly apparent in the theatres of cruelty staged by Shakespeare and his contemporaries. Indeed the coalescence of cruelty and theatrical success persists throughout the early Stuart period, as the success of later tragedies such as Webster's *The Duchess of Malfi* illustrates.

The efficacy of punishment invoked and then undermined by Shakespeare and Jonson emerges also in *The Duchess*, a play which unlike *Titus* or *Macbeth* straddles the generic boundary between domestic tragedy and tragedy of state. *The Duchess* also differs from the above tragedies in locating its violence in the martyr-like death of its female protagonist. In a horrifying scene that constitutes an emendation to his sources, which record the Duchess's disappearance after her capture by her brothers thus merely suggesting her death at their hands, Webster dramatizes her death on-stage as a torturous and drawn-out affair orchestrated by Ferdinand and enacted with initial relish by Bosola.

Bosola even presents the Duchess's death to her as punishment devised by authority (her brothers) for her sins. As in other Renaissance tragedies, Webster's play performs punishments on-stage as an enactment of patriarchally sanctioned authority but nevertheless demonstrates that enactors of violence such as Bosola frequently provoked not fear and anguish in their victims but contempt and pity. Disguised as an old man, Bosola engages the Duchess in a conversation that seems intended to provoke fear of death and dying; his manner and tone have their desired effect on Cariola who resists and pleads for her life but the calm resignation with which the Duchess faces her end baffles Bosola. Announcing himself as a tomb maker ready to design hers, he asks her to choose a design. The Duchess condemns fashion in death as a pointless distinction not recognized by death: 'Why, do we grow fantastical in our death-bed? / Do we affect fashion in the grave?' (IV, ii, ll.151–152). Bosola responds by describing two kinds of elaborate monuments to Princes erected on their tombs, neither of which presumably is available to those of the meaner sort:

> Most ambitiously. Princes' images on their tombs
> Do not lie as they were wont, seeming to pray
> Up to Heaven: but with their hands under their cheeks,
> As if they died of a toothache; they are not carved
> With their eyes fix'd upon the stars; but as
> Their minds were wholly bent upon the world,
> The self-same way they seem to turn their faces.
>
> (IV, ii, ll.153–159)

In a gruesome show of authority and a parody of state ceremony, the executioners then enter carrying a coffin, cord and bell. Cariola and the Duchess immediately recognize the import of these tools but the Duchess responds to Cariola's anguished cry with 'Peace; it affrights not me' (IV, ii, l.170). She then proceeds to enquire after the manner of death to be employed by her executioners. The conversation that follows between Bosola and the Duchess simultaneously sacralizes the Duchess's actions and reduces Bosola's role, despite his power to kill her, to that of a helpless agent caught up in political machinations beyond his control. Unable to comprehend the Duchess's remarkable calm despite his morbid shows of power, Bosola asks her again and again if death does not frighten her. Her continued calm draws him to remind her of the manner of her death: 'Yet, methinks, / The manner of your death should much afflict you, / This cord should terrify you?' (IV, ii, ll.209–211). The Duchess responds to this query with her most vocal denunciation yet of hierarchies in dying:

> Not a whit:
> What would it pleasure me, to have my throat cut
> With diamonds? or to be smothered
> With cassia? or to be shot to death, with pearls?
> I know death hath ten thousand several doors
> For men to take their *Exits*.
>
> (IV, ii, ll.212–216)

The actions that follow provide a visual reiteration of the contrasting attitudes towards death described by Bosola in his description of Princes' tombs. The Duchess dies a saintly death on her knees looking heavenward:

> Pull, and pull strongly, for your able strength
> Must pull down heaven upon me:
> Yet stay, heaven gates are not so highly arch'd
> As princes' palaces: they that enter there
> Must go upon their knees.

(IV, ii, ll.226–230)

Cariola, on the other hand, despite her earlier assertion that she would die with the Duchess, panics and falls apart trying several arguments to save her life. Unlike a court of justice which would have commuted or delayed her sentence until she could be examined to verify her claim that she is with child, Bosola and the executioners see her pleas merely as delaying tactics and strangle her immediately. The dramatist clearly intends us to see the two deaths as contrasts along the lines suggested by Bosola earlier, the Duchess willingly looking heavenward and Cariola stringently concerned with worldly affairs and survival. But the lasting impact of the scene emerges in the Duchess's condemnation of degrees of dying according to one's rank and social status. In her death the Duchess thus reiterates once again her total disregard for hierarchies of state. Like victims on the scaffold who expertly reversed their roles from that of passive objects awaiting an imprint of the State's power on their bodies to that of heroes to be emulated for their bravery and martyrdom, the Duchess thus converts the scene of Bosola's and Ferdinand's Machiavellian villainy into one of triumphant martyrdom and nobility. As Frances Dolan demonstrates, however, women's elevation to martyrdom also required that their final moments transcend bodily suffering; their martyrdom could be effected only by the effacement of their bodies and their sexuality (Dolan 1994 p.159). Webster's conscious contrast between Cariola and the Duchess demonstrates Dolan's point; the Duchess whose sexuality had been foregrounded until now is transformed into a figure of heavenly piety and devotion, while Cariola draws attention to her sexuality in a vain attempt to save herself from death. Her case provides a parallel to the actual execution of Margaret Clark that Dolan treats in detail; commenting on why Clark did not plead her belly, Dolan notes that 'To plead her belly, to redirect attention to her body, would move Clark into a carnivalesque script, one which rarely shapes accounts of women's executions, and which, when it does, works to discredit and dismiss rather than heroize them' (Dolan 1994 p.176). Cariola's insistent pleading of the belly places her death in the carnivalesque genre; the play thus calls attention to the Duchess's martyrdom by contrasting it to her servant's more ignominious end. The complete effacement of the Duchess's body is further reiterated for us by Ferdinand's reaction to it: 'Cover her face. Mine eyes dazzle: she di'd young' (IV, ii, l.259).

Webster's tragedy thus provides a vivid instance of the ambivalent role of the scaffold, especially as it staged women's executions; Dolan, who explores the ambiguities that surrounded women's executions, argues that invariably 'the scaffold becomes not only a locus of domination and oppression, but also an arena of boundary crossing, negotiation, and possibilities for agency. Specifically, in the processes of subjectification that representations of executions make visible, the condemned is at once spectacularly acted upon and an agent' (Dolan 1994 p.157). Undoubtedly, Dolan's point applies to Webster's play, for the lasting effect of the Duchess's staged death ensues from her ability to convert the ritual of oppression into one of triumphant martyrdom.

A similar transformation occurs in another popular tragedy, Massinger's *The Virgin Martyr*, which because it explores the ambiguities of state-sanctioned death within the context of decadent Rome, might be more appropriately discussed with Jonson's and Shakespeare's Roman tragedies, *Sejanus* and *Titus*, respectively.

As we have seen, defiance of authority, whether by martyr figures such as the Duchess or villains such as Aaron, permeates Renaissance enactments of punitive practice. Despite the irreverent treatment of punitive practices, however, the enacted violence of these tragedies points to the persistent appeal of the gallows as a source of entertainment to theatre-goers in Renaissance England. In these plays we see theatre's ability to successfully poach on punitive practices and at the same time to undermine, question and challenge the efficacy of these practices.

Notes

1. Whether James Burbage's Theatre in Shoreditch was the first public playhouse is a matter of some dispute. See, for example, Herbert Berry's argument for the Red Lion (which critics such as Chambers have regarded as an inn) as an earlier playhouse deliberately ignored by Cuthbert Burbage because of an earlier falling out between his father, James Burbage, and Brayne, the owner of the Red Lion. But as Berry himself acknowledges, the Red Lion 'must have been a very pale shadow of the Theatre. . . . So far as one can see, it had no walls or roofs, and the turret was to rest on plates on the ground rather than on secure footings, along with, one might guess, the stage and galleries' (Berry 1989 p.145). The 'secure footing' at least was provided only with the erection of the Theatre in 1576.
2. I include both executions and hangings somewhat inaccurately under the term scaffold but the distinction between these two forms of punishment is important: executions were reserved for the upper classes and important criminals, while criminals of the lower classes were hanged.
   For recent readings of connections between punitive practices and Renaissance theatre, see Karin Coddon (1989), Karen Cunningham (1990) and Frances Dolan (1994).
3. The Earl of Strafford, originally leader of the House of Commons, had been raised to the position of Lord Deputy of Ireland in 1628 at William Laud's suggestion and had returned to England in 1639 when Charles elevated him to an earldom. The Earl's earlier policies in Ireland had antagonized many at court and several stories of his arrogance and cruelty circulated in London, making him extremely unpopular with the people in general. Charles's open favouritism towards him (in 1640, he bestowed upon him the highest honour in England, the Order of the Garter) only increased the general ill-feeling. But Charles could do little to save Strafford when he was imprisoned in the Tower and brought to trial on 22 March at a crowded

Westminster Hall. Charles signed the Bill of Attainder against Strafford on 10 May and the earl was executed on the noon of 12 May. Dense crowds greeted the execution with rejoicing as they did William Laud's a few years later.

4. For the conventions of the Elizabethan revenge tragedy see Bowers (1940) and Charles and Elaine Hallett (1980).

5. Recent Renaissance criticism has shown particular interest in the self-reflexive and subversive aspects of drama in the sixteenth and seventeenth centuries and established the fragility of distance between spectacle and spectator, especially in Shakespeare's plays. Greenblatt redefines this sense of distance in the dramaturgy of successful playwrights such as Marlowe and Shakespeare as the creation of anxiety. Anxiety in the theatre also accompanies the evocation of delight: 'the whole point of anxiety in the theater is to make it give such delight that the audience will pay for it again and again. And this delight seems bound up with the marking out of theatrical anxiety as represented anxiety – not wholly real, either in the characters on-stage or in the audience' (Greenblatt 1988 p.135). In characteristic privileging of the Shakespearean text, he describes 'a kind of perfection' in the manipulation of anxiety, 'a startling increase in the level of represented and aroused anxiety' in Shakespeare (Greenblatt 1988 p.133). My readings suggest that the manipulation of anxiety in Shakespeare's works typifies a tendency that permeates Renaissance drama. A similar tendency characterizes the work of later playwrights such as Webster, Massinger, Middleton and Ford; in fact, in their plays this experimentation with boundaries intensifies. Mary Beth Rose seems to point to this difference between Shakespeare and his contemporaries when she argues that 'given the variety of conceptual options in Jacobean culture, he [Shakespeare] often chooses the conservative ones, a pattern that becomes obvious when we view him not on his own, but in relation to his fellow dramatists' (Rose 1988 p.173).

6. The exception to this might be Horatio's account of Don Andrea's death to Bel-imperia, though it also raises questions of authenticity by modifying two earlier accounts we have heard, the first by Don Andrea's ghost and the other by the Spanish general. Discrepancies among the earlier narratives should caution us, however, that the scene provides yet another tale glossed by the teller to satisfy Bel-imperia, a listener with different allegiances than the King and Viceroy.

7. In the eighteenth century, official concern about the efficacy of public executions and hangings in re-enforcing royal and social authority became especially acute as these occasions increasingly provided excuses for rioting and general merrymaking (Foucault 1979 p.68).

3
Theatre and cruelty: Renaissance notions of alterity in Roman tragedies

Dramatizations of decadent Rome in Shakespeare's *Titus Andronicus*, Jonson's *Sejanus* and Fletcher's *The Virgin Martyr* present vivid explorations of Renaissance notions of alterity while still exploiting the value of death as entertainment.[1] These tragedies begin by carefully constructing a dichotomy between moral and civilized Self and violent and decadent Other but they inevitably conclude by destabilizing this dichotomy, by blurring the boundaries between these poles.

I approach these plays which epitomize conceptions of alterity through another text, Samuel Purchas's account of India. Purchas's vivid description of the great Mogoll in India, narrated through the voice of Captain William Hawkins, epitomizes Renaissance England's vision of alterity as simultaneously horrible and fascinating. And yet this distant world of horrid excesses seems little different in texture and flavour from the England formulated for us by native writers such as John Stow or foreign travellers such as Thomas Platter. Purchas invites us to regard Indian court customs as horrific but presents Western habits only thinly disguised within an appropriately exotic setting: the sentence passed on guilty criminals, for example, presents a modified version of the custom of drawing and quartering quite familiar to English crowds: 'hee [the king] delighteth to see men executed himselfe, and torne in peeces with Elephants' (Purchas 1905 p.38). The ceremonies that accompany punitive procedures also resemble English customs, though Purchas intensifies his account by multiplying numbers. Traditionally a single hangman witnessed court trials in England and by positioning his axe with the blade facing outward after a guilty verdict, he symbolically reiterated the ominous nature of the sentence passed on the prisoner. Platter records this practice in an account of his travels in England: 'We then proceeded to the lieutenant's apartments where we saw the axe which is carried before the judge at a trial: if he pronounces death sentence the axe blade is turned toward the malefactor, if the latter is not guilty or is set free, the blade is turned away from the malefactor' (Platter 1937 p.163). In Purchas's India the legal procedure exaggerates and grotesquely parodies its English counterpart:

> In the middest of the place, right before the King, standeth one of his Sheriffes, together with his Master Hangman, who is accompanied with forty hangmen, wearing on their heads a certain quilted cap different from all others, with a Hatchet on their

shoulders; and others with all sorts of Whips being there, ready to do what the King commandeth.

(Purchas 1905 pp.45–46)

This carnivalesque world of exaggerated excesses differs only in degree from English spectacles of monarchical authority enacted in the Renaissance courts. Purchas's description of the exotic, initially presented as a diversionary tactic intended to provoke curiosity in 'Otherness', instead emerges as a camouflage for the self-indulgent reiteration of familiar routines.

But I do not want to suggest merely that Purchas's India presents a version of England already familiar to its readers; more importantly, Purchas's vividly brutal exposition of Mogul practices as intrinsically violent and horrible exploits his reader's interest in the excesses associated with Otherness (in what one critic describes as 'emblems of exoticism' which typify characterizations of the Other) even as it undermines his/her reliance on spectacles of excess for entertainment (Khare 1992 p.1). I am especially interested in the myth of the Other as more violent and horrible than the Self that texts such as Purchas's initially exploit and then completely deconstruct. Purchas's text typifies a *modus operandi* that characterizes Renaissance depictions of alterity; Shakespeare's early Elizabethan tragedy, *Titus Andronicus*, written some years before Purchas's text, presents a dramatic version of the same.[2]

Though there is considerable speculation about the dating of *Titus Andronicus*, Jonson's claim in his 'Induction' to *Bartholomew Fair* (1614), 'Hee that will sweare, *Ieronimo* or *Andronicus* are the best playes, yet, shall passe vnexpected at, heere, as a man whose iudgement shews it is constant, and hath stood still, these five and twentie, or thirtie yeeres', suggests that it may belong to the same period as *The Spanish Tragedy*, the reference to Ieronimo being generally understood to refer to the revenger in Kyd's play (Jonson 1960 p.11). Certainly in its reliance on the spectacle of death, it resembles Kyd's play though it accentuates the dismembered body to a greater degree. It also exploits the value of death and dismemberment as entertainment even as it undermines the efficacy of physical public punishment.

As in the case of Kyd's play, *Titus* has been seen traditionally as a strictly academic exercise in Senecan drama by an immature playwright. E. M. W. Tillyard voices this view as does Muriel Bradbrook who notes that '*Titus Andronicus* is a Senecan exercise; the horrors are all classical and quite unfelt, so that the violent tragedy is contradicted by the decorous imagery. The tone is cool and cultured in its effect' (Tillyard 1944 pp.137–138; Bradbrook 1935 pp.98–99). Critical opinion since Tillyard and Bradbrook has continued to corroborate this stand, though the play has received considerable critical attention in recent years.[3] A remark made by Dover Wilson, however, suggests at least a recognition that it is not merely a Senecan exercise and that Shakespeare may have been drawing equally on the spectacle of death visible daily in and around London through events such as hangings and executions; Wilson insists that the play is 'like some broken-down cart, laden with bleeding corpses from an Elizabethan scaffold, and driven by an executioner from Bedlam dressed in cap and bells' (quoted in Maxwell 1968 p.xxxiv). His remark captures with vivid accuracy the effect of the play and its roots in carnivalesque public punishment, a version of which Nashe exploits with equal dexterity in his *Unfortunate Traveller* and which Kyd demonstrates with brilliant effect in Pedringano's hanging and the concluding play-within-the-play.[4] Despite critical dismissal of the amateurish status of the play, *Titus* seems to have enjoyed considerable theatrical success in the Renaissance; its popularity, like that of *The Spanish Tragedy*, may be attributed to the author's ingenious transference of the spectacle of death and dismemberment from Tyburn and other such precincts to the theatrical arena. As in most Renaissance depictions of alien customs, though the play proposes to present activities in decadent Rome, Roman mores remain recognizably English. And as in Purchas's account of distant India, though initially drawn into a complacent vision of excesses authorized and sanctioned by corrupt and ineffective rulers, we ultimately confront a horrific world with punitive practices not unlike those held at Tyburn or Tower Hill. *Titus*, in short, epitomizes Renaissance conceptions of alterity as simultaneously horrific and attractive, alien and familiar.

Titus thus stages a metacritique of itself by simultaneously enacting violent excesses and at the same time undermining its audience's reliance on these for entertainment; as in Purchas's account, a crucial element that contributes to this undermining of our complacency is our clear recognition of the play's horrors as excessive and over-indulgent. Shakespeare's critique of Elizabethan punitive practices, defamiliarized by the veneer of exaggeration and overindulgence, provide a typical instance of dramatic self-reflexion and self-evaluation evident also in other Renaissance histories of decadent Rome such as Jonson's *Sejanus* and Massinger's *The Virgin Martyr*.[5]

However, the Self does not completely subsume the Other in these depictions; on the contrary, these texts purporting to transcribe Roman experiences can be seen as the site for a 'reciprocal representation' of Self and Other. To recognize this element of reciprocity in these texts is not to deny that they privilege the dominant discourses of Renaissance England, for Shakespeare's tragedy also provides a vivid illustration of R. S. Khare's caution about studying 'Otherness': 'to recognize the Other . . . is also to examine the unresolved issues of one's own self-identity, especially as we privilege self via different critical accounts. . . . But such privileging processes have a cost: they increase ethnocentrism, alienate the Other, and produce "a crisis of representation" ' (Khare 1992 pp.1–2). *Titus*, like many Renaissance plays set in other lands such as Spain and Italy, might be described as producing such an effect, for despite the play's attempted erasure of differences, Lucius's Rome continues to assert its ethnic superiority over Goths and Moors. *Titus* begins by asserting polarities, proceeds to undermine them by collapsing boundaries that separated Self from Other and yet concludes with an attempted reiteration of those very polarities that had proved so fragile. Thus in the concluding scene, despite Lucius's new alliance with the Goths, the new Emperor speaks with the voice of the old as he orders the concluding funeral arrangements: Saturninus, despite his passive complicity in the play's central actions, receives a royal burial and internment in the grave of his ancestors; Tamora despite her royal status will feed vultures; Aaron whose villainy remains inextricably linked to his status as a Moor is reserved for a more torturous punishment.[6] As Khare insists, 'Some cultures may actually so formulate their ideal and philosophical positions on the Self–Other dichotomy that they are able to (consciously or unconsciously) "decenter" (but neither neutralize nor remove) the politics of privilege' (Khare 1992 p.2). Precisely such a decentring of punitive cultural practices occurs in *Titus*, for the play closes with an elision of categories initially established as polar opposites but central characters such as the newly crowned Lucius continue to rely, especially in their exercise of punitive authority, on the Self–Other dichotomy in order to legitimize their power and control. One might even argue that the 'politics of privilege' reasserted by Lucius at the end of the play receives greater reinforcement through this process of decentring. The play's pattern of asserting differences in order to undermine and then reassert them with greater vengeance may indicate a fundamental aspect of Renaissance depictions of alterity and the experience of theatre-goers in Renaissance England as they subsidized productions whose success rested on an exploration of the Self–Other dichotomy. The play begins by reiterating the dominant discourses of triumphant Rome, presented as a sharp contrast to barbaric Scythia, but by the final scene barbaric Goths have invaded Rome and placed the exiled Lucius on the throne. The carefully constructed polarities between Self and Other have been effectively erased and rendered worthless.

Inevitably therefore, these categories of Self and Other continually compromise and realign themselves in the course of *Titus* and we move through the play's invocation of horror as if through a series of frames of gathering intensity: from the world of Romans such as Titus and Marcus who at least partially share the world-view of Renaissance England with its concerns with patriarchal and monarchical hierarchies, to the captured Goth Tamora who subverts these hierarchies from the very start, to Aaron the complete outsider recognized and categorized as such by characters within the play and the audience without. And yet precisely at the moment at which we encounter the full horror of Aaron's evil presented through Lucius as a hallmark of his outsideness (during the last stages of the play as he mounts the scaffold and reiterates his commitment to evil), we also see him as a typical figure of the Renaissance scaffold, one of several criminals celebrated in popular ballads and broadsheets as they defied authorities through their braving speeches and bold demeanour during their last moments. The most Otherly of the play's characters thus becomes, at the very moment at which he celebrates his Otherness publicly, quite clearly a version of the Self; a similar movement occurs in Purchas's account where the Mogul emperor's strategies for consolidating power seem finally indistinguishable from Tudor and Stuart political strategies. Indeed the popularity of Purchas's text and Shakespeare's early tragedy might be attributed to the authors' ability first to defamiliarize and thus to reintimate their audience with the horrors of Renaissance social practices, to exploit and then undermine their audience's reliance on spectacles of horror for entertainment. My reading focuses on the reciprocal representation of Selfhood and Otherness in *Titus*, especially as it manifests itself in depictions of punitive violence.

But unlike *The Spanish Tragedy* which presents quick and sudden deaths, *Titus* lingers on the spectacle of death as slow and torturous. Shakespeare's Roman world, like Purchas's India, emphasizes the attraction of torture rather than death as entertainment.[7] Though torture was never legally recognized by the common law in England, it was nevertheless, as George Ryley Scott points out, used frequently and justified under the name of discipline and punishment (G. R. Scott 1940 p.86). Interestingly 'judicial torture reached its greatest ecumenity in the reign of Elizabeth', as Scott documents, and this perhaps explains Shakespeare's reliance on the spectacle of torture in this Elizabethan tragedy and his later departure from it to an exploration of torture in plays such as *Macbeth* and *King Lear* (G. R. Scott 1940 p.89).[8] But *Titus* more than any other of Shakespeare's plays dwells on the spectacle of dismemberment and mutilation. The play's particular concern with mutilation and Shakespeare's later departure into explorations of pain may have much to do with popular Tudor practices and evolving changes in popular attitudes. Pieter Spierenburg points out that mutilation, common among the Tudors became less popular in the course of the seventeenth century, the early Stuart period even registering what he describes as an increasing revulsion against mutilation (Spierenburg 1984 p.77). Scott also draws attention to the fact that officially judicial torture ended in England in 1640 and in Scotland by Act of Parliament in 1708 (G. R. Scott 1940 p.136). It is reasonable to assume that in the late Elizabethan and early Stuart periods new attitudes towards the use of torture as punishment and discipline were emerging, though these changes reached the legal books only in 1640. In Shakespeare's clear association of villainy with sadistic pleasure in prolonged punishment, we might discern a record of this growing scepticism about the value of torture as discipline or punishment.

Titus opens with the spectacle of multiple deaths, Titus's arrival in Rome with the bodies of his twenty sons killed in battle. Titus's ceremonious speech emphasizes the ritual of death as a combination of public mourning and celebration, in this case because these deaths occurred as a result of encounters between Roman conquerors and barbarous Goths. Every subsequent death or violence in the play occurs as a byproduct of public ceremony and celebration. Alarbus's burning, conducted by Lucius to appease the common people as much as the gods, provides ritual public revenge, Bassianus's death occurs during the course of a ceremoniously conducted royal hunt and the multiple deaths of the concluding scene occur in the midst of a royal feast.

From the very start, the play dramatizes the ironies that typified public punitive measures. Alarbus's burning, a public ritual of celebration to the Romans, is presented through Roman eyes as a moderate and necessary response to the losses suffered by the Andronici; this attitude is effectively compromised by the presence of Tamora and the Goths, the Others in this scene, though Tamora's initial pleas for her son's life emphasize her similarity with the Romans as a parent: 'Stay, Roman brethren! Gracious conqueror, / Victorious Titus, rue the tears I shed, / A mother's tears in passion for her son: / And, if thy sons were ever dear to thee, / O, think my son to be as dear to me' (I, i, ll.104–108). In a reciprocal representation of alterity, the play dramatizes the irony and falseness of the Self–Other binary most vividly in this opening scene as Tamora and her sons, seen by the Romans as barbaric and violent, in turn decry the Roman spectacle of retaliation and vengeance as primitive and inhuman. To Titus's summary claim that religious rites demand a sacrifice, Tamora responds 'O cruel, irreligious piety!' and her son adds 'Was never Scythia so barbarous!' (I, i, ll.130–131). Thus from the very start, the play dramatizes the ironies that typified public punitive practices and this opening scene which began by reiterating the polarity between Self and Other, Roman and Goth, moves swiftly through a series of events that emphasize instead the slippery margins between these axes: Titus, after bemoaning the loss of his sons at the hands of the Goths, kills Mutius in a fit of passion; Tamora's role shifts abruptly from enemy and prisoner to Empress of Rome; the Andronici, hailed as Roman heroes, are shortly after condemned as traitors. If one of the central elements in the Self–Other dichotomy remains the Self's desire to convert and civilize the Other, Tamora's absorption into the Roman system through marriage to Saturninus and her subsequent concentration on emulating the Roman example of vengeance and retribution effectively deconstruct these binaries yet again.

Alarbus's death and mutilation may be seen to inaugurate this deconstruction in a variety of ways. Foucault illustrates that the ceremony of public punishment in early modern Europe enacted the terror of monarchical authority; 'the public execution,' he argues, 'is to be understood not only as a judicial, but also as a political ritual. It belongs, even in minor cases, to the ceremonies by which power is manifested' (Foucault 1979 p.49). J. A. Sharpe makes a similar point about executions in England: 'Every public execution was . . . a spectacular reminder of the powers of state, doubly effective because of its essentially local nature' (Sharpe 1983 p.142). Equally frequently, as we have seen, it remained open to manipulation by the condemned (Foucault 1979 p.61). The deaths in *Titus* invariably expose the inefficacy of law and monarchical authority rather than its omniscience and accuracy. Alarbus's burning, for example, takes place in a 'headless' Rome where combatants are still arguing about succession to the emperorship. In its enactment as a vacuous ritual, performed by the Andronici themselves before the issue of succession to the throne has been decided, Alarbus's death and mutilation graphically illustrate the nature of all subsequent deaths in the play as enactments of private revenge conducted without royal or legal approval.

Public death, in other words, becomes in *Titus* not an illustration of monarchical power but an exposition of its hollowness. In the two instances where the Emperor Saturninus orders such deaths, his sentences constitute gross miscarriages of justice; the innocent boy bearing Titus's letter is ordered by Saturninus to be hanged for his role as messenger in the employ of his enemy, and Titus's two sons, wrongly accused of murdering Bassianus, are beheaded on false evidence carefully manufactured by Tamora and Aaron. The death of the Clown provides a grotesque parody of public punishment not unlike that enacted by Kyd in his depiction of Pedringano's death though, unlike Pedringano, the Clown is entirely innocent and simply carries out orders for a fee from Titus. His summary disposal by the Emperor and his inability to understand the sentence of death passed on him – 'How much money must I have?' he asks in response to the death sentence – emphasize Saturninus's inefficacy as emperor. The Clown's death, a marginal event in comparison to other rituals of public death in *Titus*, nevertheless carries the same general import as the mutilation of Alarbus; it reiterates the hollowness of Roman authority as manifested through the figure of the Emperor.[9] A similar atmosphere of grotesque parody pervades Titus's desperate attempts to free his sons by sacrificing his hand to Aaron. Like the boy in Kyd's play who enjoys the 'merry jest' as he watches Pedringano go to his death, Aaron derives infinite glee from tricking Titus; as he admits later, he could scarcely contain his laughter at Titus's angry realization on receiving his sons's heads after the execution that he has been duped by Aaron. Through incidents such as these, Shakespeare like Kyd, exploits the value of death and dismemberment as entertainment to his Elizabethan audience.

The play's emphasis on mutilation, especially in the form of execution, is symbolically reiterated throughout by the image of Rome itself as dismembered and headless. Marcus invites Titus to ascend the throne in the opening scene by depicting the crisis in these terms: 'Be *candidatus* then, and put it [the crown] on, / And help to set a head on headless Rome' (I, i, ll.185–186). Despite the early resolution of this crisis through the crowning of Saturninus, however, the image persists throughout the play. Saturninus's very first act as monarch emphasizes his weakness; when Tamora insists that the Andronici need to be publicly forgiven, Saturninus gives in immediately despite his natural inclinations to the contrary. In fact it is Tamora who addresses the audience with a politic speech of diplomacy and stratagem, now speaking as a full-fledged Roman: 'Titus, I am incorporate in Rome, / A Roman now adopted happily, / And must advise the Emperor for his good' (I, i, ll.462–464). The scene which began so ceremoniously with assertions about patriarchy and male jostling for power, ends ironically with Tamora (the Other in terms of race and gender) determining the course of events.

The image of Rome as headless even dominates the concluding scene, thus presenting the ominous possibility that tragedies will continue and that Lucius's crowning simply presents a superficial solution similar to Saturninus's at the beginning of the play. As Lucius ascends the throne we are reminded constantly of the extent to which actions in this last scene duplicate events in the opening scene. The 'common voice' hails Lucius as emperor even as it had done Titus in the opening scene; Marcus again appears as a spokesperson for the commoners in their choice; and Lucius's return to Rome as a successful warrior repeats Titus's similar entry earlier. Even as we perceived Saturninus as an inappropriate choice because of his feud with his brother and his first act of revenge once in power manifested by his choice of Lavinia for wife, we are reminded of Lucius's role as revenger in the opening scene. It was he who first initiated revenge against Tamora by demanding a sacrificial prisoner from the Goths to appease the spirits of the slain Andronici. In that scene he also orchestrates the sacrifice of Alarbus and returns with tokens of his deed to revel in Tamora's humiliation as he announces its successful operation with vivid detail: 'See, lord and father, how we have perform'd / Our Roman rites: Alarbus' limbs are lopp'd, / And entrails feed the sacrificing fire, / Whose smoke like incense doth perfume the sky' (I, i, ll.141–145). Thus his election to the emperorship remains suspect because of his complicity in central tragedies of the play; he might be regarded as the author of all vengeful acts, for he sets the precedent and presents revenge as an acceptable mode of behaviour against abuses to oneself or one's kin.

The irony of Rome's headlessness at the end of the play is further underscored by the presence of powerful outsiders, the Goths who have helped to place Lucius on the throne and the talking head of Aaron, the only part of his body visible to the public, still mocking the Andronici for their vulnerability to his schemes and boasting about his successes against them. Lucius orders Aaron's punishment as a spectacle of royal power and authority: 'Set him breast-deep in earth and famish him; / There let him stand and rave and cry for food. / If any one relieves him or pities him, / For the offense he dies. This is our doom' (V, iii, ll.179–182). But Lucius underestimates Aaron's intelligence, assuming that his utterances while thus immersed under earth will consist of pleas to be fed, freed or pitied. Aaron's response to his punishment undermines Lucius's naive assumption: 'Ah, why should wrath be mute, and fury dumb? / I am no baby, I, that with base prayers / I should repent the evils I have done' (V, iii, ll.184–186).

Lucius's experiences with Aaron thus far should have enabled him to expect such a response. The play presented a parallel situation earlier when Aaron's reaction to Lucius as he faced imminent death consisted not of desperate pleas for life, but clever manipulation of Lucius's mind. On encountering Aaron with his bastard child, Lucius while on his way to Rome determines to hang him and the infant immediately. He orders the ladder to be brought and the audience is promised an on-stage hanging quite in the manner of Kyd's tragedy: 'First hang the child, that he may see it sprawl – / A sight to vex the father's soul withal' (V, i, ll.50–51). Indeed, the ladder is brought on-stage and Aaron even ascends the ladder, though he soon manages to reduce the sentence passed on him by promising to 'show thee [Lucius] wondrous things / That highly may advantage thee to hear'. In a gradual reversal of roles, it is Lucius who bargains with the victim, promising to nourish and bring up Aaron's child in exchange for details of villainies at court. Aaron's eagerness to talk about his misdeeds reveals his primary goal hereafter in the play, namely, to inflict psychological torment on his hearers by recounting their vulnerability to his villainies. He revels in this power as he turns Lucius's own words against him: 'why, assure thee, Lucius, / 'Twill vex thy soul to hear what I shall speak' (V, i, ll.61–62). Aaron waxes so eloquent and expresses such a lack of contrition for his misdeeds that Lucius finds himself commuting the sentence even further and ordering that Aaron be retained for torture rather than be allowed so easy and 'sweet a death as hanging'

(V, i, l.146). Aaron's response to the sentence is revealing for it suggests that Lucius has simply acceded to his victim's priorities; Aaron would like to live so that he might torment the Andronici with reminders of his villainies against them: 'If there be devils, would I were a devil, / To live and burn in everlasting fire, / So I might have your company in hell, / But to torment you with my bitter tongue!' (V, i, ll.147–150). Lucius's recognition of Aaron's power to use language as a means of psychological torment is immediately apparent in his response: 'Sirs, stop his mouth, and let him speak no more' (V, i, l.151); Lucius's attitude here might be compared with Cutwolf's similar response to Esdras as he shoots to silence his victim. But Aaron's ascendancy has been effectively demonstrated by his manipulation of Lucius's authority. The scene testifies to the fact that a change which Karin Coddon traces to the early seventeenth century was already emerging in the late sixteenth; arguing a similar point about the inefficacy of executions in *Macbeth*, she notes that 'In seventeenth-century England, the spectacle of punishment was clearly becoming as equivocal as the "fiendish" nature of its treasonous objects, a demonstration of sovereignty's impotence as well as power' (Coddon 1989 pp.499–500). And if, as Douglas Hay argues, the death sentence was 'the climactic emotional point of the criminal law – the moment of terror around which the system revolved', the initiative for enacting terror has transferred at least partially in this instance from Lucius to Aaron, from an agent of justice to his victim who, despite being captured red-handed, has managed to contrive a temporary reprieve (Hay 1975 p.28). The survival of Aaron's baby further accentuates the Self–Other dichotomy, for it foregrounds the primacy of familial bonds to Aaron, a sharp contrast to the violence against kin that Romans have enacted for us in scene after scene, starting with Titus's killing of Mutius and concluding with his killing of Lavinia. Aaron's natural cunning in ensuring the survival of his line thus separates him from the Romans and adds to our perception of him as simultaneously horrific and fascinating.

In this remarkable scene where Aaron climbs the ladder, we encounter the format of a typical Elizabethan hanging, including the eloquent and unlimited speech by the victim on the scaffold. Spierenburg describes the scaffold speech as a particularly English custom: 'From Tudor times on the authorities actively encouraged the condemned to address himself to the public with a moralistic story, explaining how he had sinned and deserved his punishment' (Spierenburg 1984 p.63). However, though such speeches were intended to present a repentant criminal reiterating the power of law, this was not always the case. Spierenburg cites travellers such as Balthazar Becker who 'on a visit to England, had noted the custom with surprise. The convict resembled a minister on the pulpit, Becker wrote, were it not for the rope around his neck' (Spierenburg 1984 p.63). The speech delivered on the scaffold by the victim provided an especially suitable opportunity for manipulation and defiance; intended to reinforce the power of justice, it frequently questioned rather than emphasized legal efficacy. Certainly Aaron's vaunting speech on the scaffold may be regarded as typical of numerous such defiant ones recorded in broadsheets and ballads detailing Renaissance scaffold proceedings. As in many such situations, Aaron refuses to cooperate

with the authorities by expressing apt contrition but rather subverts the authority
of those who accuse him by revelling in his misdeeds:

> Even now I curse the day, and yet, I think,
> Few come within the compass of my curse,
> Wherein I did not some notorious ill:
> As kill a man, or else devise his death;
> Ravish a maid, or plot the way to do it;
> Accuse some innocent, and forswear myself;
> . . .
> But I have done a thousand dreadful things
> As willingly as one would kill a fly,
> And nothing grieves me heartily indeed
> But that I cannot do a thousand more.
>
> (V, i, ll.125–144)

In fact the speech presents dramatic argument for curtailing victims's rights on
the scaffold, a view expressed by John Chamberlain and cited earlier (Birch 1849
p.215).

Interestingly Aaron's punishment, which constitutes a form of public imprisonment and torture, presents an obverse rather than equivalent condition to that
reserved for the worst criminals in Elizabethan England. In Newgate, the most
notorious of the London prisons, for example, the worst offenders suffered
isolation; Father Garnet, the Jesuit priest imprisoned there on suspicion of
treason, describes the punishment in one of his letters: 'Newgate is the worst
of the twelve prisons in London and Limbo is the worst place in it, being
underground and without any breathing hole to admit air or light, and that is
reserved for the worst malefactors' (Father Gerard 1898 p.41). Aaron, by contrast, suffers a very public humiliation and imprisonment, a sentence which,
though intended as prolonged torture, instead provides him with yet another
opportunity to use his considerable talent for persuasion. Elaine Scarry defines
torture as 'the invariable and simultaneous occurrence of three phenomena
which, if isolated, would occur in the following order. First, pain is inflicted on
a person in ever-intensifying ways. Second, the pain, continually amplified
through the person's body, is also amplified in the sense that is objectified, made
visible to those outside the person's body. Third, the objectified pain is denied as
pain and read as power' (Scarry 1985 p.28). In Aaron's extended imprisonment,
intended by Lucius as a deterrent and negative example, *Titus* both enacts torture
as this three-fold phenomenon and deconstructs its validity as an enactment of
power. But Lucius's perception that a sentence on Aaron needs to be augmented
by an equally ferocious sentence against any who might come to Aaron's aid
hints at the Emperor's misgivings in choosing torment over hanging, contrary to
his natural inclination. Aaron's own preference for a punishment whereby he
retains his ability to rail at the Andronici adds an ironic dimension to Lucius's
sentence. Though the concluding scene demonstrates the Andronici's victory over
Aaron, it also deconstructs the validity of Lucius's sentence as a decisive enactment of power.

The image of Aaron as a talking head left to torment Lucius and the Roman public in general by reminding them of his past victories over the Andronici even dominates our final impression of the play. Rome continues to remain dismembered, headless because of its ineffective emperor and tormented by an articulate head constantly reminding her of the tragedies that an outsider had managed to inflict upon its leading citizens. Thus Aaron at least partially subverts the intention of the authorities as they make a spectacle of his torment; he even becomes a version of the numerous heads on poles that greeted visitors to London and whose subversive effects Platter records in a description of his visit. Bemused irony marks Platter's recognition of the inherent subversive potential in such public displays of authority:

> At the top of one tower almost in the centre of the bridge, were stuck on tall stakes more than thirty skulls of noble men who had been executed and beheaded for treason and for other reasons. And their descendants are accustomed to boast of this, themselves even pointing out to one of their ancestors' heads on this same bridge, believing that they will be esteemed the more because their antecedents were of such high descent that they could even covet the crown, but being too weak to attain it were executed for rebels; thus they make an honor for themselves of what was set up to be a disgrace and an example.
>
> (Platter 1937 p.155)

The complementary image of Rome's headlessness and Aaron's talking head further deconstructs the Self–Other dichotomy which opened the play, for in the end noble Rome and the barbaric Moor retain their identities as polar opposites and yet remain functionally (dysfunctionally may be more appropriate in this context) similar because of their incomplete nature. Aaron, mocking and still gleeful about his successes, reiterates the extent to which images of disjuncture and dismemberment pervade the play; his mockery dominates our final impressions. Gillian Murray Kendall, who sees in the play's conclusion a failed attempt at the traditional ordering of state typical in Shakespeare's tragedies, makes a crucial point when she insists that the play ends 'with a focus on Aaron that leaves him forever awaiting his punishment, forever speaking, the state forever fragmented. . . . The violence in *Titus Andronicus* promises never to cease' (Kendall 1989 p.316). If as Foucault insists, public punishment 'did not re-establish justice; it reactivated power', Lucius's show of authority constitutes a failed attempt at reactivating power, for the concluding vision of Aaron's talking head reiterates the inadequacy of his punishment and the potential dangers that face Lucius who has effected only a temporary peace.

In this sense the silenced and mutilated Lavinia, a figure who retains much of our attention despite her silence, best represents the plight of Rome.[10] In her inarticulate vocality, Lavinia visibly illustrates a connection between language and violence that Elaine Scarry underscores and which I cited earlier, the reversion of individuals in pain to a state anterior to language (Scarry 1985 p.4). The play's opening battle for the emperorship between Saturninus and Bassianus transforms easily and immediately into feuding for Lavinia's hand, and her fate seems from the very beginning to be intricately connected with that of Rome. As a body ravished and mutilated by the outsiders, Demetrius and Chiron, her plight captures in miniature the enslavement and degradation of Rome, though Romans, Goths and the Moor are implicated in her tragedy. As an emblem for Rome itself, she even embodies the conundrum of the Self–Other dichotomy through her plight as a commodity of considerable value ('that changing piece' as Saturninus categorizes her) transferred by Titus to Saturninus, subsequently snatched by Bassianus, Demetrius and Chiron in succession, and then left to wander in the woods until picked up by Marcus and returned to her father. But by now she is almost unrecognizable and Marcus's words as he presents her to Titus – 'This was thy daughter' – emphasize her transformation and alienation most vividly. It might be argued that by the end of the play Rome, now hospitable to the Goths and its royal family eliminated, has similarly lost its identity. Thus Titus's wanton erasure of his daughter in the final scene reiterates the inadequacy of the apparent restitution ceremoniously proclaimed by Lucius's ascension, an ascension which simply re-enacts the hollowness of monarchical authority demonstrated in detail by Saturninus in the course of the play.

The play's focus on monarchical power and succession perhaps underscores a central concern in Elizabethan England in the 1590s governed by a virgin queen with no heir. In this sense Bruce Boehrer's claim about *Hamlet* must extend equally to *Titus*: '*Hamlet* enacts the promised end of Tudor imperial culture: an end feared and contemplated by the English monarchs and subjects at least since Henry VIII divorced Catherine of Aragon, and an end that was by 1599 almost inevitable' (Boehrer 1992 p.77). The jostling for power which begins the play perhaps even mimics similar plots and controversies in the England of the early and mid-1580s, a relative security being reached only after Elizabeth's reluctant execution of Mary Queen of Scots after nineteen years of imprisonment on English soil. Tamora, a name that does not exist in Shakespeare's source, may even be a deliberate attempt on the author's part to anagrammatically suggest Mary as an analogue. Like Tamora, Mary occupied a precarious and problematic position as outsider and kin, enemy and potential heir to the throne, and like her fictional counterpart, Mary remained vulnerable to recurring charges of whoredom; rumours even persisted that she had delivered twins during her captivity (Frazer 1971 pp.533–538). In Tamora Shakespeare perhaps personifies the challenge that the crown faced for nineteen years by the unsolicited presence of a neighbouring queen who was not wanted by her countrymen but whose witch-like charms were reputed to seduce many men into supporting her. Tamora, like Mary, is ultimately outwitted by counterplanned wiles and scheming.[11] This political analogy, like the mythical ones that permeate the text of *Titus* (Tereus–Philomel, Phaedra–Hipolytus, and Atreus–Thyestes, for example), also stresses the Self–Other dichotomy and the invariable elision of these categories that marked Renaissance political manoeuvring.

This ellipsis of categories is symbolically and literally reiterated in the play by the survival of Aaron's baby whose multiple ethnic status as Roman, Goth and Moor and dual social status as royalty and slave, suggests the danger of his presence; Lucius, having promised to 'save, nourish, and bring him up', presumably intends to keep his promise. Marcus even makes a spectacle of the baby, presenting him to the public as proof of misdoings at court: 'Behold the child; / Of this was Tamora delivered, / The issue of an irreligious Moor, / Chief architect and plotter of these woes' (V, iii, ll.119–122). His 'tawny' presence further undermines the play's restitution of order and the Roman state's ability to define it. Derek Cohen argues that the baby's male gender remains crucial, for 'he is invested with the chief value of males in patriarchal social groups' (D. Cohen 1992 p.90). The play seems to imply that such gendered power will inevitably provide another instance of the connections between patriarchy and violence enacted so vividly in scene after scene. But as Cohen also demonstrates, Aaron's progeny remains curiously allied to female vulnerability, for it provides a 'kind of symbolic counterpart to Lavinia; innocent like her, it becomes a target of violence from the start' (D. Cohen 1992 p.90). The play's collapse of categories thus receives its most vivid demonstration in the final spectacle of Aaron's child held up for public scrutiny by the triumphant Andronici.

Shakespeare's concluding verdict on monarchical power is not unlike Purchas's wry illustration of the illusion of authority demonstrated by the Mogoll emperor, who on being told by an astrologer that his brother's children rather than his own will succeed to power, forcibly converts his nephews to Christianity so that they might be hated and rejected by their countrymen. Political security seems to depend on a separation of Self from Others and on a clear demarcation of the zone between. And yet, as Purchas's text suggests, Self and other constitute slippery poles and the Mogul emperor's act ensures that his sons will be displaced by their cousins for 'God is omnipotent, and can turne the making of these Christians unto a good ende, if it be his pleasure' (Purchas 1905 p.47). The political strategies that underlie the Mogul Emperor's religious choices simply rehearse Renaissance monarchical practices already familiar to its audiences. John Hayward, we might recall, records the change in faith that occurred at Elizabeth's ascension with a wry awareness of the political expediency that necessitated it (Bruce 1840 p.5). Elizabeth's religious preference is as much a calculated political move as the Mogoll emperor's and as much a strategy for defining Self and Otherness. Mary's embrace of Catholicism makes her the political Other quite distanced from the will of her father and Elizabeth's continuation of her father's intentions raises her to the stature of a true heir. Like Purchas, Hayward seems acutely aware of the protean nature of the Self–Other dichotomy, ever subject to change, substitution and absorption. While political security in Titus's Rome, Purchas's India, and Elizabeth's England seems to have depended on a clear separation of Self from Other, this separation seems also to have become increasingly hard to maintain.

In the social realm, victims on the scaffold encapsulate this crisis of definition equally vividly. Intended by authorities as clear examples of 'Otherness', a threat to social well-being and order, they frequently became figures of interest to the popular imagination and were celebrated in print and sometimes even heralded as heroes on the scaffold. Texts such as *Titus*, through their focus on the issue of political security and their fascination with the representation of public punitive practices, record the threat that this process of self-definition increasingly faced in Renaissance England; Shakespeare's early experiment in Roman tragedy provides a metacritique of the process of self-definition as inevitably elusive and inadequate.[12]

In Gregory Bateson's terms, the play's concerted undermining of the efficacy of punishment, a quality it shares with *The Spanish Tragedy*, places it within the category of works which pose the question 'Is this play?' rather than assert the statement 'This is play'. As we have seen, Shakespeare returns to this issue with greater efficacy in his later tragedy, *Macbeth*, but Jonson's rather different treatment of the issues of monarchical power and public punishment in his Roman tragedy, *Sejanus*, may be worth some notice.

Sejanus even presents itself as a lesson for traitors; the 'Argument' prefaced to the play concludes by insisting on this moral purpose:

> This we do advance as a mark of terror to all traitors, and treasons; to show how just the heavens are in pouring and thundering down a mighty vengeance on their unnatural intents, even to worst princes: much more to those, for guard of whose piety and virtue, the angels are in continual watch, and God himself miraculously working.
>
> (Jonson 1966 p.8)

In other words, Jonson's text presents a version of scaffold proceedings intending by the terror of their example to deter onlookers from imitating treacherous behaviour. Our anticipation of viewing enacted punishments is reiterated by the characters who open the play, Sabinus and Silius, honest onlookers contemptuous of court flattery and deceit and longing to see Sejanus justly punished for his arrogant appropriation of the Emperor's powers. Silius condemns Sejanus's agents in violent language that matches similar condemnations of their enemies by characters throughout the play: 'there be two, / . . . whose close breasts / Were they ripped up to lightly, it would be found / A poor and idle sin, to which their trunks / Had not made fit organs' (I, i, ll.24–28). Arruntius, who shares their desire and suspects Sejanus of plotting the deaths of the royal family, even envisions himself as a potential hangman wreaking vengeance:

> By the gods,
> If I could guess he had but such a thought,
> My sword would cleave him down from head to heart,
> But I would find it out: and with my hand
> I'd hurl his panting brain about the air,
> In mites, as small as atomi, to undo
> The knotted bed –
>
> (I, i, ll.252–258)

This desire to see punishment enacted on traitors is expressed by various characters and permeates the play. Drusus, for example, desires to see Sejanus's body publicly abused and punished, a desire for which he pays the price shortly after: 'I'll advance a statue / Of your own bulk; but 't shall be on the cross: / Where I will nail your pride, at breadth and length, / And crack those sinews, which are yet but stretched / With your swoll'n fortune's rage' (I, i, ll.570–574). And Nero's similar desire to punish Satrius and Natta who spy on Agrippina, "Twere best rip forth their tongues, sear out their eyes, / When next they come', meets with Sosia's immediate approval (II, iii, ll.477–479). A desire to see brutal punishments enacted on others permeates the play and characters reiterate this desire again and again.

Sejanus concerns itself with topical issues in the England of the early seventeenth century. Like Shakespeare's Roman tragedy, the play is obsessed with the issue of succession which would have been a pressing concern in England in 1603. The play's particular interest in reiterating monarchical power even when absent may even have its roots in England's own plight during the last years of Elizabeth's reign, when the ailing queen continued to maintain an enigmatic silence on the issue of succession. Treason looms large on every one's mind, a result perhaps of Jonson's own encounter with the law and narrow escape from prosecution for satiric attacks on influential persons in *Poetaster* only a few years earlier. Indeed a cynical view of treason permeates the play; as the unfortunate Silius notes early 'Our looks are called to question and our words, / How innocent soever, are made crimes; / We shall not shortly tell our dreams, / Or think, but 'twill be treason' (I, i, ll.67–69). By the end, as character after character is accused of treason and led off to be punished, Arruntius can only exclaim cynically on the sentence: 'The complement of all accusings? that / Will hit, when all else fails' (IV, iv, ll.345–346).

Public vengeance reaches its climax in the vicious dismemberment of Sejanus himself at the hands of infuriated crowds who react with unabated fury immediately after the axe falls. Terentius describes their violence in vivid detail:

> which [Sejanus's head] no sooner off,
> But that, and th' unfortunate trunk were seized
> By the rude multitude; who not content
> With what the forward justice of the State,
> Officiously had done, with violent rage
> Have rent it limb, from limb. A thousand heads,
> A thousand hands, ten thousand tongues, and voices,
> . . .
> These mounting at his head, these at his face,
> These digging out his eyes, those with his brain,
> Sprinkling themselves, their houses, and their friends;
> Others are met, have ravished thence an arm,
> And deal small pieces of the flesh for favours;
> These with a thigh; this hath cut off his hands;
> And this his feet; these fingers and these toes;
> That hath his liver; he his heart: . . .
> What cannot oft be done, is now o'erdone.

> (V, vi, ll.809–831)

Vivid in detail, the passage nevertheless points to a fundamental difference between Shakespeare's Roman text and Jonson's. While *Titus* may be regarded as a concerted effort to demonstrate that the will of the people remains important and even consistent, Jonson depicts the masses as fickle, brutal and uncontrollable. *Titus*, we might remember, highlighted the democratic process with Marcus announcing the will of the people in the opening and concluding scenes. In both cases, the Romans support the Andronici's right to the throne over hereditary claims by Saturninus and Bassianus. We might even argue that tragedy occurs only because Titus thwarts the will of the people by refusing to take the crown in the opening scene. The Roman masses emerge in the course of *Titus* as astute and capable citizens quite different from the fickle crowds in *Sejanus* who blindly proclaim Tiberius's glory as he moves from favourite to favourite. Most striking is their passion for violence demonstrated in their cowardly treatment of Sejanus and his family. Nuntius describes the extent of their frenzy in extending their punishment to innocent members of Sejanus's family:

> A son, and a daughter, to the dead Sejanus,
> . . .
> Have they drawn forth for farther sacrifice;
> . . . And because our laws
> Admit no virgin immature to die,
> The wittily, and strangely cruel Macro,
> Delivered her to be deflowered, and spoiled,
> By the rude lust of the licentious hangman,
> Then, to be strangled with her harmless brother.
>
> (V, vi, ll.842–857)

In *Sejanus* public punishment presents itself as a mockery of authority, its nature and intensity determined entirely by the emotional pitch of hysterical masses who even top the villainies of the criminal in their role as adjudicators of justice. In the scene describing Sejanus's mutilation, the boundaries that separate dangerous criminals from law-abiding citizens who wish to ensure that society is purged of socially disruptive characters dissolve quite completely. Equally striking remains the play's insistence that the violent excesses of the masses simply mirror the excesses of their absent emperor. Tiberius, Arruntius tells us, has retired to Capri to indulge his appetite for deviant sex and torture:

> He hath his slaughter-house in Capreae:
> Where he doth study murder as an art;
> And they are dearest in his grace, that can
> Devise the deepest tortures. Thither, too,
> He has his boys, and beauteous girls ta'en up
> Out of their noblest houses, the best form'd,
> Best nurtured, and most modest; what's their good,
> Serves to provoke his bad. Some are allured,
> Others threaten'd; others, by their friends detained,
> Are ravish'd hence, like captives, and, in sight
> Of their most grieved parents, dealt away
> Upon his spintries, sellaries, and slaves,

> Masters of strange and new commented lusts,
> For which wise nature hath not left a name.

> (IV, v, ll.388–401)

The crowds' decision to see Sejanus's innocent daughter raped by the hangman duplicates Tiberius's similar treatment of the beauteous boys and girls he collects on his island of pleasure. The boundaries between socially ranked individuals and hysterical masses, between legal figures of authority and deviant subjects, dissolve quite completely.

Most importantly, the state's punishment of removing Sejanus from power does little to eliminate treachery and evil from the court. Macro at the end of the play assumes the role played by Sejanus at the beginning and Tiberius remains an absent monarch governing his state by proxy, though he has now substituted a new minion. Arruntius even predicts that Macro's rise and fall will outdo Sejanus's fate: 'I prophesy, out of this State's flattery, / That this new fellow, Macro, will become / A greater prodigy in Rome, than he / That now is fall'n' (V, vi, ll.753–756). The play registers a cyclical pattern that increases in intensity at each turn, thus implying that treason cannot be annihilated, merely arrested for a time. The so-called 'lesson for traitors' thus emerges as an ironic commentary on the inefficiency of judicial systems rather than a reiteration of moral norms.

As we have seen, the message recurs in another play of the period also obsessed with treason and monarchical authority, Shakespeare's equally violent tragedy, *Macbeth*. While exact analogies between the court of Tiberius and that of Elizabeth or James might be hard to draw, the rise and fall of favourites in Elizabethan and early Stuart England must certainly have added topical relevance to the actions of Jonson's play. By refusing to demonstrate that the intent that Tiberius perceives in Cordus's history of Brutus and Caesar is false and by foregrounding Tiberius's suspicion about history writing in general, Jonson even renders suspect his own choice of history as the subject of his tragedy. The 'lesson for traitors' that Jonson dramatizes thus includes critical commentary on the masses who wish to see extreme violence enacted on the bodies of criminals; indeed, the playwright's own narrow escape from the gallows in 1598 with only a branding of his thumb with the letter 'T' for Tyburn renders this dramatic exploration of the subject of public punishment and torment especially interesting.

Massinger's Roman tragedy, *The Virgin Martyr*, delivers an equally complex message on the issue of state authority and public punishment. Set in the nineteenth year of Dioclesian's rule during Rome's final persecution of Christians, Fletcher's tragedy perhaps more than *Titus* or *Sejanus* focuses on the Self–Other dichotomy by opposing Roman violence against Christian suffering. Lotman's ideas about centre and boundary cited earlier may be particularly useful in reading Massinger's persistent engagement with alterity in this tragedy; Lotman notes that 'every culture begins by dividing the world into "its own" internal space and "their" external space. How this binary division is interpreted depends on the typology of the culture' (Lotman 1990 p.131). In *The Virgin Martyr* space is initially divided and defined by the empire along religious, sexual and class lines with the Roman state representing patriarchal authority, masculine power and the machinery of legal sanction. We begin the play at a moment when all of the above face threats of invasion and inversion by Christians who are led by women and whose response to a Roman show of force consists of passive suffering and martyrdom. Lotman argues that 'the stage of self-description is a necessary response to the threat of too much diversity within the semiosphere: the system might lose its unity and definition, and disintegrate' (Lotman 1990 p.128); Massinger's tragedy registers just such a movement, from Rome's conscious self-description in the opening scenes to impending disintegration at the end. Self-description in the opening scenes involves a reassertion of Rome's past glories and a rededication of her allegiance to the ancient gods, policies administered by proxy during Dioclesian's absence by Theophilus and Sapritius; Dioclesian's absence from central actions recalls Tiberius's similar role in *Sejanus* and already implies Rome's impending decline despite the confidence with which the emperor asserts Roman values at the end of the play. His confidence at the end recalls his earlier oblivion to fissures within the state, a stance he adopts to justify his own continued absence from it:

> So: at all parts I find Caesarea
> Completely govern'd; . . .
> The ancient Roman discipline revived,
> Which raised Rome to her greatness, and proclaimed her
> The glorious mistress of the conquer'd world;
> But above all, the service of the gods
> So zealously observed . . .

(I, i, p.4)

Theophilus and Sapritius, figures of authority in the political and domestic realms, face rebellion on both fronts in the course of the tragedy, their declining familial command symbolically heralding their declining political power.

The play's central actions involve the martyrdom of Dorothea which occurs alongside the secondary plot involving the persecution of Callista and Christeta by their father Theophilus. Theophilus's zealous persecution of Christians and his ultimate transformation to Christianity through Dorothea's martyrdom provide the main plot of the play, his transformation from one extreme stand to the other quite obviously suggesting such figures as Saul. *The Virgin Martyr*'s excessive violence matches that of *Titus* and, despite the stand of such eminent editors as Gifford who strains to account for its success, the play's popularity may be similarly attributed to the repeated enaction of spectacles of death and dying. Gifford's charge against the play might, in fact, be levelled against many successful Renaissance tragedies including Shakespeare's; 'with respect to the subject [of *The Virgin Martyr*],' he notes, 'it is undoubtedly ill chosen. Scourge, racking, and beheading, are circumstances of no very agreeable kind; and with the poor aids of which the stage was then possessed, must have been somewhat worse than ridiculous' (Massinger 1860 p.31). Despite poor theatrical aids,

Renaissance audiences patronized these tragedies of cruelty with great regularity, suggesting the possibility that like stagings at Tyburn and Tower Hill their enactments of violence remained far from ridiculous and absurd.

The play's focus on cruelty is further augmented by narrated accounts of gruesome tortures that punctuate the staged violence. Theophilus's ingenious tortures devised for the Christians and described for us by him and by various characters during the early scenes of the play set the stage for later enactments such as the on-stage murders of Callista and Christeta, the execution of Dorothea and punishments inflicted on Theophilus himself after his transformation. The play might be regarded as a series of progressively intense enactments of violence reaching their climax in the last and most violent torture of Theophilus by Dioclesian. The State's determination to continue its persecution of the Christians in the final scene remains muted by the play's emphatic dissolution of boundaries between persecutors and victims, between male figures of authority and female subjects of transgression; this dissolution, registered vividly through five acts of intensifying action, dominates our final impression.

At the beginning of the play, Theophilus's steely heart, capable of ordering violence against his own daughters who have embraced the new faith, has the support of an evil spirit Harpax; in an early paean to Harpax, Theophilus describes his role as persecutor in vivid detail:

> O my Harpax!
> Thou engine of my wishes, thou that steel'st
> My bloody resolutions; thou that arm'st
> My eyes 'gainst womanish tears and soft compassion;
> Instructing me, without a sigh, to look on
> Babes torn by violence from their mothers' breasts
> To feed the fire, and with them make one flame;
> Old men, as beasts, in beasts' skins torn by dogs;
> Virgins and matrons tire the executioners;
> Yet I, unsatisfied, think their torments easy.

(I, i, p.4)

In these opening scenes, Theophilus as an agent of Dioclesian reflects his emperor's relish for ingenious tortures but even the latter's stand seems by comparison political, arbitrary and more moderate. Indeed, in a speech that parallels James I's attitude towards Cobham, Markham and Grey cited earlier, Dioclesian insists on the monarch's need to temper justice with mercy and evoke both terror and respect for the law from his subjects; of course, the audience recognizes that his conviction arises from mistaken confidence in Rome's political security:

> In all growing empires,
> Even cruelty is useful; some must suffer,
> And be set up as examples to strike terror
> In others, though far off: but when a state
> Is raised to her perfection, and her bases

> Too firm to shrink, or yield, we may use mercy,
> And do't with safety.

(I, ii, p.6)

Ironically, Rome's bases remain vulnerable to threats from within, though the state directs its cruelty not against neighbouring kings who challenge it politically but against women such as Callista, Christeta and Dorothea whose challenge to its authority poses a far greater threat. The wealthy and powerful Dorothea and Antoninus, who has fallen in love with her, remain beyond Theophilus's reach and the target of his extreme frustration from the very start:

> Have I invented tortures to tear Christians,
> To see but which, could all that feel hell's torments
> Have leave to stand aloof here on earth's stage,
> They would be mad 'till they again descended,
> Holding the pains most horrid of such souls,
> May-games to those of mine: has this my hand
> Set down a Christian's execution
> In such dire postures, that the very hangman
> Fell at my foot dead, hearing but their figures;
> And shall Macrinus and his fellow-masker [Antoninus]
> Strangle me in a dance?

(II, ii, p.12)

At the end of the play after his conversion, the pleasure that Theophilus derives from torturing Christians converts as easily into ecstasy at being tormented by the most ingenious means. Indeed he pleads that his tortures might be extreme beyond any devised until then: 'My suit is, you would have no pity on me. / In mine own house there are thousand engines / Of studied cruelty, which I did prepare / For miserable Christians; let me feel / The horrid'st you can find' (V, ii, p 31). As the guard proceeds to use various instruments of torture on him, Theophilus continues to demand more:

> Weak tormentors,
> More tortures, more: alas! you are unskillful –
> For heaven's sake, more; my breast is yet untorn:
> . . .
> The irons cool, – here are arms yet, and thighs;
> Spare no part of me.

(V, ii, p.31)

The play relies almost entirely on staged violence for its dramatic effect, even suggesting through incident after incident that only a thin line separates torment from ecstasy. Theophilus's joy in suffering at the end, for example, remains hardly distinguishable from Dioclesian's pleasure in inflicting pain. Antoninus's sexual desire for Dorothea similarly transforms into religious ecstasy at the very moment of her torture and execution, the pain of which he suffers vicariously as he dies alongside Dorothea: 'I feel a holy fire, / That yields a comfortable heat within me' (IV, iii, p.26). His language, which collapses passion and religious fervour, parallels Dorothea's similar response to Angelo:

> Thy voice sends forth music, that I never
> Was ravish'd with a more celestial sound.
> . . .
> In golden letters down I'll set that day,
> Which gave thee to me. Little did I hope
> To meet such world of comfort in thyself,
> Thy little, pretty body; when I, coming
> Forth of the temple, heard my beggar-boy,
> My sweet-faced, godly beggar-boy, crave an alms,
> Which with glad hand I gave, with lucky hand! –
> And when I took thee home, my most chaste bosom,
> Methought, was fill'd with no wanton hot fire,
> But with holy flame . . .
>
> (II, ii, p.10)

In his last moments, Theophilus responds to Dorothea's martyrdom with a similar invocation of her 'ravishing' power and his death in turn provokes admiration and notice from his persecutors though it also steels their determination to continue their persecution and increase their vigilance against Christians; Dioclesian, though amazed at Theophilus's constancy, nevertheless vows to continue the struggle:

> I think the centre of the earth be crack'd,
> Yet I stand still unmoved, and will go on:
> The persecution that is here begun,
> Through all the world with violence shall run.
>
> (V, ii, p.31)

The model deaths of Callista, Christeta, Dorothea and Theophilus promise to provoke more violence in the future; the violence in this play, as in many Renaissance tragedies of blood and gore, promises to never end.

The climactic collapse of the Self–Other dichotomy occurs, of course, when Theophilus the most dedicated of persecutors transforms into the most committed supporter of the new faith; but the play continually dramatizes the fact that concepts of Self and Other remain unstable and flexible except in the minds of the politically motivated for whom power can only exist through an assertion of differences. The most extended treatment of this issue occurs in the scene where Dorothea is brought before Antoninus to be raped. In scenes such as this one, the play shows its complete reliance on violence for theatrical effect; even when violence is not actually staged, the play thus sustains its energy by presenting the potential for violence or by promising to top itself in dramatizing cruelty.

Love-sick for Dorothea, Antoninus languishes in despair while his worried father Sapritius and his dedicated friend Macrinus hire several doctors to cure him. Antoninus, as the doctor and Macrinus indicate, provides a classic case of hysteria; primarily a female disease, hysteria was seen as the result of excess sperm in the body, sexual gratification providing the only cure for it. In keeping with a long tradition of Galenic thought, physicians continued to recommend physical relief as the only cure for it; in the fourteenth century, John of Gaddesden recommends the following:

> the woman should get together and draw up a marriage contract with some man. If she does not or cannot do this, because she is a nun and it is forbidden by her monastic vow or because she is married to an old man incapable of giving her due, she should travel overseas, take frequent exercise and use medicine which will dry up her sperm. . . . If she has a fainting fit, the midwife should insert a finger covered with oil of lily, laurel or spikenard into her womb and move it vigorously about.
>
> (quoted in Leyser 1995 pp.96–97)

Macrinus more than the others recognizes Antoninus's condition explicitly as hysteria or a version of disease called 'the suffocation of the mother', for he insists that only a midwife can cure his friend of his deep melancholy; in response to Sapritius's bewildered response to this suggestion and consequent query about whether his son is with child, Macrinus describes the only remedy that can keep Antoninus from death:

> Yes, with child;
> And [he] will, I fear, lose his life, if by a woman
> He is not brought to bed.
> . . . let him hear
> The voice of Dorothea, nay, but the name,
> He starts up with high colour in his face:
> She, or none, cures him.
>
> (IV, i, p.21)

Antoninus demonstrates the validity of his friend's claim by his hysterical veering between extremes of emotion, intense despair and unbridled anger. Sapritius, in the meantime, determined to cure his son by any means available to him, drags Dorothea in by the hair and presents her to Antoninus with the following 'fatherly' injunction:

> Break that enchanted cave; enter, and rifle
> The spoils thy lust hunts after; I descend
> To a base office, and become thy pander,
> In bringing thee this proud thing: make her thy whore,
> Thy health lies here; if she deny to give it,
> Force it: imagine thou assault'st a town's
> Weak wall; to't 'tis thine own, but beat this down.
>
> (IV, i, p.22)

Then in an extraordinary display of voyeurism, he suggests that he and Macrinus witness the scene from another room: 'Come, and unseen, be witness to this battery / How the coy strumpet yields' (IV, i, p.22). This multiple frame within the play in a scene of imminent violence, where the audience views Sapritius and

Macrinus as they in turn view Dorothea and Antoninus (who are also being watched by Angelo), recalls similar stagings of cruelty in plays such as *The Spanish Tragedy* and *The Revenger's Tragedy*. In fact, as in the earlier plays, the playwright uses tactics of delay, deferment and suspense to carry us through the scene. At first the scene propels us towards imminent disaster as Antoninus seems agreeable to his father's suggestion; as Dorothea cries to the heavens for help, Antoninus ominously suggests 'When a tiger / Leaps into a timorous herd, with ravenous jaws, / Being hunger starved, what tragedy then begins?' (IV, i, p.22). 'I must' he continues, 'climb that sweet virgin tree . . . and pluck that fruit which none, I think, e'er tasted.' Impatient at his delay and lack of action, Sapritius and Macrinus in the other chamber express their frustration in language that suggests their real reasons for staging the rape, voyeuristic and vicarious interest rather than a selfless desire to see Antoninus cured of his frenzy. Not surprisingly, when deprived of such pleasure by Antoninus who decides finally that 'pleasures forced / Are unripe apples; sour not worth the plucking', their energy shifts to ensuring that Dorothea's rape be staged by any means at all. Thus the theatrical effect of the scene seems equally poised between the tragedy of violence on the one hand and the comedy of a multiple *coitus interruptus* on the other. Sapritius's frustration at the delay speaks volumes for his vicarious interest in the rape:

> thou'rt no brat of mine;
> One spark of me, when I had heat like thine,
> By this had made a bonfire: a tempting whore,
> For whom thou'rt mad, thrust e'en into thine arms,
> And stand'st thou puling! . . . but thou shalt curse
> Thy dalliance, and here, before her eyes,
> Tear thine own flesh in pieces, when a slave
> In hot lust bathes himself, and gluts those pleasures
> Thy niceness durst not touch.
>
> (IV, i, p.22)

When the British slave from a nation famous 'for true whoring' is called forth to complete the task, the scene threatens to take us once again through acts of cruelty and voyeurism with an added audience this time, for the rape now about to be staged is partly for the benefit of the unfit Antoninus. The scene dissolves once again into semi-comedy as the slave refuses to commit so base an act as rape, insisting that he will not be reduced to so base a state: 'I am, as yet, / But half a slave; but when that work is past, / A damned whole one, a black ugly slave, / The slave of all slaves' (IV, i, p.22). The pattern of potential violence and deferment thus repeats yet again. By the end of this scene, the focus has shifted entirely from the love-sick Antoninus to his frustrated father, who has transformed from a figure of authority to an object of contempt even from the slaves and who now exhibits the classic symptoms of hysteria. Antoninus recognizes the shift and remarks on it: 'Good sir, give o'er: / The more you wrong her, yourself's the vex'd more.' Sapritius's fury remains unabated, however, and he directs his passion entirely towards Dorothea, whom he now wishes to see raped at any cost: 'thus down I throw / Thy harlot, thus by the hair nail her to the earth. / Call in ten slaves, let everyone discover / What lust desires, and surfeit here his fill. / Call in ten slaves' (IV, i, p.23). Ten slaves are summoned to ravish her but it is Sapritius who falls down in an excited frenzy, frustrated beyond measure and unable to victimize Dorothea despite the best efforts of all the males around him. The scene ends with Dorothea being dragged off stage presumably to be raped by ten slaves, though we learn at her death that she has remained a virgin nevertheless. The pattern of imminent violence, delay and deferment has thus repeated yet again.

The climax of the play features Dorothea's execution with Sapritius, Theophilus, Antoninus and Angelo as onlookers. The 'Roman customs' that Theophilus invokes proves to be little different from the punishment often meted out to deviant women in Renaissance England. Dorothea is first tied to a pillar and beaten and then executed upon a scaffold specially constructed for the event; she is even allowed a scaffold speech and like numerous female victims in Renaissance England, she dexterously converts the moment of her death into a martyrdom. Her heavenward-looking speech provides a standard text for numerous Christian martyrs in Renaissance England:

> What is this life to me? not worth a thought;
> Or, if it be esteem'd, 'tis that I lose it
> To win a better: even thy malice serves
> To me but as a ladder to mount up
> To such a height of happiness, where I shall
> Look down with scorn on thee, and all the world;
> Where, circled with true pleasures, placed above
> The reach of death or time, 'twill be my glory
> To think at what an easy price I bought it.
>
> (IV, iii, p.25)

She dies a self-conscious death, aware of her role as martyr and symbol for future generations of Christians:

> O! strike quickly;
> And, though you are unmoved to see my death,
> Hereafter, when my story shall be read,
> As they were present now, the hearers shall
> Say this for Dorothea, with wet eyes,
> She lived a virgin, and a virgin dies.
>
> (IV, iii, p.26)

Massinger thus provides in her death a dramatic equivalent of prose exhortations on how to die well popular in the Renaissance. Dorothea's death provokes almost immediate emulation from those who witness it. Antoninus dies in the same scene, finally experiencing the ecstasy he had so desired, though his emotions have now transmuted into divine rather than physical passion: 'See! I can stand, and go alone; thus kneel / To heavenly Dorothea, touch her hand / With a religios kiss' (IV, iii, p.26). And as we have seen, Theophilus also emulates Dorothea in his death during the last scenes of the play. The play thus partakes of Renaissance folklore concerning the hanged or executed individual's mystical powers (Hay 1975 pp.109–110). Like Kyd, Shakespeare and Jonson, Fletcher dramatizes the elusiveness of state authority and the ability of victims to reinvent themselves at the very moment of their ignominy; Dorothea shares with numerous Protestant and Catholic victims on the Renaissance scaffold an ability to convert the moment of her public shame into a moment of personal triumph and martyrdom. Despite Dioclesian's resolve to continue his torment of Christians, the play suggests the possibility of more conversions, for even the doggedly determined Sapritius remarks with admiration on Theophilus's constancy in death. Thus the play repeatedly dramatizes the conversion of Others into Selves, even suggesting the inevitability of such change as new systems displace the old. *The Virgin Martyr* does not simply sanction youth over age, women over men, subjects over figures of authority and female solidarity over male division and strife, it erodes the boundaries between these polarities emphatically and absolutely: the language of sexual energy remains indistinguishable from the vocabulary of religious ecstasy; Roman valour symbolized by Antoninus, the warrior newly returned from successful campaigns abroad, merges with womanly power to subject oneself to patient suffering; proud persecutors become enthusiastic supporters of the cause they opposed; class distinctions and social demarcations collapse as slaves overcome masters through dignified non-action; and as in Kyd and Shakespeare, victims on the scaffold expertly convert the moment of their ignominy into triumphant martyrdom.

These Roman tragedies by leading playwrights of the period may be regarded as Renaissance explorations of alterity which also demonstrate the fragility of power as it rests on public demonstrations of torment to sustain itself. By their invocation of violence as a source of entertainment, these plays expose the value of the scaffold as a perpetual site of theatrical energy; by explicitly condemning violence as a mark of the Roman state in decline while also suggesting affinities with the Renaissance world, Shakespeare, Jonson and Fletcher also implicate the audience within the condemnation levelled at decadent Others.

Notes

1. See Gary Miles (1989) for a sustained discussion of Renaissance conceptions of Romanness.
2. I am aware that there may be causal links between Elizabethan drama and later travel literature such as Purchas's but my interest here lies in exploring an identifiable Renaissance perception of other worlds that these texts share.
3. Among these might be listed Maurice Hunt (1988), Eugene Waith (1984) and Douglas E. Green (1989).
4. For an early analysis of a specific connection between a hanging and Shakespeare's *Comedy of Errors*, see T. W. Baldwin (1931). I am grateful to Douglas Bruster for drawing this book to my attention.

5. For a recent study of Senecan elements see Gordon Braden (1985).
6. For studies of Aaron's role in the context of Renaissance attitudes towards Moors, see Emily Bartels's essay (1990) and her book (1993) for a study of Renaissance notions of Otherness; for studies that focus specifically on Moors in drama, see Anthony Gerard Barthelemy (1987) and Elliot H. Tokson (1982).
7. This is especially true about villainous characters such as Aaron. Titus in fact remains unique among the characters in the play in his early desire to fight enemies immediately and kill them quickly and efficiently.
8. For historical studies of torture and punishment in the Renaissance, see John Laurence (1960), John Langbein (1977) and Gail Kern Paster (1992); William Harrison remains an useful Renaissance source (1587). For a discussion of physical and psychological torment in *The Tempest* within the context of official strategies for coping with treason, see Curt Breight (Breight 1990).
9. Barker invests this scene with considerable cultural significance. 'The episode,' he argues, is a marginalized "representation" which but barely represents ... both in extent and intensity, the death by hanging among the ludic rustics and non-elite clowns of early modern England and Wales – the real dead. ... The lack of effect associated with the demise of the Clown in *Titus Andronicus* makes it casual ... part of the routine, "natural" landscape and lifescape of the poor' (Barker 1993 pp.191–192).
10. For an absorbing discussion of Lavinia's significance in the construction of Titus's character, see Douglas E. Green (1989).
11. While she languished in prison, Mary had become the focus of several Catholic conspiracies to replace Elizabeth and had finally been trapped into exposing her alliances by Walsingham's intrigues. The Throckmorton plot was uncovered in 1583, and the Babington plot which led to Mary's execution had mostly unravelled by 1587.
12. Of course not all texts that deal with the issue of Otherness reveal the same degree of ironic self-reflexiveness. A pamphlet of 1676 'Great Newes from the Barbadoes', for example, though written considerably later in the period, registers the more conventional attitude when it glorifies English acts of genocide as acts of self-preservation sanctioned by God. The author describes with obvious relish what appears to have been a feeble attempt at rebellion by natives and the resulting mass hysteria that led to the capture and violent deaths of nearly a hundred of them. With genuine conviction, the author concludes his narrative by noting that 'Thus escaped from Eminent dangers, this flourishing and fertile island, or to say more properly Spatious and profitable Garden, one of the chiefest of his Majesties Nurseries for Sea-men' (Anon. 1676 p.13). The sexual vocabulary itself establishes the close connection between the civilizing project and rape of virgin lands in order that they might yield future profits.

4

Theatre and carnival licence: exploring the boundaries of comic freedom and tragic excess

Theatre's interest in carnivalesque excess, in crossing the limits of comic licence and tragic dignity, emerges in several plays of the early Stuart period. In the early seventeenth century, both comedy and tragedy seem to test the limits of their genre. These plays demonstrate a close relationship between theatre's interest in crossing the boundaries of comic form and tragic dignity and the sociopolitical crossing of boundaries that emerged shortly after in the events of the mid-century. Theatre both reflects and contributes to a pattern of violations that emerge during this period, violations that lead ultimately to a clear desacralizing of traditional structures of social and political behaviour that had characterized society until now.

Many plays test the limits of genre and gender simultaneously and the first half of this chapter focuses on texts which combine these transgressions. Bruce Boehrer argues that 'in a social formation that ascribes rank, wealth, and identity genealogically, family structure is always already macropolitical; to write or rewrite the family is to write or rewrite the state' (Boehrer 1992 p.4). Ira Clark insists that this symbology remains especially valid in the Caroline period when 'sociopolitical hierarchy was inseparable from family hierarchy' (Clark 1994 p.20). Comic and tragic rewritings of the family in several Renaissance plays suggest the political dimensions of Renaissance drama's concern with issues of gender and domestic hierarchy. Ultimately, gender transgressions in Fletcher's *The Woman's Prize or the Tamer Tamed*, Beaumont and Fletcher's *The Maid's Tragedy* and Webster's *The Duchess of Malfi* may be seen as a result of theatre's successful poaching of carnival transgression and a fascination with the central images of carnival, topsy-turviness and the woman-on-top. Middleton and Rowley's *The Changeling*, Middleton's *Women Beware Women* and *The Bloody Banquet*, a play whose author is known only by the initials T. D., reveal their indebtedness to carnival through a persistent engagement with the process of debasement; unlike in earlier tragedies, the central action in these plays might be described as a process of debasing and desanctifying aristocratic bodies. *The Bloody Banquet* might even be described as an extended carnival which stages the crowning and uncrowning of numerous Carnival kings.

Comic freedom and the politics of festivity in *The Woman's Prize or the Tamer Tamed*

Some plays even announce their violation of limits as a conscious rewriting or extension of Elizabethan texts. This is certainly the case with *The Woman's Prize* which remains especially interesting because it presents its discussion of gender as a revision of Shakespeare's farcical comedy, *The Taming of the Shrew*. Its comic plot also invokes carnival festivity and transgression directly.

Critical evaluations of Shakespeare's *The Taming of the Shrew* have frequently centred on the issue of patriarchy and on whether the play reiterates or undermines gender-based social expectations.[1] Interestingly, critics on both sides of this issue target the same theatrical space for their scrutiny, namely, Kate's final speech; however, unlike modern critical readings focusing on gender, John Fletcher's commentary on Shakespeare's text, voiced in his sequel *The Woman's Prize*, does not concentrate on the final scene in *The Shrew*, though it does rewrite that scene along entirely different lines.[2] Critics have for the most part either ignored or minimized Fletcher's pervasive commentary on Shakespeare. George Ferguson, for example, dismisses the play's relationship to the earlier text as superficial and tenuous:

> Beyond these rather general hints [direct references in the text] there is little else to remind the reader of the Shakespeare play except the Italian names, but only three of them are to be found in *The Taming of the Shrew*. Of these three – Petruchio, Tranio, and Byancha – only Petruchio bears any resemblance to the characters of Shakespeare's play.
>
> (Ferguson 1966 p.12)

Even modern notices of Fletcher's play dismiss its importance as little more than a passing reference to Shakespeare's concluding vision.[3] On the contrary, characters and situations in *The Woman's Prize* seem closely modelled on *The Shrew* and Fletcher's calculated intertextual glance comments, rewrites and undermines the ideological assumptions in Shakespeare's.

The play's more radical stand on the issue of gender may account in part for the attitude of Sir Henry Herbert, the Master of Revels, when he suppressed a scheduled performance in 1633. The play's use of 'oaths, profaneness and ribaldrye' seems to have been the target of his censure but his choice of words in reiterating the need to censure old plays points to other equally serious transgressions posed by earlier texts and presumably *The Woman's Prize* as well: 'All auld plays ought to bee brought to the Master of Revells, and have his allowance to them, for which he should have his fee, since they may be full of offensive things *against church and state*' (quoted by Ferguson 1966 p.23 [italics added]). One suspects that at least part of his concern about 'offenses to church and state' centred on the threat posed by the play's clearly anti-patriarchal theme.

In fact Fletcher's sequel provides more than a farcical continuation of Shakespeare's plot; Fletcher comments on Shakespeare's text in a variety of ways and provides an example of the ambivalent and problematic nature of Renaissance attitudes towards gender roles. Jean Howard insists that 'early modern England was not only permeated by well-documented social mobility and unsettling economic change, but by considerable instability in the gender system as well' (Howard 1988 p.425); Fletcher's play provides one gloss on this social instability and resolves its conflicts in entirely different ways than Shakespeare's text did in the previous century.[4] In this sense *The Woman's Prize* demonstrates an aspect of Fletcher's dramaturgy that has only recently received critical attention, namely, its critical and frequently subversive engagement with topical issues of the day.[5]

The explicitly farcical nature of Fletcher's play probably bears some responsibility for its comparative critical neglect, though similar charges against *The Shrew* have not detracted from its interest. Recent revaluations of farce, however, have moved towards recognizing the genre's ability to subvert and criticize under cover of excessive play. Alice Rayner's point about comedy in general may apply equally to farce and to *The Woman's Prize* in particular: 'For all its playfulness, it engages moral and ethical material which it appears either to trivialize or mock. . . . comedy consistently appears to have a didactic purpose, suggesting an ethically better world' (Rayner 1987 p.5). Peter Berek, speaking of *The Shrew* as an example of farce, makes a similar point: 'the conventions of farce seem to be a way of treating matters that might well be seen as highly important, such as sex, money, and power, but doing so in a way that pretends they are unimportant'. He insists that farces do more than provoke laughter: 'such plays are striking for the way they veil their own complexity' (Berek 1988 p.99).[6]

In this sense farce as a literary entity bears a generic resemblance to carnival as a cultural activity. As in carnival, farce enacts excesses of comic freedom and the exaggerated nature of these excesses seems to render them innocuous as political or social criticisms. Farce, in other words, constitutes a clear form of 'play' and its inversions of social norms seem to pose no threats. But as observers of carnival have repeatedly recognized, the excessive play of carnival festivity could provide a façade for real threats to the officialdom that sanctioned it. Indeed, as Peter Stallybrass argues, 'elements of carnival and charivari were central to the symbolic repertoire of political subversion in early modern England' (Stallybrass 1989 p.51). The nearest generic kin to carnival on the stage, farce more than any other genre could force a revaluation of the cultural practices it inverts and mocks. Leah Marcus makes a similar point when she insists on the normative and revisionist aspects of festival; 'seemingly lawless topsy-turvidom,' she points out, 'can constitute a process of adjustment within a perpetuation of order' (Marcus 1986 p.7). The argument may be especially true about a play such as *The Woman's Prize* which invokes carnival and skimmington explicitly through the taming of Petruchio and all the men in the village by Maria and her friends. In its reliance on metaphors of topsy-turviness, Fletcher's seventeenth-century farce shares aspects with carnivalesque Renaissance activities such as May day celebrations which, as Stallybrass notes, provided 'a privileged time for gender inversions' (Stallybrass 1989 p.54). The central figure in these inversions, which often included a procession led by women, was 'unruly Marion', 'a figure often used to legitimate political action by the powerless' (Stallybrass 1989 p.55).

Such was the case in the Essex food riots in 1622 and 1629, where the format of the rebellion differed little from that depicted in the play. Anne Carter who led the revolt in 1629 even assumed the title of 'Captain' as Maria does in Fletcher's play (Stallybrass 1989 pp.54–55). And it may be no accident that the carnivalesque procession by women in Fletcher's play is led by the aptly named Maria whose name inevitably suggests Marion. The resemblance of actual later riots to circumstances depicted in the play suggests the extent to which Fletcher's text registers real possibilities in seventeenth-century England rather than merely literary, artificial and impossible inversions traditionally seen as the domain of farce.

Even the women's mode of attack in the play resembles those used successfully by rebels in Renaissance England. In 1549 crowds that had gathered for July celebrations got together under the leadership of Robert Kett and marched on Norwich. By 23 July they had actually taken the city, but as Stallybrass notes, 'the defenders were overpowered not by weapons but by the naked arses and obscene gestures of the rebels' (Stallybrass 1989 p.53). The incident has its parallel in *The Woman's Prize* when the country wives and the city wives march through the streets led by Maria. Tranio recounts this clearly carnivalesque display of female authority to the bewildered men in vivid detail:

> Arme, arme, out with your weapons,
> For all the women in the Kingdom's on ye;
> They swarme like waspes, and nothing can destroy 'em,
> But stopping of their hive and smothering of 'em.
> . . .
> They heave ye stoole on stoole, and fling Potlids
> Like massive rocks, dart ladles, tossing Irons,
> And tongs like Thunderbolts, till overlayd,
> They fall beneath the waight; yet still aspiring
> At those Emperious Codsheads, they would tame 'em.
> There's nere a one of these, the worst and weakest,
> (Choose where you will) but attempt the raysing
> Against the sovereign peace of Puritans,
> A May-pole, and a Morris, maugre mainly
> Their zeale, and Dudgeon-daggers: and yet more,
> Dares plant a stand of battering Ale against 'em,
> And drinke 'em out o'th Parish.

(II, iv, ll.33–67)

Tranio here explicitly links the rebellion to May day festivities, thus evoking memories of legendary rebellions such as Kett's. The men, surprised by the attack, resort to spying and peeping through windows to ascertain the women's agenda. The details provided by Jaques of the women's activities recall the equally successful mode of attack adopted by Kett and his followers in 1549:

> They have got a stick of Fiddles, and they firke it
> In wondrous waies, the two grand Capitanos,
> (They brought the Auxiliary Regiments)

Daunce with their coats tuck't up to their bare breeches,
And bid the Kingdom kisse 'em, that's the burden;
They have got Metheglin and audacious Ale,
And talk like Tyrants.

(II, vi, ll.36–42)

Modes of rebellion and festivity merge quite completely as the women usurp male roles and perform a perfect imitation; Petruchio, we might recall, had been categorically referred to as a 'tyrant' in the early scenes of the play.

Audiences of the seventeenth century would have seen the tactics adopted by the women and the nature of the rebellion, not as an entirely farcical improbability simply to be enjoyed within the artificial confines of the theatre, but as a genuine possibility similar to numerous such revolts that occurred and were occurring in Renaissance England. Commenting on the close relationship between festivals and revolt, Yves-Marie Berce insists that 'like the festival, revolt noisily proclaimed its beginnings to the sound of bells and drums, both traditional instruments of alarm and symbols of the major collective disturbances. Like the festival, it interrupted day-to-day normal existence, led men abruptly into another system. It procured a sort of utopian time-scale in which the ordinary workings of society ceased . . .' (Berce 1987 pp.116–117). No doubt, those Renaissance figures who argued vigorously for the curtailing of sports and festivities instinctively recognized the close connection between festival and revolt. Even in 1580 in Edmund Assheton's objection to May games conveyed in an official letter to William Ffarington, one senses an awareness of the licence from tradition that festive occasions invariably provided, especially to women:

> I am sure Right Worship you have not forgotten the last yere stirres att Brunley about Robyne hoode and the May games. Nowe consideringe that it is a cawse that bringeth no good effecte, being contrary to the beste, therefore a number of the Justices of Peace herein in Salford Hundreth have consulted with the Commission to suppresse those Lewde sportes, tendinge to no other ende but to stirre opp of freiyle natures to wantonness; and meane not to allowe neither olde custome.
>
> (Assheton 1580 p.128)

This close relationship between festivity and revolt is vividly illustrated in *The Woman's Prize*. The raucous festivities of the play with all the traditional accompaniments of rough music, images of topsy-turviness and carousing constitute an orchestrated communal revolt by women who remain determined to correct the inequities of the past, a past which seems explicitly to include lessons taught by Shakespeare's consideration of gender issues in *The Taming*.

However, in its successful enactment of the taming of Petruchio by Maria, the play goes considerably farther towards social subversion than Shakespeare's play had done. If Shakespeare's *Shrew*, as Richard Hillman argues, 'beyond any other work in the canon, has value as a tensely poised paradigm of subversion's power and its suppression', Fletcher's enactment carries the argument a step farther (Hillman 1992 p.25); Fletcher presents subversive power as a realizable goal rather than as an idea to be debated and then contained. In this sense *The*

Woman's Prize presents a revision of Shakespeare's argument; in 1613 Fletcher rewrites the gender debate to force a more liberal outcome than was perhaps possible in the theatre of the 1590s.

But Fletcher goes beyond simply reversing earlier themes and instead takes Shakespeare to task for his inadequate representation of gender conflicts. The prologue initiates this contention by deliberately targeting female members of the audience and announcing this preference as a deviant but more appropriate practice than the customary nod to males.[7] *The Shrew*, on the other hand, as Shirley Garner argues, is performed for the male characters in the Induction, an audience which reveals 'its own erotic fantasies', for the play they witness 'is intended to have the same salacious appeal as are the paintings proposed for his [Sly's] enjoyment' (Garner 1988 p.115). Indeed Fletcher's differentiation between male and female audiences in his prologue may be treated as tongue-in-cheek commentary on Shakespeare's catering to salacious male tastes, for despite Fletcher's suggestion that we should not look for intellectual argument and debate in his play, Maria's final victory, as I hope to illustrate, results from highly original and intellectually stimulating verbal battles with Petruchio.

The author's suggestion that his play might function as 'physick' to cure one's melancholy also recalls the outer frame of Shakespeare's text where the Lord tricks Sly and makes a similar claim about the effects of comedy. The prologue's invocation of this motif implicitly aligns the audience with the deluded Sly in the earlier play, and posits that Fletcher's text either undoes the psychological damage enacted by the earlier play or provides the closure explicitly denied by it.

Fletcher's play opens some years after Kate's death, with Petruchio's marriage to a shy and demure young maiden named Maria. Maria, however, with the help of her cousin Biancha, resolves to tame Petruchio; her reputation as a spokesperson for women's rights soon spreads and she receives help from several city and country wives who desire similar freedom from their husbands. Their rebellion against the men takes a farcical turn as the women march up the streets with pots and ladles, wear breeches, drink ale and carouse to music and stick their arses out of windows calling to the men to kiss them.[8] This concerted rebellion achieves a temporary conclusion in Act III when Petruchio, desperate to restore his marriage to normalcy, signs a contract containing diverse demands drawn up by Maria.[9]

Fletcher's opening scene between Tranio and his friends, Moroso and Sophocles, who gossip about Petruchio's just-concluded wedding, blatantly deconstructs the nominal closure constructed by Shakespeare's play. While *The Shrew* had concluded with a recanting speech by Kate describing the subservient role of women, Fletcher insists that Kate had never been 'tamed'. In the course of her tempestuous marriage, she converted Petruchio to her own ways, 'turn'd his temper, / And forced him blow as high as she' (I, i, ll.19–20). Her influence has been so total that Petruchio apparently still lives in terror of her, as Tranio explains:

For yet the bare remembrance of his first wife
(I tell you on my knowledge, and a truth too)
Will make him start in's sleep, and very often
Cry out for Cudgels, Colstaves, any thing:
Hiding his breeches, out of feare her Ghost
Should walk, and weare 'em yet.

(I, i, ll.31–36)

This opening scene clearly responds to Shakespeare's concluding vision and reverses the pattern of the earlier work. Is Fletcher targeting Shakespeare's text as unnatural in its concluding transformation? Certainly his reading suggests that Shakespeare may have sacrificed veracity for dramatic convenience. The close parallels between the plays force us to consider that Fletcher's text projects the author in a dual role, as dramatist and theatre critic at once.

Similarities between the texts are numerous. The just cited speech by Tranio, for example, recalls the men's similar show of sympathy for Petruchio just before his marriage to Kate; as in the earlier play, Petruchio is once again marrying the older of two daughters; the younger daughter Livia has an old wealthy suitor Moroso who, like Gremio in Shakespeare's play, has the initial approval of her father; her true love Rowland, the young and learned suitor, ultimately wins her through the machinations of Biancha and Tranio (the latter, one recalls, had coordinated a similar union between Bianca and Lucentio earlier). Petruchio's friends even take a wager that marriage to Petruchio will take Maria to her grave within three weeks, a veiled suggestion perhaps about Kate's plight as a result of constant verbal battles with her husband. They even suggest that the only way for Maria to survive in her marriage would be by outmatching Petruchio's tyranny; Tranio, who has presumably seen Petruchio adopt a tyrannical attitude towards Kate, explains the sole means by which Maria might cope with her tyrant husband:

I would learn to eate Coales with an angry Cat,
And spit fire at him: I would (to prevent him)
Do all the ramping, roaring tricks, a whore
Being druncke, and tumbling ripe, would tremble at:
There is no safety else, nor morall wisdom,
To be a wife, and his.

(I, i, ll.25–30)

Biancha, Maria's cousin, echoes the same sentiments and advises a similar course of action and this is precisely what Maria proceeds to do. Thus Fletcher insists on reading Kate's transformation speech ironically or as an unfelt repetition of learned platitudes. Fletcher's comedy emphasizes the fallacy of claims such as Peter Berek's recent one that 'ironic readings of the sexism in the play have to be regarded as ahistorical' because 'Elizabethan audiences do not seem to have perceived Kate as kidding when she thanks her husband for his support' (Berek 1988 p.98).[10] On the contrary, the popularity of Fletcher's play with later audiences suggests that ironic re-readings of Kate's transformation may have been a

commonplace of the theatrical experience for many early audiences.[11] Petruchio
himself acknowledges that Kate had never been tamed and that his marriage had
been a perpetual hell:

> Had I not ev'ry morning a rare breakfast,
> 'Mixt with a learned lecture of ill language,
> Louder than Tom O'Lincoln; and at dinner,
> A dyet of the same dish? was there evening
> That ere past over us, without thou knave,
> Or thou whore, for digestion?

(III, iii, ll.158–162)

Even Fletcher's choice of Biancha as the instigator of women's rebellion could
not be merely accidental and hardly at odds with Shakespeare's portrayal of her
as 'the mild sister of Katharina' as Ferguson claims (Ferguson 1966 p.12). As
'engineer' to the rebellion, Biancha functions as an extension of Shakespeare's
manipulative Bianca who seemingly poses no threat to the males until she shows
her hand overtly at the end of the play by making her own choice of husband
and then by refusing to be available at his beck and call. Biancha's role simply
continues Shakespeare's depiction of her during the last scene where she causes
Lucentio to lose his wager.

The earlier play and Kate in particular are invoked by Fletcher at several points.
Kate's memory looms large over the events in *The Woman's Prize*: Petruchio in
the first half of the play mistakenly compares Maria's behaviour to Kate's, though
he ultimately recognizes that their motives differ radically; Maria, on the other
hand, when presented with the comparison by Biancha, reacts with disdain,
denying any parallel and asserting her superiority and clearly communal agenda:
'Shee was a fool, / And took a scrvy course: let her be nam'd / 'Mongst those
that wish for things, but dare not do 'em' (I, ii, ll.142–144). Unlike Kate, Maria
wishes to be 'chronicled' and go down in history as a selfless liberator of women.
This aspect of her character invokes the Marion figure of May day celebrations
and suggests the play's links with actual revolts of the sixteenth and seventeenth
centuries. By contrast Shakespeare's text provides a successful skimmington, a
model explicitly designed as social schooling by officialdom, its lessons to be
absorbed and then used to control unruly women who deviate from the norm.

Of course Fletcher's intertextual glance extends beyond these discussions of
Kate's role to involved metaphors that recall similar ones in Shakespeare. The
central metaphor of falconry invoked by Petruchio as an analogy for his triumph
over Kate in Act III, Scene i, for example, is expertly reversed by Maria:

> Hang these tame Eyasses, that no sooner
> See the lure out, and heare their Husbands call,
> But cry like Kites upon 'em: the free Haggard
> (Which is that woman, that hath wing, and knowes it,
> Spirit, and plume) will make an hundred checks,
> And look out every pleasure; not regarding
> Lure nor quarry, till her pitch command

What she desires, making her founderd keeper
Be glad to fling out traines, and golden ones,
To take her down again.

(I, ii, ll.148–158)

By allying herself with the haggard, a type of falcon that cannot be trained, Maria reiterates her individuality and value. The bestial metaphor suggested by Shakespeare's title is also adeptly reversed to propound a more radical philosophy; Maria insists that 'that childish woman / That lives a prisoner to her husbands pleasure, / Hath lost her making, and becomes a beast, / Created for his use not fellowship' (I, iii, ll.136–140). Fletcher thus posits an entirely new argument about gender relationships, though his invocation of *The Shrew* at every stage suggests that he is simultaneously rewriting Shakespeare's text. Maria's choice of words in describing marriage as mutual 'fellowship' reflects attitudes that dominated contemporary Puritan discourse on the subject. In this context we might recall that Fletcher 'secured the patronage of Henry Hastings, fifth earl of Huntingdon, a member of a family that had been staunch defenders of Puritanism during the reigns of Elizabeth and James' (Hamilton 1992 p.168). Though Mary Beth Rose does not treat *The Woman's Prize* in her study of what she regards as an evolving 'heroics of marriage' on the Renaissance stage, Fletcher's play best illustrates her point regarding this movement; in plays which propound 'a heroics of marriage', as Rose points out, women become 'powerful agents of cultural change', as Maria certainly does (Rose 1988 p.9).

Fletcher also rewrites the gender debate as a literal text rather than an oral one; marriage partnership in *The Woman's Prize* emerges as a direct result of texts first proposed by males and then rescripted by females: Maria insists on a signed contract from Petruchio after his suggestion that she draw up conditions; Livia's marriage to Rowland is accomplished by duping the men (her father, Moroso and Rowland) into signing two separate documents devised by Biancha; the women talk about being chronicled and thus providing a textualized precedent for future generations of women; Petruchio himself concludes the play by promising to keep to his text hereafter in his treatment of Maria. In the women's insistence on written records to authenticate their marital agreements, we see a record of the increasing currency in seventeenth-century England of the written text.[12] The following extract from a newspaper account demonstrates the reliance on the written word that typified seventeenth-century attitudes and habits: 'In these days the meanest sort of people are not only able to write, but to argue and discourse on matters of the highest concernment and thereupon do desire that such things which are most remarkable may be truly committed to writing and made public' (cited by Friedman 1992 p.422). Maria insists on a text that can be circulated and used as a model by others who choose to follow her example. Fletcher's association of the women's movement with the ascendancy of the written word over the oral, which men prefer and find quite satisfactory, constitutes the most radical revision of the Shakespearean vision. His persistent depiction of the women's struggle as a revision of texts also emphasizes his own role as a revisionist playwright and implicitly argues for the primacy of literary revision over the oral tradition of communally accepted norms on which the earlier play had relied.

Fletcher's more serious agenda emerges most vividly in his depiction of Maria. She does evoke the Marion figures of carnivalesque revolts staged by women but she is not simply a farcical figure of unruliness and excess, a claim more appropriate to the country wives and city wives who support her cause. Maria's victory over Petruchio, established only in Act V, emphasizes the inadequacy of farcical and temporary illusions of power acquired at the end of Act III by the women's rambunctious march and revelry; in fact, Maria insists that Kate's previous victory (marked by her ability to turn Petruchio into a shrew) remains inadequate as an example to other women for precisely this reason and that she herself plans to move beyond simple concessions by males to genuine equality between the sexes and to a rewriting of gender relations along entirely different lines than had been conventional practice.[13] That we are to take Maria more seriously than we do the other women emerges most clearly in the marked difference in her attitude towards such ideas as 'love', 'marriage' and 'duty'. While the men see all three items as closely dependent on the ability of women to satisfy men sexually, the women recognize the efficacy of withholding sex as a means of getting the attention of men. On the advise of Biancha, who most vehemently supports such exertion of power, Maria begins her rebellion by withholding sex but moves well beyond such a monolithic interpretation of male–female relationships. In Fletcher's delineation of Maria as simultaneously a figure of rebellion and a serious champion of liberty, we perhaps glimpse the cultural transition of Marion that Stallybrass discusses from a figure of misrule who dominated early representations to the virtuous and noble maid we recognize today (Stallybrass 1989 pp.45–76).

The second half of the play, which Ferguson sees as a mere continuation of the farcical battle between the sexes with no surprises in plot, is crucial in establishing Maria's more serious intent to win respect and equality from her husband. To a baffled Petruchio, who believes the battle over once he signs the contract containing concessions, Maria's continued unwillingness to 'behave as other wives do' remains perplexing. In response to Sophocles's suggestion that he might try force on her because 'some women love to struggle' (III, iii, l.10), Petruchio notes in bewilderment that he did and that it proved ineffective, for 'She swore my force might weary her, but win her / I never could, nor should until she consented; / And I might take her body prisoner,' but 'her mind' would remain unconquered (III, iii, ll.12–15). Maria's choice of words suggests her serious purpose and prevents us from regarding Fletcher's play as simply a farcical staging of a *coitus interruptus*. Petruchio's second attempt at force receives similar treatment and Maria threatens to take back her love for him:

> I defie you.
> And my last loving teares farewell: the first stroke,
> The very first you give me, if you dare strike,

> Try me, and you shall find it so, for ever
> Never to be recall'd: I know you love me,
> Mad till you have enjoyed me; I doe turne
> Utterly from you, and what man I meet first
> That hast but spirit to deserve a favour,
> Let him bear any shape, the worse the better,
> Shall kill you and enjoy me.

(IV, ii, ll.143–151)

She thus undermines the importance of appearance as a criterion for love and emphasizes instead the need to 'deserve' love in order to receive it. Her attitude is typical of Marion figures on the Renaissance stage. Maria, the heroine in *The Family of Love*, another Jacobean play which treats the subjects of licence and women's freedom, reacts in similar language when her uncle keeps her locked up: 'My body you may circumscribe, confine / And keep in bounds; but my unlimited love / Extends itself beyond all circumspection' (I, i, ll.32–34). Like *The Woman's Prize*, the play posits a more liberal ideology, for it 'tends to institutionalize sexual license rather than remove it'; as Simon Shepherd points out, 'the development of the comedy has led us into desiring a liberation of sexual relationships of the play, and has thus jokingly made us approve something with which the Family of Love supposedly shocks us' (Shepherd 1979 p.iii).

The third and fourth acts of *The Woman's Prize* pit the couple against each other in a series of arguments which have a similar outcome. Petruchio again and again echoes conventional notions about marriage and women, only to be taunted and effectively chided for such mindless repetition. Petruchio's demand that 'due obedience' should follow her marriage to him, for example, meets with an emphatic denunciation of such platitudes:

> Tell me of due obedience? what's a husband?
> What are we married for, to carry sumpters?
> Are we not one piece with you, and as worthy
> Our own intentions, as you yours?
> . . .
> Take two small drops of water, equall weighed,
> Tell me which is heaviest, and which ought
> First to descend in duty?

(III, iii, ll.97–103)

Petruchio's response indicates that he recognizes that he has lost the argument, for he retracts quite completely from his original point about duty. Maria had earlier won a similar exchange on the issue of beauty by arguing for the natural beauty of independent women:

> And we appear like her that sent us hither,
> That onely excellent and beauteous nature;
> Truly ourselves, for men to wonder at
> But too divine to handle; we are Gold,
> In our own natures pure; but when we suffer

> The husbands stamp upon us, then alayes,
> And base ones of you men are mingled with us,
> And make us blush like copper.

(I, iii, ll.239–246)

Fletcher's invocation of platitudes through Petruchio and his subversion of them through Maria recall Shakespeare's play as it mimics the pattern of the final scene where Kate seemingly parrots Petruchio's philosophy with precision; in *The Woman's Prize* Maria's subversive doctrine, at first rejected by Petruchio as preposterous, is similarly absorbed and then rehearsed before an admiring audience in the last scene.

The play concludes with Petruchio's avowal that he will never turn tyrant again and thereby cause his wife to resort to taming him a second time. Contrary to being an abrupt and dissatisfying conclusion, as Ferguson claims, Maria concludes the taming only after Petruchio has acknowledged that he is 'new born'. While Maria's claim that 'I have tamed you, / And now am vowed your servant' (V, iv, ll.45–46) may jar modern sensibilities, one must remember that neither Maria nor the play rejects notions of duty altogether; both illustrate the mutual responsibility of couples in marriage and Maria's reversion is decidedly qualified by Petruchio's oath that he will never give her cause to complain about his behaviour. In her reiteration of her love for him, she insists on reminding him of his responsibility in the partnership: 'all my life / *Since ye make so free profession*, / I dedicate in service to your pleasure' (V, iv, ll.57–59; emphasis added). Indeed Petruchio concludes by suggesting, as Kate had done earlier, that he will use his acquired learning to correct others who misbehave as he had done in the past: 'Well, little England, when I see a husband / Of any other nation stern or jealous, / I'll wish him but a woman of thy breeding' (V, iv, ll.61–63). In his desire to provide an example to other men, he imitates Maria's earlier claim that succeeding generations of women will use her example to free themselves from male tyranny.

This mutual validation of their roles as examples for the future, reminiscent of *The Shrew*, also emerges in the 'Epilogue' which announces that the author proposes 'To teach both sexes due equality'. But one recalls that the ultimate outcome of the debate remains entirely in favour of women.[14] In the course of the play, women 'tamed' the entire male populace in the town, including Petruchio, and concluded the schooling only after the men acknowledged their inherent weakness and promised not to assert their authority in tyrannical fashion. Thus Fletcher's conclusion, despite the 'Epilogue's' attempted moderation, seems equally as one-sided as the outcome in *The Shrew* had seemed.[15]

In his presentation of power struggles between men and women, Fletcher thus draws on the same folk roots as Shakespeare but converts them to different purpose. As in Shakespeare, the central images of the world-upside-down and the woman-on-top in *The Woman's Prize* derive from popular cultural activities such as the skimmington, but unlike the conventional skimmington which purported to teach women their place in the ordained hierarchy and men how to impose such order, Fletcher's play targets male tyranny and expectations by invoking the potential for subversion that always existed in carnivalesque activities. In Fletcher's play the tone of mocking laughter which always accompanied skimmingtons in practice quite clearly targets males.[16]

This difference between the comedies may reflect emerging changes in cultural attitudes, changes which have been noted by historians such as Natalie Davies, who has shown that in England during the sixteenth century skimmingtons invariably directed themselves against aggressive women who beat their husbands, whereas in the late seventeenth and early eighteenth centuries, recorded cases of skimmingtons involved men who beat their wives (Davis 1975 p.150). In the mid-century, for the very first time, Parliament even considered legislation to prevent husbands from treating their wives cruelly; the author of *The Parliament Scout* in early December 1644 records the consideration of this legislation by the Commons in language that registers sympathy for women in unfortunate marriages: 'we hope hereafter care will be taken . . . to punish the exorbitancies of the husband to the wife: if a Master strike a servant as is not fit, there is a remedy, but if a husband be never so cruell to the wife, unlesse to death, we know not where relief is to be had' (Raymond 1993 p.161). Major differences between Fletcher's play and Shakespeare's more conservative comedy suggest that changes in cultural attitudes might already have been in the making in the early seventeenth century. It might even be argued that in Fletcher's play, we witness the prior enactment in the theatre of a cultural change that would reach the record books only considerably later. It may also be no accident that this play with its radical revaluation of marriage was composed during a period when not only patriarchy, but its equivalent in the political realm, monarchy, figured as subjects of public discourse and debate. Like the equally radical *Maid's Tragedy* written by Fletcher in collaboration with Beaumont, *The Woman's Prize* was written in the period between 1609 and 1614 when, as Hamilton points out, 'the oath of allegiance controversy ran at its peak' (Hamilton 1992 p.11). Not surprisingly, the carnivalesque challenge to male authority springs from the socially transgressive space of the tavern; as Berce records, 'the social role of the tavern needs little explanation. People went there to gamble, to gossip, drink, and amuse themselves. . . . At the risk of sounding blasphemous, we may fairly say that tavern and church were the twin poles of village life' (Berce 1987 p.35). The play's movement from church to tavern in the staging of revolt may itself point to its participation in sociopolitical issues. Fletcher's plays, in fact, inevitably convert topical matters into theatrical discourse, a fact that has remained unrecognized until recently.

Linda Boose, who consistently explores the extent to which Shakespeare's *The Shrew* represents a romanticized version of contemporary practices for controlling the unruly woman, has noted a similar change in official records between the early seventeenth and later seventeenth centuries; she concludes her essay by speculating on the virtual absence of any mention of scolds in church records after 1642. Citing T. N. Brushfield, who in 1858 commended women in Cheshire for being true ladies unlike the scolds of Shakespeare's England, Boose posits that his text records 'the social process by which women of one generation . . . were shamed, tamed, and reconstituted . . . into the meek, amiable, softspoken ladies he so admires in his own time' (Boose 1991 p.213). It is equally likely that scolds disappear from record books and that skimmington practices changed in the later century because of an emerging recognition among at least some segments of English society that male tyranny and female silence do not constitute universally desirable social norms; perhaps plays such as *The Woman's Prize* record the beginnings of this dawning recognition. The very popularity of Fletcher's play in later years may indicate its currency and topical relevance. Alan Sinfield suggests that invariably the movement in Shakespearean comedy is towards the transformation of bold and sprightly women into submissive obedient wives – Katherine, Rosalind, and Beatrice come to mind (Sinfield 1992 pp.54–55); the opposite applies to Fletcher's comedy where the meek and mild Maria is transformed by the experience of marriage to rectify its inequities.

Tragic excess and the politics of gender in *The Maid's Tragedy* and *The Duchess of Malfi*

Tennenhouse's sensational assessment of early Stuart drama in which he sees the emergence of assaults on female aristocratic bodies on the Jacobean stage suggests figures such as Middleton's Beatrice Joanna or Ford's Annabella (Tennenhouse 1989 p.77). On closer examination, this claim and his insistence that 'the theatre was never more political than when it called attention to the body of an aristocratic female' appear highly questionable as a *carte blanche* summary of early Stuart theatrical practices. After all early Stuart drama enacts equal violence on male aristocratic bodies: several of the Duke's sons are beheaded or murdered in *The Revenger's Tragedy* and the multiple masques at the end of the play result in the deaths of four male figures, the Duke's violent death at the hands of his mistress Evadne is staged with a relish for detail that dominates our memory of Beaumont and Fletcher's *The Maid's Tragedy*, Alonso Piracquo's dismembered body figures prominently in the actions on-stage in *The Changeling* and Giovanni's gored body remains on-stage at the conclusion of *'Tis Pity*. Equally questionable is Tennenhouse's insistence on the importance of the aristocratic body; after all, most if not all Renaissance tragedies focus on aristocratic bodies and the very nature of tragedy dictates its staging of violence.[17] In other words, the assault on aristocratic female bodies that Tennenhouse develops into a political rereading of early Stuart theatre appears highly suspect as a doctrine of theatrical practice for the entire period, though in individual plays tied to particular and localized contexts we might very well discern political concerns staged through the enactment of violence and, in particular cases, this political statement may even be tied to the issue of violence directed at females. *The Maid's Tragedy* and *The Duchess of Malfi* provide just such examples.

The Maid's Tragedy, a play perhaps intimately concerned with Jacobean politics because of its authors' connections with the court, and Webster's later

Jacobean tragedy *The Duchess of Malfi* provide examples of works which do indeed reconceptualize the male body politic along new lines, but this reconceptualization emerges not through assaults on female aristocratic bodies (though this certainly occurs in these plays) but as a refiguring of male power as feminized, fragile and weak. These plays present male figures of authority in decidedly feminized terms even as they ascribe masculine strength and determination to their central female figures. They thus prove to be interesting counterparts to tracts of the period and suggest a possible solution to the query posed recently by Laura Levine regarding the general instability of gender in the Renaissance: 'Why do these tract writers become steadily more obsessed with the idea of the effeminized man? Why do the images of androgynous breakdown – of boys with breasts and man–woman monsters – multiply from 1579 to 1642?' (Levine 1994 p.24).

All the main male figures in *The Maid's Tragedy*, the Duke, Melantius and Amintor, may be described as undergoing a process of feminization during the course of the play. Even minor characters such as Aspatia's twin, who never appears in the play though Aspatia later disguises herself as her brother, are represented in 'androgynous rather than masculine terms; Melantius describes him as a soldier with a face 'as womanish as hers' (I, i, l.109). And our early introduction to Diphilus suggests his reluctance to fight in battle for Rhodes, though he uses the king's command as his excuse for not joining Melantius on the field.

Of the main male figures, Melantius clearly represents the most masculine, a military leader renowned for his bravery on the field and much admired by youths desirous of emulating his prowess. Even before we meet Amintor, for example, we hear about his youthful admiration of Melantius's achievements in battle; Melantius himself describes Amintor's fascination in vivid detail:

> When he was a boy,
> As oft as I return'd (as, without boast,
> I brought home conquest), he would gaze upon me
> And view me round, to find in what one limb
> The virtue lay to do those things he heard;
> Then would he wish to see my sword and feel
> The quickness of the edge, and in his hand
> Weigh it. He oft would make me smile at this.

> (I, i, ll.50–57)

The play opens with emphatic reiterations of his difference from other male characters such as Diphilus or Amintor, and Melantius proudly recognizes that he is ill at ease within the world of court masques and wooing: 'These soft and silken wars are not for me: / The music must be shrill and all confus'd / That stirs my blood, and then I dance with arms' (I, i, ll.41–43). Melantius thus sees himself as different from the courtiers at Rhodes, even using the charge of effeminacy in his verbal battles against figures such as Calianax (I, i, l.63). The actions that follow dramatize his ultimate assimilation into the system that he so much despises at the beginning of the play. The play dramatizes the erosion of Melantius's masculine traits and what might be described as his increasing feminization within the world of courtly behaviour and custom.

Confronted with the King's adulterous relationship to his sister, Melantius's initial reaction appears to be well in keeping with his role as a man of action rather than words; he upbraids Amintor for his sorrow and advocates instead a course of vengeance:

> Dry up thy wat'ry eyes
> And cast a manly look upon my face,
> For nothing is so wild as I thy friend
> Till I have freed thee; still this heaving breast.
> I go thus from thee, and will never cease
> My vengeance till I find thy heart at peace.
>
> (III, ii, ll.198–203)

Despite this firm resolution, Melantius's concern soon degenerates into ensuring his own safety in accomplishing revenge: 'I hope my cause is just; I know my blood / Tells me it is, and I will credit it. / To take revenge, and lose myself withal / Were idle' (III, ii, ll.287–290). Unlike revengers such as Vindice in *The Revenger's Tragedy* who recognize that they will pay for revenge with their lives, Melantius wishes to accomplish revenge without implicating himself. The valiant soldier who would fight any who challenged his honour thus transforms into a figure more concerned with hidden revenge and self-preservation.

The scenes that follow show him enlisting Evadne to commit the murder and his manoeuvrings hereafter constitute an attempt to gain the fort to ensure his own safety. He outsmarts Calianax in open court by using his verbal rather than physical prowess and even boasts of his more adept use of the tongue, a traditionally feminine weapon: 'You cannot blast me with your tongue, and that's / The strongest part you have about ye' (IV, ii, ll.231–232). In the last scene, which shows him with Lysippus who has apparently pardoned him, he tries to kill himself over Amintor's death and Diphilus chides him for his unmanly behaviour. His final lines ensure that his transformation is complete and that he will, as Lysippus describes it, be 'curs'd' for he retains no interest in living hereafter; his role at the end recalls Aspatia's at the beginning.

While Melantius's transformation occurs on-stage, Amintor from the very beginning remains an effeminate and vulnerable figure evoking contempt from characters such as Evadne. His lack of 'manly' courage presents itself most vividly in his initial confrontation with his wife where he discovers her infidelity. The scene begins with Evadne telling Amintor she hates him and desires his death and ends with Amintor pleading that she take pity on him and kill him in order to end his grief. In his confrontation with the King a few scenes later, he similarly pleads to be killed. Only in the last scene, when confronted with the suicides of Evadne and Aspatia, does Amintor find the courage to kill himself as he had desired at the beginning of the play.

But Beaumont and Fletcher's strongest indictment of male effeminacy and weakness emerges in their depiction of the monarch at the centre of the play's actions. Even early in the play, we witness the King's inability to make his courtiers accede to his wishes; his attempts to effect a reconciliation between Calianax and Melantius, for example, meet with strong resistance and we see the King simply acknowledge his inability to command. His dependence on Evadne emerges most vividly in his jealous visit to the newly married couple's bedchamber and his petulant reactions to Amintor's account of the night's actions. Invoking his authority as king, he threatens to punish Evadne for her betrayal but Evadne responds to his show of authority with contempt: 'Why, it is in me, then, / Not to love you, which will more afflict / Your body than your punishment can mine' (III, i, ll.188–190). His dependence on her love ensures her ability to kill him easily and efficiently.

The scene of the King's murder constitutes the play's most emphatic depiction of gendered topsy-turviness, for it emphasizes the King's effeminacy and weakness and Evadne's equally monstrous usurpation of male authority and power. Melantius, we might recall, resorted to physical threats in order to get Evadne to undertake the murder but, despite her earlier reluctance, she now expresses both fear and pleasure as she approaches her task, even justifying her decision by the joy she feels at the prospect: 'I must kill him, / And I will do't bravely: the mere joy / Tells me I merit in it' (V, i, ll.27–29). She then proceeds to tie the King up and, in a grotesquely humorous turn, he awakens with keen anticipation of this new sexual strategy devised by his lover: 'What pretty new device is this, Evadne? / What, do you tie me to you by your love?' (V, i, ll.47–48). The scene that follows mimics the violence of the sexual act as Evadne, presumably atop the prone and helpless King, stabs him numerous times; his cries for help could as easily be mistaken for sexual rapture and Evadne emphasizes the collapse of sex and death as she notes, 'we must change more of these love-tricks yet'. The gentlemen of the bedchamber who presumably hear the King's cries, nevertheless wait until Evadne leaves to enter and check on the King. The sequence of events recalls the play's early reminder through the concluding song of the wedding masque that sex and violence are intimately linked and that the bride's cries of ecstatic pain on her first night should remain unheeded:

> Stay, gentle Night, and with thy darkness cover
> > The kisses of her lover.
> Stay and confound her tears and shrill cryings,
> Her weak denials, vows, and often-dyings;
> > Stay and hide all,
> > But help not though she call.

(I, ii, ll.229–234)

Evadne's murder of the King recalls the advice in minute detail: the King denies his crimes, pleads for his life several times and then dies a prolonged death of 'often-dyings' as Evadne stabs him a dozen or more times. His effeminacy is most emphatically reiterated by his bridal role in this final encounter with Evadne even as she has usurped the male role of aggressive sexual violence. After discovering the murder, the gentlemen of the bedchamber even recognize that they will have a hard time convincing others that a woman had done the deed: 'this will be laid on us: who can believe / A woman could do it?' (V, i, ll.126–127), and Cleon's surprised reaction – 'Her act! A woman!' – reiterates the gendered topsy-turviness of the events we have just witnessed.

This refiguring of the monarch (or male authority) as effeminate and the simultaneous allocation of effeminacy to court circles may be read as a direct response to ambiguities that surrounded James I's sexual preferences. Many at court were familiar with James's choice of handsome young men as favourites. His early notice of Robert Carr and his later elevation of George Villiers were founded entirely on the young men's handsome appearance and charming qualities; contemporaries even imply that the Queen and others with her deliberately provided an occasion for James to meet George Villiers in 1614 as part of an attempt to orchestrate the fall of Carr who had grown overconfident and arrogant. The orchestration even took into account that Villiers (who later became the Duke of Buckingham) would transform, as Carr had done, from an agreeable youth to an arrogant figure of authority. John Nichols, commenting on Villiers's meeting with the King, notes that the favourite's 'fortune was not actually made until he had been exhibited before the King at Cambridge in March 1614–15' and adds that 'the rise of Villiers was certainly accelerated by the efforts of Archbishop Abbot and the Queen, who, being justly offended by the arrogance of Somerset and his undue influence over the King, adopted the resolution of, as it has been termed, "driving out one nail by another"' (Nichols 1828 p.20). Nichols also describes James's interest in Villiers: 'The King, as in the case of Carr, was attracted by admiration of his handsome exterior, it being one of our Monarch's most remarkable foibles, that he was delighted, almost to fascination, by a fine figure and countenance, and a graceful carriage' (Nichols 1828 p.19). James himself seems to have been acutely aware of rampant rumours concerning his interest in handsome courtiers; in a letter to his Queen, Anne of Denmark, written shortly after his succession to the throne of England, he goes to considerable trouble to quell such rumours and reiterate his love for her:

> I thank God I carrie that love and respecte unto you quhich, by the law of God and nature, I ought to do to my wyfe and mother of my children, but not for that ye are a King's dauchter, for quither ye waire a king's or a cook's dauchter, ye must be all alike to me, being once my wyfe. . . . God is my witness I ever preferred you to all my bairnes, much more then to any subjects; but if you will ever give place to the reports of everie flattering sicophant that will perswade you that when I account well of an honest and wise servant for his true fathful service to me, that it is to compare, or prefere him to you, then will nather ye or I be ever at reste at peace.
>
> (Nichols 1828 pp.153–154)

The Maid's Tragedy may thus be read as a dramatic rendering of the Jacobean court's tendencies, though these tendencies have been appropriated to serve the extreme ends of tragedy; in this sense the play's depiction of male authority provides another gloss of courtly life such as we receive from letters and diaries of the time. But the issue may be even more complicated; the fluid nature of gender in this play and in others of the period may indeed demonstrate what Laura Levine sees as a fundamental aspect of Renaissance drama, 'a kind of *a priori* sense of powerlessness that springs from precisely the fear that there is no real masculinity, no masculine self' (Levine 1994 p.8). The play's invocation of court life is immediately apparent in the opening scene which stages preparations for a lavish but typical wedding masque and in the subsequent scene where the King enters the newly married couple's bedchamber invoking the privilege of patriarchal authority.[18] The first decade after James's ascension saw the performance of numerous masques at court; at certain times of the year, courtiers hardly had time to move from performing one masque to preparing another. On 26 February 1607, for example, Rowland Whyte writes from Whitehall to the Earl of Shrewsbury that 'The great Maske intended for my Lord Hadington's marriage is now the only thing thought upon at Court' and in a letter on the 29th, he adds that 'no sooner had he Ben Jonson made an end of these *The Masque of Beauty*, but that he undertook a new charge' for a masque at Viscount Hadington's marriage (Nichols 1828 p.175).

Strato's condemnation of the masque to be staged in *The Maid's Tragedy* directs an attack at the Jacobean court that is hard to miss; asked by Lissipius if the masque will be a good one, Strato responds by invoking the artificial nature of masques in general: 'they must commend the King, and speak / In praise of the assembly, bless the bride and groom / In person of some god: they're tied to rules / Of flattery' (I, i, ll.9–12). The masque that follows remains true to convention, but the central figures in the masque, Cynthia the androgynous goddess of the hunt and chastity and the Protean gods of the sea, encapsulate the play's central theme of breaking boundaries, both with regard to gender and morality. The play may indeed be read as an example of what Foucault terms 'the great transformation of sex into discourse' (Foucault 1988–90 p.22).

A similar point might be made about Webster's collapse of gender boundaries in *The Duchess of Malfi*, a play which insists on conveying Ferdinand's feminization by implicitly allying his evil with witchcraft and by focusing on his lycanthropy in the later scenes. His lycanthropy, a malady sometimes afflicting pregnant women, emerges as a demented state caused by his sister's fertility. Though Frank Whigham's reading of the play solely in terms of class issues and his claim that Ferdinand's incestuous passion constitutes a pose might be extreme, his recognition that Ferdinand's character reveals a propensity for hysterical reaction may hold considerable truth; Whigham argues that Ferdinand is 'a threatened aristocrat, frightened by the contamination of his ascriptive social rank, and obsessively preoccupied with its defense. . . . Ferdinand's incestuous inclination toward his sister is a social posture, of hysterical compensation – a desperate expression of the desire to evade degrading association with inferiors' (Whigham 1991 p.266). Ferdinand seems to suffer from classic symptoms of hysteria, traditionally a female disease linked directly to sexuality. As Ilza Veith demonstrates, the Galenic theory about hysteria as a result of the retention of semen caused by sexual abstinence still dominated Renaissance thinking about

NOTE

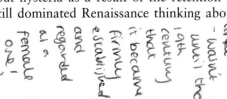

the disease (Veith 1965 pp.120–154). Ferdinand's hysteria manifests itself most vividly in the scene with the Cardinal where he rants about the Duchess's recently discovered liaison with Antonio; the Cardinal seems to recognize his brother's malady, registering considerable perturbation throughout at the implications of Ferdinand's passionate outbursts. In response to his brother's caution against creating 'so wild a tempest', Ferdinand erupts into a violent rage whose sexual undertones are unmistakable: 'Would I could be one, / That I might toss her palace about her ears, / Root up her goodly forests, blast her meads, / And lay her general territory as waste, / As she hath done her honour's' (II, v, ll.19–23). His obsession with seeing his sister in his imagination 'in the shameful act of sin' 'with some strong thig'd bargeman' lends some credence to Whigham's point about his concerns regarding contamination by mixture with the lower class, but the passion of his outbursts suggests that his sexual obsession hardly constitutes a posture. If anything, Ferdinand's concern about class contamination presents itself as an exaggerated posture intended to mask his incestuous passion for his sister.

Paracelsian notions about the cause of hysteria, especially a form of the disease that Paracelsus calls *chorea lasciva*, provide a clue to Ferdinand's state of mind as it obsesses over his sister's sexual liaisons:

> Thus the cause of the disease, *chorea lasciva*, is a mere opinion and idea assumed by the imagination, affecting those who believe in such a thing. This opinion and idea are the origin of the disease both in children and adults. In children the cause is also an imagined idea, based not on thinking but on perceiving, because they have heard or seen something. The reason is this: their sight and hearing are so strong that unconsciously they have fantasies about what they have seen or heard. And in such fantasies their reason is taken and perverted into the shape imagined.
>
> (cited by Veith 1965 p.106)

Ambrose Pare's extensions on the subject of hysteria, which figure in his work as a female disease of the mind, further elucidates Ferdinand's behaviour:

> For some accidents com by suppression of the terms, others com by corruption of the seed, but if the matter bee . . . of a choleric humor, it causseth the madness called *furor uterinus*, and such a pratling, that they speak all things that are to be concealed; and a giddiness of the head, by reason that the animal spirit is suddenly shaken by the admixture of a putrefied vapour and hot spirit: but nothing is more admirable, then that the diseas taketh the patient sometimes with laughing, and sometimes with weeping, for som at the firt will weep and then laugh in the same diseas and state thereof.
>
> (cited by Veith 1965 p.114)

Pare's description aptly summarizes the state to which Ferdinand degenerates after the Duchess' death.

Ferdinand's association with witchcraft also adds to this general impression of feminization; when he hires Bosola to serve him, to watch the Duchess for he 'would not have her marry' as he puts it, Bosola suggests the analogy by describing his own role as that of a witch's 'familiar', 'a very quaint invisible devil in flesh' (Act I, ii, ll.199–200). Protestant notions of witchcraft, as Allison

P. Coudert demonstrates, unlike the Catholic view demonstrated in detail in the *Malleus Malleficorum*, concentrated not on the sexual liaison between witch and devil but on the witch's opposition to holy, heterosexual matrimony (Coudert 1989 p.80). Unable to actually dissolve the knot of holy matrimony, however, witchcraft directed itself through charms and spells to cause separation and rift between partners. Thus in Middleton's *The Witch*, Sebastian discovers that his betrothed has married another while he was away fighting in the wars and enlists the help of witches to prevent sexual union between Isabella and Antonio. The activity of the witches throughout this play directs itself specifically against holy matrimony, though their power, as they themselves recognize, remains limited in this regard:

> we cannot disjoin wedlock;
> 'Tis of heaven's fastening. Well may we raise jars,
> Jealousies, strifes, and heart-burning disagreements,
> Like a thick scurf o'er life, as did our master
> Upon that patient miracle [Job]; but the work itself
> Our power cannot disjoint.
>
> (I, ii, p.133)

In this context it might be worth recalling that the activity of the witches in *Macbeth* also results in discord and emotional divorce between Macbeth and Lady Macbeth who are initially represented as close and loving.

As Sigrid Brauner also demonstrates, for Protestant thinkers who took their theories about witchcraft from Martin Luther, the witch as one opposed to holy matrimony thus represented the opposite of the pious Christian wife (Brauner 1989 p.29). And this is precisely the opposition that Webster elaborates in his play. By contrast to Ferdinand's obsessive compulsion to obstruct the Duchess's desire to marry which he sees as lustful and intemperate, the Duchess herself speaks of matrimony in religious terms, though not without implications of sexual union and propagation. The exchange between the Duchess and Antonio in the scene of their contract emphasizes the sanctity and naturalness of their union:

> *Duch.* Bless, Heaven, this sacred Gordian, which let violence
>   Never untwine.
> *Ant.*   And may our sweet affections, like the spheres,
>   Be still in motion.
> *Duch.* Quic'ning, and make
>   The like soft music.
> *Ant.*   That we may imitate the loving palms,
>   Best emblem of a peaceful marriage,
>   That nev'r bore fruit divided.
> *Duch.* What can the Church force more?
>   . . .
>   How can the Church build faster?

> We now are man and wife, and 'tis the Church
> That must but echo this.
>
> (I, ii, ll.393–406)

As we have also seen earlier, Webster goes to considerable trouble to detail the Duchess's death in terms that suggest devout Christianity, while Ferdinand remains throughout the play in direct opposition both to his sister and the Cardinal who, despite his villainy, seems to represent organized religion. In our very first encounter with Ferdinand, he voices his opposition to seeing his sister married in terms that suggest his unnatural mental state and obsession with the subject. In their first encounter with their sister, the Cardinal and Ferdinand both exhort her to remain a widow but it is Ferdinand who reveals an unnatural obsession with sexuality as he warns her against marriage. His vulgarity and explicit references to male sexuality – 'And women like that part, which like the lamprey, / Hath nev'r a bone in it' – shock the Duchess considerably. Interestingly too, Webster is not the only Renaissance playwright to link witchcraft and incest. In *The Witch* Middleton suggests an incestuous relationship between Hecate and her son Firestone through Hecate's jealousy at not being able to share her son's bed every night; 'You're a kind son,' she laments, 'But 'tis the nature of you all; I see that / You had rather hunt after strange women still / Than lie with your own mothers' (I, ii, p.130).

The Protestant view of witchcraft, as I have already suggested, shared with the Catholic the notion that witchcraft is gender specific (Brauner 1989 pp.32–33). By defining Ferdinand exclusively in terms of his opposition to his sister's marriage whether it be to Antonio or anyone else, Webster inevitably suggests his effeminacy and unnaturally gendered state. The association is emphasized throughout the play in obvious ways. Ferdinand also demonstrates a preoccupation with human body parts, especially limbs, another factor often associated with witchcraft. The witches' brew in *Macbeth*, we might recall, has a plentiful supply of these – a Jew's nose and the finger of a babe strangled after being ditch-delivered. Equally pervasive was the belief that these body parts figured in conjurations intended to kill or torment devout Christians. The belief was pervasive enough to warrant legal action by the authorities; on 9 June 1604, for example, a statute was passed which enacted that

> if any person shall practise or exercise any invocation or conjuration of any evil or wicked spirit, or take up any man, woman or child out of his, her, or their grave, ... or the skin, bone, or any other part of any person to be employed or used in any manner of witchcraft, ... or shall ... practise ... any witchcraft ... whereby any person shall be killed, pined, or lamed in his or her body or any part thereof, such offender shall suffer the pains of death of felons without benefit of clergy or sanctuary.
> (quoted from Reginald Scott by Bullen 1964 note on p.125)

As Ferdinand acknowledges to Bosola, he wishes to bring the Duchess to a distraction and, in his first attempt, pretends to shake her hand and make peace. Only when the Duchess calls for lights fearing that her brother's cold hand presages an illness does she realize with horror that he has presented her with a

dead man's hand; the association with witchcraft is explicit in her reaction to
the macabre event: 'What witchcraft doth he practise, that he hath left a dead
man's hand here?' (IV, i, ll.54–55). But Ferdinand has only just begun his torment
and Bosola opens the curtains to reveal the artificial figures of Antonio and his
children which the Duchess mistakes for their dead bodies. The vision seems to
produce the intended effect, for the Duchess lapses into intense despair thereafter
and pleads to be killed herself:

> Good comfortable fellow
> Persuade a wretch that's broke upon the wheel
> To have all his bones new set: entreat him live,
> To be executed again. Who must despatch me?
> I account this world a tedious theatre,
> For I do play a part in't against my will.

(IV, i, ll.79–84)

Ferdinand's use of wax and/or clay figures itself suggests his association with
witchcraft; a common charge levelled against witches was that they used such
artificial figures of their enemies to cause torment or to induce their death.
Ferdinand's desire to see the Duchess' family suffer a gruesome death reveals the
intensity of his hatred:

> I would have their bodies
> Burnt in a coal-pit, with the ventage stopp'd,
> That their curs'd smoke might not ascend to Heaven:
> Or dip the sheets they lie in, in pitch or sulphur
> Wrap them in't, and then light them like a match:
> Or else to boil their bastard to a cullis,
> And give't his lecherous father, to renew
> The sin of his back.

(II, v, ll.69–72)

And his artificial figures begin the course of his vengeance against Antonio and
his children. Though the following so-called confession about witchcraft earlier
in the period shows a somewhat different use of wax and clay figures, it shares
with Ferdinand's methods a basic desire to cause harm to one's enemy:

> He bein further demanded to what end the spirits in the likeness of toads and the
> pictures of man in wax or clay do serve, he said that picyures made in wax will cause
> the party (for whom it is made) to continue sick two whole years. . . . And as for the
> pictures of clay, their confection is after this manner. They used to take the earth of a
> new-made grave, the rib-bone of a man or woman burned to ashes. . . . And after all
> ceremonies ended, they put a prick, that is a pin or a thorn, in any member where
> they would have the party grieved. And if the said prick be put to the heart, the party
> died within nine days.

(Quoted by Bullen 1964 note on p.128)

Interestingly, while Webster goes to considerable trouble to paint Ferdinand's
feminized nature as monstrous and unnatural, he depicts the Duchess, despite
her dominant role in marriage, in the most positive light. His tragedy thus differs

considerably from Beaumont and Fletcher's experimentation with twin-gendered individuals, though the inspiration for his concern with feminized masculinity might have been provoked by the same sociopolitical environment.

Tragedy and carnival: the debasement of aristocratic bodies in *The Changeling*, *Women Beware Women* and *The Bloody Banquet*

The Changeling, *Women Beware Women* and *The Bloody Banquet*, plays that were composed during the 1620s, also invoke carnival inversion and transgression, though along rather different lines than *The Maid's Tragedy* or *The Duchess of Malfi*. The process in all three plays constitutes a debasement of its central characters, Beatrice Joanna in the first, the Duke of Florence in the second, and Tymethes and the Tyrant's Queen in the last.

Middleton's tragedies also foreground sexual transgression by staging rapes as part of their central actions. In *The Changeling*, Beatrice Joanna employs De Flores to murder Alonzo Piracquo only to find herself having to pay with sex for the murder; in *Women Beware Women*, Bianca finds herself locked in a room in Livia's house with the Duke of Florence who proceeds to seduce her. While critics have generally recognized that the latter scene stages rape, few have seen Beatrice Joanna's relationship with De Flores (perhaps because of her culpability in the murder of Alonso Piracquo) as similarly rooted in rape. The language suggests, however, that despite the change of heart by Bianca and Beatrice Joanna after the rapes, we are to see the scenes in similar terms as sexual violations. As the Duke embraces Bianca despite her protests in *Women Beware Women*, he remarks on her breasts panting like a turtle dove and assures her that she will grow to love what she now holds in awe and dread, vocabulary which recurs in *The Changeling* as De Flores insists on his due payment from Beatrice Joanna: ''Las how the turtle pants! Thou'lt love anon / What thou fear'st and faintest to venture on' (III, iv, ll.170–171). Thus at the very centre of these plays stands a carnivalesque misalliance between high and low; Bakhtin describes this essential aspect of carnival in some detail: 'All things that were once self-enclosed, disunified, distanced from one another by a noncarnivalistic hierarchical world view are drawn into carnivalistic contacts and combinations. Carnival . . . combines the sacred with the profane, the lofty with the low, the great with the insignificant, the wise with the stupid' (Bakhtin 1984 p.123). The alliances that emerge between Beatrice Joanna and her servant De Flores and between the Duke of Florence and Bianca might be described as just such a carnivalistic commingling of the high and the low.

Both women emerge from the rape with similar attitudes towards their seducer. Bianca transfers her anger to Guardiano who facilitated the rape but acknowledges her newly awakened desire for the Duke: 'I'm made bold now, / I thank the treachery; sin and I'm acquainted, / No couple greater; and I'm like that one, / Who, making politic use of a base villain, / He likes the treason well, but hates the traitor' (II, ii, ll.444–447). Beatrice Joanna similarly transforms from one who detested the very sight of De Flores to one who relies on him to direct her actions hereafter: 'I'm forced to love thee now', she tells him as he evolves the plan to rescue her from discovery by Alsemero. The radical transformation that occurs in both women immediately following the rape epitomizes the carnivalesque movement of these plays and the audience's ultimate perception of its central characters as monstrous and contaminated rather than beautiful and pure, aspects emphasized during the early scenes of the plays. The central movement in both plays thus constitutes a debasement of its central characters, Beatrice Joanna in the former and the Duke and Bianca in the latter.

Peter Stallybrass makes a similar point about *The Revenger's Tragedy* where we move from socially sanctioned activities such as marriage to carnivalesque acts of consumption; he argues that 'the reordering of social boundaries and the construction of genealogies through marriage is displaced by the ordering/ disordering of eating and the kiss' (Stallybrass 1987 p.210). But the movement from high to low, from the normal to carnivalesque excess in the form of physical and sexual consumption in that play is far less profound than in either of Middleton's tragedies. *The Revenger's Tragedy*, we might recall, already opens on the borders of transgression with Vindice holding the skull of his beloved and providing a running commentary on members of the Ducal family as they pass by. The members of this family are hardly distinguishable from each other as they conjunctively embody a variety of vices, among them lechery, lust and ambition. Vindice himself, as his name signifies, embodies an attitude and a type rather than an individual. In this our first introduction to central characters in the play, we thus view bodies already in states of corruption and decay. *The Revenger's Tragedy* announces its generic affiliation with carnivalesque excess at the very beginning and its subsequent staging of sexual and physical excesses comes as no surprise. The movement in *The Changeling* and *Women Beware Women*, on the other hand, is considerably more dramatic. In both plays we move from visions of 'classic' bodies to deformed and corrupted ones, from purity to contamination.

The distinction between the classical and grotesque body that theorists on carnival such as Bakhtin and Stallybrass elaborate might be worth recalling in this context. The classical body presents a static form and as Stallybrass points out, 'we gaze up at the figure in wonder. We are placed by it as spectators to an instant – frozen yet apparently universal – of epic or tragic time' (Stallybrass 1987 p.210). The grotesque, a fundamental aspect of carnival transgression, presents a body in flux, 'multiple, split, mobile'. Rather than gaze up in wonder and awe, we look down to focus on the lower bodily stratum (Bakhtin 1984 pp.21–22). Both *The Changeling* and *Women Beware Women* dramatize a movement from the classical to the grotesque.

The Changeling opens with Alsemero's paean to Beatrice Joanna's beauty associated in his mind with the church where he first saw her:

> 'Twas in the temple where I first beheld her
> And now again the same. . . .

> The place is holy, so is my intent:
> I love her beauties to the holy purpose;
> ...
> The church hath first begun our interview,
> And that's the place must join us as one;
> So there's beginning and perfection too.
>
> (I, i, ll.1–12)

The tragedy closes with our vision of Beatrice Joanna as contaminated blood; as Vermandero approaches his daughter in anguished disbelief at the tragedy that has unfolded, she cautions him: 'O come not near me, sir; I shall defile you! / I am that of your blood was taken from you, / For your better health; look no more upon 't, / Let the common sewer take it from distinction / Beneath the stars' (V, iii, ll.150–155). We have moved through the course of the play from purity to contamination, from the beautiful to the monstrous, from Church to the common sewer, in short, from a classical to the grotesque view of the body.

Middleton and Rowley emphasize this movement by invoking a potent symbol of transmutation in the Renaissance, alchemy. References to alchemy pervade the play but the metaphor receives its fullest elaboration in the concluding scene where Alsemero thrusts Beatrice Joanna and De Flores into his closet to 'rehearse again / Your scene of lust' and to produce what Alsemero later describes as 'a wonder'. The closet into which he thrusts them, the very closet where he keeps his medicines used earlier to test Beatrice Joanna's virginity, serves as the equivalent of an alchemical chamber in which substances combine to produce new elements. Alchemical descriptions frequently represent the merger of substances in a chamber or jar as coition between male and female elements. Sir George Ripley's *The Compound of Alchymie* describes the process of 'conjunction' between elements thus:

> The Chapter here followyth of secret Conjunccion;
> Whych natures repugnant joyneth to perfyt Unyte,
> ...
> And therfore Phylosophers geveth thys deffynycyon,
> Seying thus Conjunccion ys nought ells
> But of dyffeveryd qualytes a Copulacyon.
>
> (Ashmole 1967 p.144)

Elsewhere Ripley refers to the conjunction between mercury and sulphur, primary elements in alchemical experiments, as a copulation between 'male and female' (Ashmole 1967 p.145). In 'Fragments' on alchemy, Thomas Charnock similarly equates alchemical fusion with sexual union: 'With hic and haec thus may ye do, / As Husband and Wife together them wed; / Put them in a chamber both two, / And shet fast the dore when they be abed' (Ashmole 1967 p.432). The implied reference to this alchemical process is unmistakable in the concluding scene of *The Changeling* which produces a monstrous new substance unrecognizable to those who witness its emergence. Of course, unlike a sanctified alchemical union such as Alsemero had planned, the deviant carnivalesque process, orchestrated not by the alchemist himself but by a woman in collaboration with her servant, produces not a superior substance but a monstrous one.

The play's movement from the classical to the grotesque is further accentuated by its straddling of genres, by its simultaneous indulgence in tragic transgression and comic licence. Critics have long recognized the play's unstable generic stance between comedy and tragedy, attributing it traditionally to the collaboration between Middleton and Rowley. Some critics see it as an aspect of late Renaissance baroque (Huebert 1977); Raymond Pentzell explains it in terms of the Mannerist style of late Renaissance drama, though he quite misconstrues the complexity of the play's generic ambivalence by focusing on the concluding scene: 'There are two dead bodies left on-stage. No provision has been made to carry them off. They have been lying there through all the punning changes rung on "change". Now what? Either they lie in place until the whole audience files out chuckling, or else they get up, bow, and walk off. . . . Either way, our "tragedy" has ended in a grisly double take of grisly comedy' (Pentzell 1986 p.275). Many Renaissance texts present us with dead bodies in the last scene that remain on-stage while characters unravel the plot or provide homiletic advice for the audience to keep in mind as they leave the theatre. The scenario Pentzell sets up typifies many Renaissance tragedies where dead bodies at the conclusion will either have to revive and exit with the rest of the cast or remain on-stage because the written text makes no provision for their disposal. *The Changeling* blurs genre far more completely than Pentzell's reading suggests and this generic dissolution involves more than a simple contrast between comic sub-plot and tragic main plot resulting from dual authorship. All plots in the play encompass the possibilities for tragedy and comedy simultaneously: the moment of Beatrice Joanna's tragic deception of Alsemero as she fakes the effects of his virginity potion, for example, is simultaneously comic and tragic; Diaphanta's horrible death by fire, a result of her eagerness at the deception being practised on Alsemero as she usurps Beatrice Joanna's place in the bridal bed, similarly evokes dual emotions; even De Flores's insistence on his due rewards for murder, which seems to take Beatrice Joanna entirely by surprise, produces a dual effect; the sub-plot where Antonio and Francisco assume disguises in order to begin a relationship with Isabella, only to find themselves accused of murder and deceit, almost culminates in tragedy; the comic sub-plot even stages a near-rape as Antonio tries to seduce Isabella. The play thus carries generic mutation to new limits in its invocation of comic and tragic conventions; it thus belongs to the realm of carnival genres, distinguished by Bakhtin from the 'pure' genres of tragedy and epic by their ambivalence and multiplicity (Bakhtin 1984 p.127).[19]

Middleton's theatrical engagement with carnivalesque transgression and debasement emerges most fully, however, in the tragedy he composed by himself, *Women Beware Women*. No other play of the early Stuart stage, with the possible exception perhaps of *The Virgin Martyr* which I discussed earlier, explores more fully the pleasurable effects of transgressive voyeurism to a male audience than *Women Beware Women*. The play repeatedly draws attention to visuality, especially to acts of transgressive viewing. From the play's opening line 'Thy sight was never yet more precious to me' to the spectacular sights of the concluding scene, references to seeing and vision recur in a way that involves not only the players themselves as spectators and participants (as the concluding scene's erasure of the spectator–participant distinction illustrates) but the audience as well as both participants and producers of the play's visual pleasure; Frederic Jameson's claim about cinema that 'the visual is essentially pornographic, . . . it has its end in rapt, mindless fascination' is truer of this tragedy than of any other on the Renaissance stage (Jameson 1990 p.1). The play demonstrates the extent to which Laura Mulvey's claim that 'the magic of the Hollywood style at its best arose, not exclusively, but in one important aspect, from its skilled manipulation of visual pleasure' might apply equally to successful Renaissance theatre (Mulvey 1989 p.16). In what might be described as an extension of the typical perspective afforded to those nearest the stage, namely the groundlings, Middleton manipulates vision and space to direct his audience as a whole towards looking upwards only to see the underside of things.

The play's manipulation of visual pleasure is most explicitly presented in what appears to be a minor scene at the heart of the tragedy, in which the wealthy Ward conducts an extended scrutiny of Isabella to determine whether she might make a suitable wife. As in other scenes, the playwright here directs our vision upward only to draw our attention ultimately to the underside of things; the pattern, as I will indicate, recurs in other crucial scenes of the play. Sordido, the Ward's man, participates fully in this examination and his comments on Isabella – her hips, her tongue, her mouth, her nose, her form – suggest that his response caters to salacious tastes among sections of the theatre audience. The examination, which moves from an attempted inspection of Isabella's mouth to a peep beneath her skirts, invokes the commonplace Renaissance conflation of mouth and genitalia explored by Karen Newman in other contexts (Newman 1991 p.11). The Ward's invitation to Sordido to 'dab down as you see me and peep of one side, when her back's to you' signals the scene's exploitation of woman as a site for voyeuristic examination by males (III, iii, ll.103–104). The Ward and Sordido thus explicitly direct our gaze of Isabella's body inwards and from below. In response to the Ward's request that Isabella walk back and forth so that they might observe her fully on 'both sides', Sordido makes an extraordinary claim which draws attention to the play's interest in the female body as an object to be viewed, scrutinized and judged from below before it can be acquired or violated: 'And you shall find me apt enough to peeping. / I have been one of them has seen mad sights / Under your scaffolds' (III, iii, ll.118–120). Sordido's reference to viewing from beneath the scaffold thus includes the audience, or at least those immediately beneath the stage, the groundlings, in his act of gazing. His language also suggests an analogy between what he sees and the hell beneath the stage even as it alludes to the death and decay associated with punitive practices, references which come to mind particularly because the audience is aware of Isabella's incestuous relationship with her uncle Hippolyto.

The Ward's examination thus tries to achieve what Sordido had earlier underlined as an essential part of marital transactions, that is, that the groom view his prospective bride naked before entering into any alliance with her. A few lines later, having apparently 'peeped' as he had been directed to do, Sordido elaborates on what he has seen: 'I see the sweetest sight to please my master.' Sordido's language which moves from 'mad sights under the scaffold' to 'sweetness' thus fuses the monstrous and the marvellous within his transgressive glance that takes in both sides of Isabella, thus directing the audience to do the same. Middleton here stages a metatheatrical moment at the heart of his play, though of course the effects of the scene remain suggestive rather than literal; what is important here is the gestural significance implied by the Ward's and Sordido's language as they conduct this extended examination of Isabella, not that they actually see anything at all. In fact, their inability to see anything is theatrically presaged by their earlier failed attempts to look inside Isabella's mouth.

On an obvious level, this private drama between the Ward, Sordido and Isabella stages transgressive pleasure and the woman being viewed is constructed by the gazers as the Other whose very Otherness provokes curiosity and voyeuristic interest; the scene's theatrical essence lies in its provocation of fantasy, what Jacques Lacan describes as 'the idea of another locality, another space, another scene, the between perception and consciousness' (Lacan 1977 p.56). Sordido's reference to the space beneath the scaffold invites the Ward to conceive of just such another view, to visualize 'that space in which fantasy stages its mise-en-scene of desire' (Lacan 1977 p.56). In this sense, the scene recalls other transgressive looks in the play, Leantio's first vision of Bianca in a window at her parents' house and the Duke's similar vision of her at Leantio's house; in both cases, Bianca's framed and picture-like image provokes desire, functioning in a manner similar to the lewd pictures that Guardiano later strategically places for her to see as she tours Livia's house before her rape/seduction by the Duke. In all these cases, we look up with characters only to have our gaze ultimately directed downwards towards sexuality.

However, this later scene between the Ward, Sordido and Isabella remains crucial for more than Middleton's obvious manipulation of voyeuristic interests among his audience by inviting them firstly to visualize another space beyond the one they actually see and secondly to conceive of this other space as a privileged view only available to those immediately beneath the scaffold, namely, the groundlings. Equally important is the playwright's conflation of the high and the low as we are directed to envision 'mad' and 'sweet' sights at once. Yet the scene does not, despite Sordido's obvious reference to sections of the theatre audience, simply implicate males and those of the lower social orders in the pleasure to be derived from indulging the transgressive gaze. Isabella herself, having decided to marry the Ward in order to conceal her incestuous relationship with Hippolyto, willingly participates in the violation, thus complicating the issues of voyeurism and transgression that this scene so dramatically foregrounds. Isabella's role as indulgent participant even aligns her with Bianca whose dramatic transformation after her rape by the Duke similarly implicates her in the violence enacted upon her. There are three different aspects to the pleasure being staged in this scene: firstly, scopophilic pleasure shared by the Ward, Sordido and the audience whose willingness to visualize the unseen implicates them in the actions being staged; secondly, pleasure in being scrutinized, enjoyed by Isabella herself as she parades for her spectators; and most importantly, narcissistic pleasure, for as the audience in the theatre and all the participants in the play recognize, the 'sweet' sight that Sordido claims to see cannot in actuality constitute an Other space. The narcissistic pleasure that halts the Ward's examination arises not from a private joke but from a public one, a joke in which the entire audience participates as the play draws attention to the role of the actor who masquerades as a woman on-stage. In other words, what presents itself as a scene of female objectification and commodification becomes, through Sordido's reference to the view from beneath the scaffold, a metatheatrical moment when, in psychological terms, the castration complex is first rehearsed and then dispelled, and the act of looking secretly, staged initially as a violation or intrusion, degenerates into a common but reassuring theatrical joke. The scene which seemingly constructs itself as a parade of woman as an object of display and wonder ultimately has little to do with woman, much more to do with man. Mulvey's point about the sculptures and paintings of Allen Jones applies equally to Middleton's tragedy: 'Women may seem to be the subject of an endless parade of pornographic fantasies, jokes, day-dreams, and so on, but fundamentally most male fantasy is a closed loop dialogue with itself' (Mulvey 1989 p.11). In other words, the scene dramatizes, even if only for the briefest of moments, what Susan Zimmerman describes as 'the complex appeal of boy actors' on the Renaissance stage (Zimmerman 1993 p.47) and what Laura Levine characterizes as 'the degree to which in Renaissance texts masculinity itself must be staged in order to exist' (Levine 1994 p.8). In this sense, Annette Kuhn's point about crossdressing as a simultaneously problematic and safe mode of cinematic practice applies equally to Middleton's theatre: 'If crossdressing narratives always in some measure problematise gender identity and sexual difference, then, many do so only to confirm finally the absoluteness of both, to reassert a "natural" order of fixed gender and unitary subjectivity' (Kuhn 1985 p.57).

The narcissistic pleasure that this scene affords requires some qualification, however. Despite the phallic focus of the scene, and as I will suggest, the play as a whole, the narcissistic pleasure which Sordido invokes by his comment about the sweet sights is not simply a matter of one-to-one identification; after all, despite the joke in which all participate, Isabella presents on-stage the unmistakable image of woman. The joke really turns not on an exact identification between those who gaze and the phallic image that they see but from a perception of incongruity. It revolves on the play's insistence that we imaginatively visualize 'both sides' of the object, the ultimate androgyny: the woman with a penis and the man with breasts embodied in a single figure elaborately paraded on-stage through more than a hundred lines of dialogue. Francette Pacteau argues that fascination with androgyny needs to be understood not merely in physical terms but as a mental process at work, as a 'fascination with sexual ambiguity'.

'Androgyny', Pacteau insists, 'cannot be circumscribed as belonging to some being; it is more a relation between a look and an appearance, in other words, psyche and image' (Pacteau 1986 p.62). The language of sexual innuendo and the act of transgressive looking work at cross-purposes in this scene and throughout the play to emphasize the theatricality of looking itself, to demarcate the arena of the scaffold as a space designed for sexual play and fantasy. The scene, in fact, testifies to 'a culturally inscribed fascination with sexual indeterminacy' which Zimmerman attributes to Renaissance audiences in general (Zimmerman 1993 p.55) but it is a sexual indeterminacy that remains rooted within the culturally secure art of 'playing on-stage' and which constructs itself as a pro-duction of woman based on the phallic norm.

Though the scene constructs itself as catering only to sections of the audience immediately beneath the scaffold (its very status as part of the under or secondary plot adds to this impression), its theatrical import extends to all the onlookers. The vision it provides ultimately reinforces that provided by the main plot involving Bianca and the Duke. By its very nature the scene invites comparison with another elaborate tour staged for us as Guardiano directs Bianca through Livia's private rooms, a tour which culminates in her rape/seduction by the Duke. The scene of Bianca's seduction also exploits the value of voyeuristic transgression; in response to the Mother's question about what she has seen in her tour, Bianca responds 'The monument and all: . . . / ???'Faith, I have seen that I little thought to see / I' th morning when I rose' (II, ii, ll.454–459). Her response, like Sordido's, involves a joke which all those present (except the mother) comprehend. Similarly her view of the Duke's 'monument', like Sordido's view of Isabella, constitutes a view from below, both because the viewers are lower in the social order than those they view and because the object of their gaze is the lower body and its parts. Our first vision of the Duke in the opening act of the play, as Bianca and the Mother witness his stately procession through the city, had provided a very different view. However, our view of him after Bianca's rape/seduction directs itself not to his divinity, but to his 'monument' and sexual life. In the language of carnival, we move from a vision of the classical to the grotesque body but Middleton has manipulated the parameters of our gaze considerably: instead of 'looking up at the classical body in awe' Middleton arranges the earlier scene so that spatially we look down upon it as the Duke heads a procession on the street below the mother's house; we later glance upwards to the monument in the rooms above the main stage as our vision transfers permanently from the Duke's divinity to his sexuality.

Most importantly, while the actions in the main and secondary plots construct themselves as contrasts, their movement ultimately takes us in similar directions, towards viewing the same things – 'the sweet sight' and 'the monument' – in short, to the male rather than female centre of the action. One might argue that despite the play's persistent references to women in its title and its crucial scenes, man remains the real subject of Middleton's tragedy.

The idea of transgressive viewing and another space with its complementary drama of action receives its greatest elaboration in the concluding scene where nuptial celebrations and death occur simultaneously and our view is once again directed, despite the frenetic action on-stage, to the space beneath the scaffold. The concluding act, in fact, opens with an elaborate discussion between Guardiano and the Ward as they draw the audience's attention to the space beneath the trapdoor through which Hippolyto is supposed to fall to his death. The object that will accomplish his death, the galtrap or caltrap, is brought onto the stage by Guardiano and carried off by the Ward who descends the trapdoor in order to set it up. The caltrop is an instrument of war, an iron ball with four sharp spikes one of which always extends upward no matter how the caltrop is thrown. With this phallic instrument of war poised upright beneath the scaffold, Guardiano proceeds to participate in the masque on-stage which ends with all the principal characters dying through a variety of means, all involving poison. Something goes awry, however, and it is Guardiano himself who falls through the trap, thus staging a private drama of death (which the audience is invited to visualize) for the Ward whose presence beneath the trapdoor has prevented him from seeing the masque above. The elaborate ritual of drawing our attention to the caltrop at the head of this scene has ensured, however, that we do not miss this theatre beneath the scaffold, one equally as violent and fantastic as the drama above, indeed quite literally 'a mad sight under the scaffold' from which the surprised Ward, frightened by his uncle's screams, flees in horror.

We are provided with three stages of death in this concluding scene: the masque of death staged by Livia, Guardiano, Isabella and Hippolyto; the horrible private theatre of death enacted under the scaffold and only imaginatively envisioned by the audience; and the deaths of Bianca and the Duke on the upper stage in a plot of Bianca's making gone awry. The conclusion reiterates the point that the actions above, on and beneath the scaffold differ only in form not in substance. Private viewing and public theatre merge once again.

Thus the extended scene dramatizing the Ward's and Sordido's scrutiny of Isabella seemingly constructs itself as indulgence for salacious tastes of the lower orders (to which Sordido belongs) but, by suggesting events in the other plot involving the Duke and Bianca, loses its effect as a scene of such restricted interest. The scene's manipulation of visual pleasure and its general relevance to central actions contributes to the play's pervasive deconstruction of class hierarchies both within the play as characters constantly defy their social status and through the playwright's insistence that his audience view the actions of his various plots as mirror images of each other. Inevitably, the play's indulgence in playing and seeing takes us, via elaborate tours of the upper, middle and lower stages or through visions of beautiful and grotesque bodies, always to the male centre of the text; 'mad sights' merge with the familiarity of 'sweet sights'; classic works of high art in a gallery lead to a monument signifying male desire; elaborate deaths on-stage enacted by Juno and her nymphs accomplish as much as a phallic caltrop strategically placed beneath a trapdoor. The groundlings' view thus affords a special insight that they arrive at naturally as a result of their privileged position directly beneath the stage, namely, that looking up inevitably constitutes looking under; other spectators arrive at this insight only gradually through Middleton's successful manipulation of vision and space.

The typological relevance of the scene in which the Ward examines Isabella to central actions thus contributes to the play's deconstruction of class hierarchies, an essential aspect of the carnivalesque literary genre (Bakhtin 1965 p.127). In *Women Beware Women* Middleton thus experiments less with genre than with dissolving social and political hierarchies; the play shares with others of the period a carnivalesque indulgence in breaking boundaries. As I suggested earlier, such experimentation with gender, genre and familial and social hierarchy undoubtedly carried political implications; at the very least, by staging carnivalesque debasement, these tragedies question the sanctity of gendered and social hierarchies.

Renaissance drama's most explicit link with carnival emerges also in another tragedy of this period sometimes attributed to Middleton, *The Bloody Banquet*.[20] While the play's movement takes us, as in *The Changeling* and *Women Beware Women*, from the high to the low and from the classical to the grotesque, the play's most significant connection with carnival emerges in its central actions which might be described as the crowning and uncrowning of kings. Bakhtin describes this process as a central carnivalistic act: 'The primary carnivalistic act is the mock crowning and subsequent uncrowning of the carnival king. This ritual is encountered in one form or another in all festivities of the carnival type' (Bakhtin 1984 p.124). The central actions in *The Changeling* and *Women Beware Women* might be described as enacting a process of crowning and uncrowning; especially in the latter play, the Duke of Florence undergoes just such a process of debasement and humiliation. *The Bloody Banquet*, however, literally stages the crowning and uncrowning of a carnival King who presides through the course of the play over a carnivalesque world of excess and topsy-turviness.[21]

The play signifies its links with carnival by its very title which refers to the concluding scene in which Armatrites, the usurper king of Lydia, is uncrowned. The play opens with the uncrowning of the real King of Lydia and the usurpation of his throne by the King of Cilicia; it ends with the recrowning of the King of Lydia and the uncrowning of the usurper. However, the 'Induction' which prefaces the play, by staging the uncrowning of the King of Lycia by the King of Lydia, suggests that the play's central action of crowning and uncrowning constitutes an endless cycle of events likely to be repeated again in the near future.

The play itself stages the adulterous relationship between Tymethes, the King of Lydia's son and heir, and Tethis, the usurper King's young and beautiful Queen. With the aid of her servants, the Queen manages to conceal her identity from her lover; he is brought to her in darkness and woos her while she remains veiled. Curious to discover the identity of his mistress, Timothes one day steals upon her while she is asleep. The furious Queen then shoots and kills her lover, only to find herself discovered by her husband; the King enters too late to enact vengeance on Tymethes but, unable to dismiss the vision of his wife in the arms of her handsome lover, he hits upon a gruesome punishment for his wife:

> Thou shalt not die as long as this is meat,
> Thou kill'd a Buck which thou thyself shall eat.
> . . .
> Here's Deer struck dead with thine own hand,
> 'Tis venison for thy own tooth, thou know'st the relish
> A dearer place hath beene thy taster.

(ll.1647–1652)

The last scene presents us with a lavish banquet at which the usurper King and his subjects entertain the real King of Lydia and his followers who have entered the castle disguised as pilgrims. At an adjacent table sits the distressed Queen condemned by her husband to consume the flesh of her lover; Tymethes's quartered body hangs on-stage for all to see as they feast. As the usurper King notes, despite the lavish banquet set before them, none can take their eyes off the distressed Queen and her gruesome punishment: 'I perceive strangers more desire to see / An object than the fare them set' (l.1921). This Thyestean scene which concludes the play combines death and feasting, music and distress, fascination and horror in the extreme. The actions that follow continue this collapse of opposites. The pilgrims throw off their disguise and the cornered usurper proceeds to kill his Queen before he himself is stabbed to death by the pilgrims all acting at once. The usurper King dies laughing, however, even comparing his pleasure in dying with the pleasures of sex: 'ha, ha, ha. / So, laugh away this breath, / My lust was ne're more pleasing than my death' (ll.1993–1995). What follows, the reinstatement of the old King to the throne of Lydia, the miraculous return of his Queen and the equally miraculous preservation of his son and heir, makes the concluding scene what the Queen describes as a 'happy hour' sanctioned by the gods. Despite the dead bodies on-stage, the play thus concludes on a happy note; 'No storm of fate so fierce but time destroys, / And beats back misery with a peal of joys', the King notes, as he ascends his throne once again. The playwright thus presents us with a tragedy that ends happily; like *The Changeling*, the play belongs to the carnivalesque genre, a form that was not uncommon on the Renaissance stage.

In plays such as *The Woman's Prize*, *The Maid's Tragedy*, *The Duchess of Malfi*, *The Changeling*, *Women Beware Women* and *The Bloody Banquet*, theatre successfully poaches on the cultural activity of carnival as it stages assaults on generic and social conventions. These plays, as new historicist re-readings of the Renaissance have so forcefully demonstrated, provoke sociopolitical interpretations precisely because they do not present isolated cases but, rather, record a general trend.

Notes

1. See essays by Coppelia Kahn (1977), John C. Bean (1980), Kathleen McLuskie (1982), Valerie Wayne (1985) and Tita Baumlin French (1989).
2. All citations from Shakespeare's play, hereafter referred to as *The Shrew*, will be

from the Arden edition of *The Taming of the Shrew*. All citations from Fletcher's play, hereafter referred to as *The Woman's Prize*, will be from the text edited by George Ferguson.

3. Lynda Boose sees Fletcher as a dramatist who does not radically revise patriarchal ideology, but she recognizes that his engagement with the issues raised by Shakespeare itself suggests 'the kind of discomfort that *Shrew* characteristically provoked in men' (Boose 1991 p.179). Brian Morris, in his introduction to the Arden edition of Shakespeare's play, also notes Fletcher's sequel, citing it as proof of *The Shrew's* popularity in the seventeenth century (Morris 1981 p.88).

4. For other considerations of gender tensions in early modern England, especially with regard to the taming of shrews, see essays by Ruth Melinkoff (1973) and Martin Ingram (1984) and books by Alan Macfarlane (1981) and David Underdown (1985).

5. For a reading that suggests that Fletcher and Beaumont were not merely court entertainers reflecting Stuart tastes but ideologically committed dramatists involved with debating issues of the day, see Philip J. Finkelpearl's study (1990). A similar revisionist view pervades Sandra Clark's more recent book (1994).

6. A similar and extremely convincing revaluation of the genre pervades Douglas Bruster's study of Renaissance theatre (1992).

7. The controversy surrounding the authorship of the 'Prologue' and 'Epilogue' is summarized by George Ferguson in his introduction to the text (1966 pp.11–35).

8. In its format the event imitates 'rough music' or the 'skimmington' invoked also by Shakespeare's play. This metaphoric analogy becomes especially vivid and acquires a double irony in the context of Renaissance theatre, where as in the case of the 'skimmington', male actors played women's parts.

9. The list of thirteen demands Maria draws up ranges from material demands such as 'continuall moneys' to 'Musick' and the company of women 'to read French' (II, v, ll.138–143). Its focus on commodities and economic value, though it may deter somewhat from the dignity of the women's struggle, may be seen as a first step towards equality, for Maria continues her rebellion even after Petruchio agrees to these concessions.

10. A similar claim is made by Morris: 'The play is rooted and grounded in well-known, sacred, and serious expressions of the duty of wives. Shakespeare cannot possibly have intended it to be spoken ironically' (Morris 1981 p.146). Morris leaves open the possibility of ironic interpretation and concentrates on authorial intent. Fletcher's re-reading, which Morris notes in passing, seems to me to detract somewhat from such magisterial claims about authorial intention.

11. On speculations about the play's popularity in the eighteenth century, see Ferguson (1966) pp.23–24.

12. Writers who discuss the increased literacy of seventeenth-century England include the following: Joseph Frank (1961), David Cressy (1980), R. A. Houston (1988) and Jerome Friedman (1992).

13. Indeed the extent to which *The Tamer* shares the general tendency of farce to mask seriousness in the form of excessive play becomes most apparent when one considers its literary precedent, Aristophanes' *Lysistrata*, which similarly voices trenchant commentary on contemporary political and social events; as critics have long recognized, the play directs a potent argument against the state to end the demoralizing and wasteful Peloponnesian war between the Spartans and the Athenians.

14. This discrepancy between the moderate note of the 'Epilogue' and the play's content might be partly accounted for by the possibility that somebody other than the author was responsible for the 'Prologue' and the 'Epilogue', as Ferguson suggests.

15. The play's return to a seemingly conventional arrangement between Maria and Petruchio thus remains fragile and one recalls that the action had continually reiterated Maria's ability to assert her independence. Harold C. Goddard's early attempt at a feminist response to Shakespeare's play might be more appropriate to Fletcher's:

'the play is an early version of *What Every Woman Knows* – what every woman knows being, of course, that the woman can lord it over the man so long as she allows him to think he is lording it over her' (Goddard 1951 pp.68–69).

16. Shakespeare's play, by contrast, seems to direct its mockery at both males and females. Petruchio's appearance at the wedding provokes taunts from the men, as does Kate's behaviour throughout; even the final scene is fraught with ambivalence, for despite Kate's seeming conformity, the behaviour of Bianca and the Widow results in the public shaming of Lucentio and Hortensio.

17. A far more convincing political argument, such as the one made by Francis Barker about *Titus*, might rely on dramatic violence on non-aristocratic bodies, a pattern that goes against the grain of conventional tragedy (Barker 1993).

18. The allusive significance of this incident is remarkably clear; it was customary for James to insist on the privilege of a father and enter the bridal chambers of his favourites on the morning after their wedding; Carleton records such an event in January 1605. Lawrence Stone cites a similar instance years later after the wedding of John Villiers (Stone 1965 p.652).

19. Interestingly the 1553 edition of the text announces the play as a comedy.

20. See the 'Introduction' to the play for questions regarding the authorship of the play (Ferguson 1966 p.vi).

21. Shakespeare's *Hamlet* provides an earlier example of a play which stages the carnival crowning and uncrowning of kings. Michael Bristol has explored the play's crucial reliance on carnival which, as Bristol notes, 'is the liminal occasion par excellence, something that happens betwixt and between the regularly scheduled events of everyday life' (Bristol 1994 p.352). But the play's clearest link with carnival lies in the thrust of its central action which may be described as the playful crowning and uncrowning of kings, a point Bristol fails to notice. The desire to repeat this action seems to lie with the crowds who initially give Claudius their support, then see Hamlet as potential heir, later storm the palace calling for Laertes's crowning and presumably accept Fortinbras's election at the end. But the uncrowning of so many candidates simply validates Hamlet's wry recognition earlier that 'Your worm is your only Emperor for diet: we fat all creatures else to fat us, and we fat ourselves for maggots' (IV, iii, ll.20–22). This kernel truth at the heart of many Renaissance tragedies of state imposes a carnivalesque effect on the crowning of kings which often concludes these plays.

5

Theatre and transgression: secularizing the sacred and sacralizing the secular

Recently Bruce Boehrer has addressed the issue of incest in Renaissance literature, documenting its pervasive recurrence both on the stage and elsewhere. Boehrer goes so far as to argue that 'in some basic ways the English Renaissance is about incest. . . . various of the products (principally literary, but also historical, theological, and legal) of courtly culture in early modern England developed as a response to problems in the function and the structure of the family and such problems actively engage the subject of incest on both a practical and theoretical level' (Boehrer 1992 p.5).[1] The boldest treatment of incest on the Renaissance stage, John Ford's *'Tis Pity She's a Whore*, may be regarded as just such a response to the sociopolitical concerns of the 1630s.[2]

'Tis Pity simultaneously desacralizes the institution of patriarchy which had for so long maintained associations with the divine even as it sacralizes the act of sibling incest, which by its very nature constitutes a defiance of patriarchy. This simultaneous movement may be traced to Ford's dexterous appropriation and subversion of the patterns and vocabulary of traditional devotional literature, a genre in which the devotee addresses God, the ultimate patriarch. Indeed Ford's tragedy achieves its assault on patriarchy by exploiting and foregrounding the contradictions inherent in the vocabulary of devotional love, thereby evoking the disturbing effects that have traditionally characterized responses to this play.[3] I am not suggesting merely that Ford invokes the divine in presenting transgressive love; through his depiction of the Friar and Giovanni, he in fact suggests that worldly incest draws its very impulse from the vocabulary of devotional love.

Incest, politics, and the vocabulary of devotional love: Queen Elizabeth I's *Glass of the Sinful Soul*

On the one hand, incest represents the ultimate crossing of boundaries and threatens by its very nature to undermine the norms on which society is based. And yet several areas of Renaissance thought, devotional literature and political theory in particular, survived through the invocation of familial metaphors which, if transposed to the secular and private realms, would constitute incest.

Likewise in the social realm, in-marriages were frequent as the wealthy tried to consolidate their assets and prevent the dissipation of their property and monetary holdings. Thus, though one's spouse's family became one's kin and the doctrine of carnal contagion propounded by medieval theologians forbade inter-marriages between families that were already related, such alliances were not infrequent. The case of Horatio Palavicino recorded by Lawrence Stone and described succinctly by Richard Wilson, provides an extreme example of such calculated intermarriages among kin. Horatio Palavicino died in 1600, as Wilson records, leaving his lands to his son Henry, a dower for his wife Anna provided she did not remarry, a dowry of £5000 for his daughter Baptina and the rest of his capital to be equally divided between Henry and his younger brother Toby. Lady Anna, joint executor of the fortune with two Palavicino agents during her children's minority, nevertheless managed to obtain sole power as executor. In 1601 Oliver Cromwell of Hinchinbrook convinced the widow to marry him; a few years later Cromwell's daughters were married to Henry and Toby Palavi-cino, respectively, and his heir Henry then married Baptina. These triple marriages thus irrevocably secured Horatio Palavicino's fortune to Cromwell's. Certainly some theological circles, at least, might have regarded the case as a clear illustration of carnal contagion. But as Lawrence Stone points out, the Palavicino case provides an extreme example of the way in which inheritances were consolidated in Renaissance England (Stone 1965 p.171). Marc Shell cites J. H. Fowler's summary of the medieval theologian Rabanus Maurus to describe the concept of carnal contagion:

> there is something like a communicable disease metaphor involved in early medieval notions of sexuality. If one sleeps with a woman who sleeps with another man who sleeps with another woman who sleeps with me, then whether I will it or not my flesh is inextricably bound up with the flesh of that first man's. A term which continually shows up in these canons and letters to describe fornication is *contagio carnalis* – carnal contagion.
>
> (quoted by Shell 1993 pp.13–14)

Renaissance audiences may have been partially knowledgeable about the doctrine of carnal contagion for it had been a subject of much debate during Henry VIII's marital manoeuvres. Indeed the Henrician court seems to have been continuously involved with defining incest and the future Queen Elizabeth found herself constantly implicated in these redefinitions. Henry's marriage to her mother Anne Boleyn was made possible by Henry's realization that his earlier marriage to Catherine of Aragon constituted incest because Catherine had been married to his brother Arthur. Anne Boleyn in turn was accused of an incestuous relation-ship with her brother and an adulterous relationship with five men and lost her head a year after her marriage to Henry. The 1536 Act of Succession declared Elizabeth a bastard on the grounds that her mother had committed adultery and incest. But Anne Boleyn's marriage to Henry was itself regarded as incestuous by some because of Henry's prior relationship with Mary Boleyn, Anne's sister, and his rumored relationship with their mother previous to that. As Marc Shell points out, Archbishop Cranmer relied on the doctrine of carnal contagion, by which it was deemed incestuous to sleep with the sister of one's mistress, to declare Henry's marriage to Anne incestuous and Elizabeth a bastard (Shell 1993 p.10). There may be considerable truth in Boehrer's argument that the consequences of Henry's divorce of Katherine, which prompted 'the greatest official effort to define incest in Renaissance England', 'were being felt right to the Interregnum and beyond' (Boehrer 1992 p.41). Plays such as *The Revenger's Tragedy*, *Women Beware Women*, *The Unnatural Combat* and *'Tis Pity She's A Whore* participate in this ongoing Renaissance discourse on the subject of incest.

The case of Henry's third wife Anne of Cleves provides yet another example of the way in which royal authority could manipulate familial structures to its advantage. Anne, who testified that her marriage to Henry had not been consummated, chose to remain in England after her divorce and was granted the right to be regarded as Henry's sister thereafter. Catherine Howard, Anne Boleyn's cousin and Elizabeth's aunt, later became Elizabeth's stepmother through her marriage to Henry. Thomas Seymour, Elizabeth's step-uncle through his sister's marriage to Henry, also became Elizabeth's stepfather when he married Catherine Parr, Henry's last queen; Thomas Seymour was later beheaded by his brother Edward on the charge that he had attempted to seduce Elizabeth. During Mary's reign, Mary and Elizabeth vied at one point for the affections of the same man; after Mary's death, her husband, Philip II of Spain, entertained ideas of marrying Elizabeth and even proposed to her. Many prominent figures associated with Henry's court played multiple familial roles simultaneously and the Tudor court seems to have been endlessly involved in the delineation of familial ties, ties which seemed under royal prerogative to have been infinitely malleable.

Similarly, as he walked a political tightrope in expectations of succeeding to the English throne, James VI of Scotland characterized his relationship to Queen Elizabeth in numerous letters as that of a sibling or a child as the occasion demanded. His reconciliatory letter of 15 December 1586, for example, written during a period of delicate negotiations concerning the fate of his mother and the issue of his succession to the English throne, ends with a conventional invocation of siblinghood: 'Your most loving and affectionate brother and cousing. James R' (Rait and Cameron 1927 p.99). Only a short while later, however, having been informed of the arrival of the Spanish Armada, James pledges his support to Elizabeth and promises to act 'not as a stranger and foreyne prince, but as zour natural sone and conpatriot of your countrey in all respectis' (Rait and Cameron 1927 p.207). What Boehrer terms 'the highly peculiar kinship vocabulary' of King James VI's letters to Elizabeth, testifies yet again to the infinite malleability of familial relationships as they served political ends (Boehrer 1992 p.12). Such malleability, a characteristic also of devotional literature, may even have received its force from the conventional metaphors that allied monarchy and divinity.

Elizabeth herself encouraged such vocabulary and exploited its potential with equal dexterity. As Richard McCabe demonstrates, 'England's self-appointed virgin-mother, "mystically" married to the state, exploited the politics of maternity better than many of the most prolific monarchs. . . . Indeed, by arguing to act as godmother to James . . . she appropriated to herself something of Mary's relationship to the child while extending towards it the elusive prospect of succession through spiritual affinity' (McCabe 1993 p.123).

Renaissance attitudes toward physical incest were further complicated by religious thinkers who had to explain Biblical events such as the marriages of Cain and Abel or the relationship between Lot and his daughters. Some even insisted that the taboo on incest arose out of social rather than moral concerns; thus Thomas Abell argued that 'The holy patriarke Abraham married his owne sister Sara and we may not think and saye that so holy a man wolde wetingly do so grievouse a syn as to breke the law of nature' (quoted by Boehrer 1992 p.33). William Tyndale carried the argument a step further:

> the marriage of the brother with the sister is not so grievous against the law of nature . . . Moreover, the greatest cause to send the daughter out is unity and peace between divers kindreds.
>
> Wherefore, if greater peace and unity might be made with keping hir at home, I durst dispence with it: as, if the king of England had a son by one wife, heir to England, and a daughter by another, heir to Wales; then, because of the great war that was ever wont to be between those two countries, I would not fear to marry them together, for the making of a perpetual unity, and to make both countries one, for to avoid so great effusion of blood.
>
> (Tyndale 1849 p.331)

In the context of attitudes such as Abell's and Tyndale's, not uncommon in a period that grappled continually with the subject of incest, the idealized language of devotional literature with its invocation of familial ties thus emerges as considerably complex.

The supreme model of devotional love was the Virgin Mary who was at once the mother of Christ, his sister, daughter and spouse. As Shell insists, 'the term *sponsa Christi* which defines Mary's relationship to God, emphasizes a woman's marriage to Christ in a union at once extramarital (Mary is married to Joseph) and incestuous' (Shell 1993 p.23).[4] It may be true, as Lisa Jardine argues, that 'the Reformation had terminated the cult of Mary in England' but Marian images remained crucial in Elizabeth's writing and speeches as she forged her identity as virgin Queen, mother and sister of her subjects and the 'cult of Elizabeth' which supplanted the cult of Mary retained the essence of Marian topology (Jardine 1983 p.177). Thus 'Elizabeth publicly identified with Saint Elizabeth and other Marian figures, including the Elizabeth who was the niece of Saint Anne (of the Immaculate Conception) and the cousin of Saint Mary (of the Virgin Birth)' (Shell 1993 pp.317–318). Not surprisingly, therefore, spiritual ideals establishing the relationship between devotee and God in Marian terms that within a social/worldly context would constitute incest may be best studied through a royal text of the sixteenth century, Princess Elizabeth's *Glass of the Sinful Soul* (1548), a translation of Marguerite of Navarre's *Le Mirroir de l'ame pecheresse* (1533). Mary's prominence as a role model is vividly apparent in this early writing of the future Queen. The first edition with a conclusion by John Bale was printed by Dirk van der Straten in Marburg, Germany; subsequent editions appeared in London during Elizabeth's reign in 1568, 1582 and 1590. Written by Elizabeth when she was only eleven years of age, the translation throws considerable light on Renaissance devotional attitudes and conventions, which seem to have crossed Catholic/Protestant boundaries. Bale's 'Conclusion' reiterates the importance of the work not as a translation but as evidence of Elizabeth's virtue, godliness and potential for greatness:

> Such noble beginnings are neither to be reckoned childish nor babyish, though she were a babe in years that hath here given them. Seldom find we them that in the closing up of their withered age do minister like fruits of virtue. . . . They shall not be unwise that shall mark herein what commodity it is or what profit might grow to a Christian commonwealth if youth were thus brought up in virtue and good letters. If such fruits come forward in childhood, what will follow and appear when discretion and years shall be more ripe and ancient?
>
> (Bale 1993 pp.94–95)

Does Bale's cautionary remark about discretion point to his discomfort with Elizabeth's near-erotic devotional language? The text certainly reveals something of young Elizabeth's psychological reactions to disruptions at court which accompanied her father's temperamental marital choices.

The various intrigues at court involving her father's earlier marriages must have been much on Elizabeth's mind as she treats the subject of devotion between God and devotee in familial terms that suggest incest when transposed to worldly contexts. Shell goes so far as to suggest that the work concerns 'the transmutation of the desire for or fear of physical incest into desire for or fear of spiritual incest' (Shell 1993 p.7). His argument that Elizabeth's text, because it was republished several times during her reign, may have had considerable literary and social importance deserves attention: 'surely almost any work written by a reigning monarch and published in several editions during her lifetime is likely to have had some literary and/or political influence' (Shell 1993 p.6). But while critics have paid considerable attention to the influence of texts such as James's *Basilikon Doron* on Jacobean literature, they have generally tended to ignore this text as an influence on Elizabethan writing. Of course the subject of Elizabeth's text, the devotional union between Christ and his worshipper, and the fact that it is a translation of Margaret Nevarre's work, makes it considerably more difficult to assess the precise nature of its influence on Elizabethan thought and literary practices. I treat its vocabulary and language as typifying devotional literature and suggest that these emerge also in Elizabethan and early Stuart plays, especially those that treat the subject of incest.

Elizabeth prefaces her translation with a letter to her stepmother, Catherine Parr, in which she invokes the conventional metaphors of devotion:

> And therefore have I as for an essay or beginning (so following the right noble saying of the proverb aforesaid) translated this little book out of French rhyme into English prose, joining the sentences together as well as the capacity of my little wit and small

learning could extend themselves. The which book is entitled, or named, *The Mirror or Glass of the Sinful Soul*, wherein is contained how she (beholding and contemplating what she is) doth perceive how of herself and of her own strength she can do nothing that good is, or prevaileth for her salvation, unless it be through the grace of God, whose mother, daughter, sister, and wife by the scriptures she proveth to be.

(Elizabeth I 1993 p.111)

The text itself elaborates these metaphors in a variety of ways as the devotee takes us through each of these relationships in order. The transgressive potential of the text emerges most vividly in its concluding sections as the devotee moves from being sister to spouse of Christ: 'Now then that we are brother and sister together, I care but little for all other men. Thy lands are my inheritance. Let us then keep (if it pleaseth Thee) but one household' (Elizabeth I 1993 p.126). The transition from sibling to spouse is not entirely easy, however, as the tortured language of the subsequent lines suggests:

Therefore my heart hath cause to sigh always, and with abundance of tears my eyes to come out of my head. My mouth cannot make too many exclamations, for there is neither old nor new writings that can show so pitiful a thing as the same which I will tell now. Shall or dare I tell it? May I pronounce it without shame? Alas, yea, for my confusion is to show the great love of my husband; therefore, I care not if for his worship I do declare my shame.

(Elizabeth I 1993 p.127)

The text, though it moves gradually to a passionate but tortured reconciliation of the multiple familial ties that bind devotee and beloved, nevertheless reveals the junctures that render such a reconciliation problematic:

O what union is this, since (through faith) I am sure of Thee. And now I may call Thee son, father, spouse, and brother. Father, brother, son, and husband: O what gifts Thou dost give by the goodness of those names. O my father, what paternity; O my brother, what fraternity; O my child, what delection; O my husband, O what conjunction! Father full of humility, brother having taken our similitude, son engendered through faith and charity, husband loving in all extremity.

(Elizabeth I 1993 p.133)

The parallel structures that mark the devotee's delineation of her relationships reach their crescendo in the double 'O' that articulates the spousal tie; the structure at this point both retains the movement of the three earlier lines and yet breaks their pattern through the interjection of the second 'O' thus pointing to the gathering emotional intensity of the speaker. The movement of the passage thus parallels the movement of the text as a whole as it moves from sibling to filial to maternal to spousal love.

Elizabeth's text is not unique in its expression of devotion in familial terms. Saint Teresa of Avila's meditations, for example, have long been recognized for their erotic emotional fervour.[5] The inherent ambiguities in Elizabeth's *Glass* provide a context, however, for the tradition of devotional love that Ford's Caroline tragedy clearly invokes and then subverts.

Even as devotional literature did in delineating the relationship between devotee and God, political theorists articulated the relationship between monarch and realm through a complex set of familial metaphors. Thus both Elizabeth and James could speak of their relationship to the kingdom as simultaneously that of parent, spouse and child. At her coronation Elizabeth consciously established herself as virginal mother and wife of the English people, an image that would persist throughout her reign (Shell 1993 p.67). Her coronation speech provides an early glimpse of the reasons for her determined opposition to marriage throughout her reign:

> I have long since made choice of my husband, the kingdom of England. And here [showing the coronation ring] is the pledge and emblem of my marriage contract, which I wonder you should so soon have forgot. I beseech you, gentlemen, charge me not with the want of children, forasmuch as everyone of you, and every Englishman besides, are my children and relations.
>
> (Shell 1993 p.67)

At her accession Elizabeth seems to have transposed the devotional language and idealized content of *The Glasse*, in which she defined herself as the spouse of Christ, into the political realm. Thus as Shell argues, the young Elizabeth's *Glass* may have molded her later political theory and the text 'thus reflects the beginnings of a new ideal and real political organization, which, partly out of Elizabeth's own concerns with incest and bastardy, and partly out of the political exigencies of the time, England's great monarch introduced as a kind of "national siblinghood" to which she was simultaneously the mother and wife' (Shell 1993 p.7). It was a metaphoric alliance that James also embraced as he depicted the kingdom as his spouse and child.

The subject of incest, transposed from the political and religious realms to the theatrical arena, could become an potent metaphor; in the case of playwrights such as Tourneur, Middleton and Ford, it became a weapon for undermining traditional orthodoxies such as patriarchy. This is precisely the effect of plays such as *The Revenger's Tragedy*, *Women Beware Women*, *The Unnatural Combat* and *'Tis Pity She's A Whore*, which stage incest as a direct assault on patriarchal power. Dramatic engagement with the subject of incest, which Bradbrook designated as evidence of decadence on the Jacobean and Caroline stage, emerges instead as intense preoccupation with the sociopolitical concerns of early Stuart England.

Deconsecrating patriarchy and sacralizing transgression in *The Changeling*, *The Revenger's Tragedy*, *The Unnatural Combat* and *'Tis Pity She's a Whore*

The sexual transgressions staged in many Renaissance tragedies draw their impetus from the abuse of authority by patriarchal figures. It may even be argued that plays such as *The Changeling* and *'Tis Pity* stage literal and metaphoric parricides in their final scenes which, in an age that drew close parallels between patriarchy, monarchy and the divine, may indicate a growing scepticism about the sanctity of these institutions.[6] As Boehrer insists and as Renaissance scholars have increasingly recognized, 'in a social formation that ascribes rank, wealth, and identity genealogically, family structure is always already micropolitical; to write or rewrite the family is to write or rewrite the State' (Boehrer 1992 p.4). At the very least, playwrights such as Middleton and Rowley and Ford debate the issue of patriarchal authority and their works reflect a deep cultural reticence towards accepting without question the gendered hierarchies which had hitherto dominated Renaissance sociopolitical systems.

Even as they deconsecrate the hitherto 'sacred' institution of patriarchy, many of these plays also sacralize socially transgressive behaviour such as adultery and incest. The effect of this simultaneous movement produces a disturbingly carnivalesque effect; though dramatists often demarcate immoral actions as transgressive, they nevertheless prompt fascination for transgression by presenting such behaviour in vocabulary that sanctifies and sacralizes them. This dual trend in Renaissance drama towards secularizing what had been regarded as sacred and sacralizing what emerges as transgressive social behaviour receives its fullest treatment in Ford's 'Tis Pity, but an earlier play such as The Changeling already reveals this tendency. A brief look at Middleton and Rowley's Jacobean treatment of adultery in sacred terms clarifies Ford's more daring treatment of incest along similar lines on the Caroline stage.

The Changeling, we might recall, stages a metaphoric parricide in which Vermandero, who had begun the play doting on the two items that defined his role as patriarch, his daughter and his castle, is reduced at the end of the play to silence. The tragedy that unfolds in the last scene suggests that Vermandero shares at least some of the blame for the play's transgressions of which he had remained blissfully ignorant throughout. Adultery, rape and murder had occurred within his own castle walls and were orchestrated by his own daughter and trusted servant. The last lines of the play promise relief for the other characters caught in the tragedy but suggest that Vermandero's status as patriarch has been permanently destroyed.[7] Most ominously, Alsemero, who speaks the concluding lines to the audience in an Epilogue, indicates his own rise to power through a marriage never consummated. Now heir to Vermandero's fortune, Alsemero suggests that his travels have concluded and that he has found a permanent home at his father-in-law's house despite the fact that his marriage to Beatrice Joanna was never consummated. Vermandero's acquisition of a son, Alsemero points out, might mitigate somewhat his sorrow over the death of his daughter:

> All we can do to comfort one another,
> To stay a brother's sorrow for a brother,
> To dry a child from a kind father's eyes,
> Is to no purpose; it rather multiplies.
> Your only smiles have power to cause relive
> The Dead again or in their rooms to give
> Brother a new brother, father a child:
> If these appear, all griefs are reconciled

('Epilogue' ll.5–8)

In a final ironic twist, the tragedy has produced another changeling child substituted for Vermandero's real one, who is now only a painful memory to be recollected by association. Alsemero who until now has led a wanderer's life, as Jasperino informs us, has found a permanent home and Vermandero presumably has a substitute child and heir to help him recover from his recent loss.

We might recall that the initial tragedy had evolved from the introduction of Alsemero into the actions of the play. Intruding on a scene of nuptial preparations for the impending marriage between Beatrice Joanna and Alonso Piracquo, Alsemero's desire for Beatrice Joanna is presented in the opening scenes as at once holy and adulterous. Alsemero opens the play by declaring his intentions to marry Beatrice Joanna, having fallen in love with her at first sight in the temple:

> 'Twas in the temple where I first beheld her,
> And now again the same; . . .
> The place is holy, so is my intent;
> I love her beauties to the holy purpose
> . . .
> The church hath first begun our interview
> And that's the place must join us into one;
> So there's beginning and perfection too.

(I, i, ll.1–12)

He soon forgets these high sentiments and seems quite willing to hold clandestine meetings and maintain a secret relationship with her. At their first secret meeting in her bedchamber (arranged through the collusion of Diaphanta and Jasperino) Beatrice Joanna, having hit upon the idea of using De Flores to get rid of Alonso, advises caution in planning future meetings. Alsemero's response, 'You teach wisdom, lady', suggests his willingness to maintain a secret relationship despite her forthcoming marriage to Alonso. But even as they plot deceit, the lovers continue to present their affection in vocabulary that suggests sanctity and purity. As critics have regularly recognized, 'the play's vocabulary is unquestionably invested in religious terminology' (Little 1993 p.19). But the playwrights concentrate their religious terminology almost exclusively on transgressive and deviant behaviour while socially sanctioned relationships such as that of Isabella and Alibio and that of Beatrice Joanna and Alonso Piracquo remain strikingly secular in representation. Indeed the conjunction of sanctity and transgression evident in Beatrice Joanna's relationship with Alsemero in the early scenes transfers in the second half of the play to her relationship with De Flores; thus implicitly the play links Alsemero's and De Flores' adultery, forcing us to regard Alsemero with suspicion if not condemnation from the very start.

The conjunction of sanctity and transgression is most vividly apparent in one of the most arresting scenes in the play as Beatrice Joanna engages De Flores's services to murder Alonso. De Flores greets the opportunity as a 'blest occasion' and kneels to receive the privilege of murdering Alonso:

> If you knew
> How sweet it were to me to be employed
> In any act of yours, you would say then
> I fail'd and used not reverence enough
> When I receive the charge on't.
>
> (II, ii, ll.120–124)

Beatrice Joanna continues to collapse the worlds of sin and sanctity in her response: 'to such / Gold tastes like angels' food' (II, ii, ll.124–125). George William, the editor of the Regents edition, points out that her vocabulary suggests 'an extreme parallel' for it yokes 'angels' food' which is 'consubstantial with manna in the Old Testament and the body of Christ in the New' with rewards for murder.

Such extreme parallels pervade this and other plays and contribute greatly to the disturbing effect of many early Stuart tragedies. The ultimate irony emerges in the concluding scene as Beatrice Joanna and De Flores recognize that their union has been forged not in heaven but in hell. But despite the clearly transgressive nature of their love, the play grants their affair an authenticity of emotion that remains missing in other relationships. Ford's tragedy of transgression, 'Tis Pity, similarly juxtaposes the sacred and the secular while also enlisting our sympathy for characters who deliberately violate social norms. Ford goes considerably farther than Middleton and Rowley, however, for he does not merely represent transgression through the borrowed metaphors of devotion; his tragedy insists that the very basis of incest lies in the sanctioned vocabulary of devotional love.

'Tis Pity also stages transgressions as a direct result of the patriarch's inability to exercise authority over his family. Like Vermandero, Florio begins the play proud of his role as patriarch, keen to ensure the continuance of his family through an appropriate match for his daughter. In the last scene, when confronted by evidence of the incestuous relationship between his children, Giovanni and Annabella, Florio falls dead with grief and astonishment. The Cardinal, speaking as it were for all the characters on stage, describes his death as parricide jointly engineered by Annabella and Giovanni: 'Monster of children, see what thou hast done, / Broke thy old father's heart' (V, vi, ll.63–64). 'Tis Pity thus stages a more decisive assault on patriarchy than The Changeling even as it enacts a more horrifyingly transgressive act in the form of incest.

From the very beginning Giovanni expresses his love for Annabella in spiritual terms; the play opens with his passionate arguments addressed to Friar Bonaventura and justifying his love as natural devotion: 'Must I not praise / That beauty which, if framed anew, the gods / Would make a god of, if they had it there, / And kneel to it, as I do kneel to them?' (I, i, ll.20–23). He insists that their sibling relationship itself justifies their natural love for each other:

> Say that we had one father, . . .
> Are we not therefore each to other bound
> So much the more by nature? by the links

Of blood, of reason? nay, if you will have't,
Even of religion, to be ever one,
One soul, one flesh, one love, one heart, one *all?*

(I, i, ll.28–33)

Giovanni's claim that religion sanctions his love perhaps refers to the doctrine of universal siblinghood put forward by Christ through the dictum that all men are sons to his father and, therefore, brothers; the dictum taken to its extreme classifies all worldly love as incestuous. Similarly all men and women who entered holy orders were simultaneously establishing both their universal siblinghood and their spousal ties with Christ; Giovanni, who has remained under the tutelage of Friar Bonaventura for some years and whose penchant for books and tutoring from the Friar suggests that he may be grooming himself for entry into holy orders, seems to perceive this as church-sanctioned incest. Florio even hints at Giovanni's potential future in the Church when he dismisses his son as a candidate for the continuance of the family line and pins his hopes instead on Annabella. The Friar's feeble response to Giovanni's confession, that he spend his time in prayer, provides no real way out of the dilemma for Giovanni. Indeed, the very conventional nature of the Friar's advice militates against its effectiveness as a deterrent to Giovanni's passions:

Hie to thy father's house, there lock thee fast
Alone within thy chamber, then fall down
On both thy knees, and grovel on the ground:
Cry to thy heart, wash every word thou utter'st
In tears (and if't be possible) of blood:
Beg heaven to cure the leprosy of lust
That rots thy soul, acknowledge what thou art,
A wretch, a worm, a nothing: weep, sigh, pray
Three times a day, and three times a night.

(I, i, ll.69–77)

The passage differs little in intent from Elizabeth's equally conventional prayer that begins *The Glass*:

Now behold how in pain, crying, and weeping my poor soul, a slave and a prisoner, doth lie without clarity or light, having both her feet bound by her concupiscence, and also both her arms through evil use. . . . and humbly do I confess that, as for me, I am much less than nothing: before my birth, mire, and after, a dunghill, a body ready and prompt to all evil, not willing other study.

(Elizabeth I 1993 p.115)

A few lines later, Elizabeth continues the theme of her lowliness and worthlessness: 'Thou camest to me which am nothing but a worm of the earth all naked' (Elizabeth I 1993 p.116). The irony of the Friar's advice to Giovanni lies in the fact that such a prayer, if it should naturally lead his pupil into proper devotion as Elizabeth's does, will also make him confront the mystery of God's relationship to his devotee as a clearly familial and four-fold one. The Friar's prayer, in other words, provides a circular path that will merely take Giovanni back to his desires for Annabella; perverted as this desire may be, the Friar's tutelage provides Giovanni with a justification of his love for his sister, a love which in its intensity and totality replicates the fervour of religious devotion.

Not surprisingly, therefore, Giovanni's confession of love to Annabella, made after attempts at praying to God for forgiveness, invokes the authority of Nature and the Church:

> You
> My Sister Annabella; I know this
> And could afford you instance why to love
> So much the more for this; to which intent
> Wise nature first in your creation meant
> To make you mine; else't had been sin and foul
> To share one beauty to a double soul.
> Nearness in birth or blood doth he persuade
> A nearer nearness in affection.
> I have asked counsel of the holy church,
> Who tells me I may love you, and 'tis just
> That since I may, I should; and will, yes, will.

(I, ii, ll.233–243)

Giovanni's blatant assertion that the church sanctions his love has always troubled critics; after all, Ford generally represents Giovanni as honest, especially in his relationship to his sister. Clifford Leech, for example, insists that he is lying, for 'nothing that the Friar has said to him [Giovanni] could be legitimately twisted to mean this. At this moment his wooing becomes seduction' (Leech 1957 p.290). But is Giovanni blatantly lying to Annabella, implying that the Friar has sanctioned their love, or is he referring to the fact that the Friar's advice, that his pupil pray for guidance from above, has led him to the conclusion that the church sanctions sibling love? Certainly the sequence of events thus far and Ford's depiction of Giovanni as an intelligent pupil keen to carry theological arguments to their limits suggest the latter possibility.

Annabella seems to accept the Church's sanction without question and their vows of fidelity to each other made shortly after as they kneel together in a kind of holy matrimony deliberately suggests its devotional counterpart when devotees pledge themselves as spouses of Christ. The movement from tears to ecstatic union with God that characterizes devotional texts such as Elizabeth's *Glass* is also invoked in the last lines of Ford's scene as the lovers leave the stage: 'After so many tears as we have wept, / Let's learn to court in smiles, to kiss, and sleep' (I, ii, ll.266–267). Giovanni's dying lines in the last scene of the play similarly invoke religious vocabulary: 'Where'er I go, let me enjoy this grace, / Freely to enjoy Annabella's face' (V, vi, ll.106–107). It is precisely this collapse of incestuous passion and religious intensity and Giovanni's explicit argument that the former results from the latter that make the play disturbing and unsettling.

It is also this attitude that separates Giovanni and Annabella from all the other characters in the play who, whether they sanction the love as Putana does or condemn it as the Friar does, perceive their relationship as simply lustful.

Putana characterizes Annabella's love as desire for sex that might be satisfied by any and sundry:

> Nay, what a paradise of joy have you passed under. Why, now I commend thee, charge; fear nothing, sweetheart; what though he be your brother? Your brother's a man I hope, and I say still, if a young wench feel the fit upon her, let her take anybody, father or brother, all is one.
>
> (II, i, ll.45–49)

The Friar suggests fornication as the easier alternative to satisfy Giovanni's lust for ''tis much less sin' (I, i, l.62). On the other hand, as Bernard Beckerman notes, 'Ford paints Giovanni's and Annabella's love in the most attractive colors. While sensual, it is also deeply spiritual, obsessive yet somehow idealized'; by contrast, none of the other sexual relationships in the play 'has the heartfelt emotion of the forbidden passion' (Beckerman 1983 p.450).

But the play's repeated representation of bedroom scenes reveals a dramatic insistence that such intensely spiritual love is inevitably also physical, an insistence that has much to do with the troubled response that the play invariably provokes. Giovanni, though he presents his love to the Friar as divine and heavenly, does not fail to hint at its sensuous and physical dimension:

> View well her face, and in that little round
> You may observe a world of variety:
> For colour, lips; for sweet perfumes, her breath;
> For jewels, eyes; for threads of purest gold,
> Hair; for delicious choice of flowers, cheeks;
> . . .
> But, father, what is else for pleasure framed,
> Lest I offend your ears, shall go unnamed.
>
> (II, v, ll.49–58)

Giovanni's triumphant intrusion on Saranzo's feast in the last scene after killing Annabella continues the collapse of sanctity and transgression; his language continues to merge the spiritual and the physical. Annabella's bleeding heart on his dagger becomes an equivalent of the dainty feast that Saranzo has prepared for the Cardinal and his guests: 'You came to feast, my lords, with dainty fare: / I came to feast too; but I digged for food / In a much richer mine than gold or stone / Of any value balanced' (V, vi, ll.23–26). Giovanni himself has become a 'glorious executioner' effecting a transformation in Annabella that has unmistakably religious consequences: 'The glory of my deed / Darkened the midday sun, made noon as night' (V, vi, ll.22–23). The disbelieving audience, who confronts the horror of his actions only after he has reiterated it several times, may be reacting also to his insistent collapse of the sacred and the profane in his vocabulary, for Giovanni continues to invoke heaven as he glories in his deed, swearing 'on all that you call sacred' while still insisting on the 'stol'n delights' he enjoyed in 'sweet Annabella's sheets'.

Even this simultaneous insistence on spirituality and physicality has its source in devotional literature. Elizabeth's *Glass* reveals the same troubling tensions which, in the light of the author's experiences at court, make it a rich source for psychoanalytical readings that may throw considerable light on the makings of an extremely successful monarch. But what may we make of Ford's dramatic strategies as he presents incest both as a taboo and as a natural extension of the spiritual vocabulary of divine worship? An obvious and perhaps partially valid case may be made for *'Tis Pity* as a calculated attack on Catholicism and its excesses. Certainly the depiction of the Friar and the Cardinal would support such a reading. Giovanni's dramatic entry in the last scene with his sister's heart upon a dagger and the commingled allusions to blood and food that mark his speeches in this scene may be treated as a travesty of Catholic ritual.[8] But such a reading only partially addresses the complexities of the play.

More importantly, the play stages a decisive attack on patriarchy and, by extension, on monarchy. By staging incest, a controversial and malleable topic especially among the privileged classes of early Stuart England who formed the primary audience for Ford's plays and by depicting Florio's death on stage, Ford's tragedy goes considerably farther than *The Changeling* in representing the dissolution of patriarchal authority.[9] *'Tis Pity*'s more emphatic engagement with this sociopolitical issue is most apparent in its choice of subject; as Richard McCabe insists, 'Sexuality is political as politics is sexual, and incest functions as an appropriate metaphor for political disturbance by virtue of received concepts of natural law uniting private and public morality in the interests of the familial state. In the Elizabethan *Homilies* civil war is regarded, like incest itself, as a crime against kin and the association is very common in English literature thereafter' (McCabe 1993 p.120). *The Life of Jack Straw* explicitly compares civil war to incest (II, ll.603–608). The metaphor of civil war, the result of violence between siblings, appropriately describes *'Tis Pity* which ultimately stages the elimination of Florio's family as a direct result of the patriarch's ignorance and negligence.

The shocking and disturbing treatment of incest in Ford's play thus results from the playwright's conscious usurpation of the vocabulary of devotional literature to represent a relationship that flagrantly violates all social and moral codes; the play thus collapses the metaphors of divine worship and romantic love. At the juncture of this collapse in the final scene of the play, the patriarch, who has both encouraged this tragedy and remained oblivious to the logical extremes to which his dictums could be pursued, remains the most culpable figure solely responsible for the elimination of his family line. As Michael Neill demonstrates, 'Far from being a potentially castrating symbol of paternal authority, Giovanni's knife is made into an instrument and sign of his impious assault on the very foundations of patriarchal order and power' (Neill 1988 p.172). In this assault, the vocabulary of devotional love provides a metaphoric equivalent to Giovanni's knife; by violently yoking the sacred and the transgressive, *'Tis Pity* thus proffers a more radical reassessment of Renaissance ideologies than any other play of its time.[10] The potency of its assault results from drama's continuous engagement with the subjects of incest and weak or tyrannical patriarchy throughout the seventeenth century.

Though the assault is less explicit in Tourneur's *The Revenger's Tragedy*, the play provides an early example of drama's engagement with desacralizing patriarchal authority while sanctioning or desacralizing sexual transgression. In a play which constantly elides distinctions and where characters inevitably become versions of each other, the bastard son's usurpation of his father's bed simply reiterates this theme of endless duplication. In the scene of their wooing, the Duchess and Spurio choose incest specifically as an act of defiance against the Duke. The Duchess decides on this course in revenge for the Duke's inaction in saving her youngest son who, on the charge of having raped Antonio's wife, is condemned to die: 'And therefore wedlock faith shall be forgot. / I'll kill him in his forehead, hate there feed – / That wound is deepest though it never bleed' (I, ii, ll.106–108). However, her desire remains unreciprocated and she has to woo Spurio with argument, the central point of which remains his questionable birth. She wins him only after she has convinced him that the Duke's role as his father remains in doubt: 'Why th'art his son but falsely, / 'Tis a hard question whether he begot thee' (I, ii, ll.132–133). Spurio's response, 'I' faith 'tis true too', suggests that she has succeeded in arousing his anger against the Duke. She goes on to insist that even if the Duke were his father, he has undermined his role as patriarch by refusing Spurio's legitimacy:

> Let it stand firm both in thought and mind
> That the Duke was thy father: as no doubt then
> He bid fo't, thy injury is the more;
> For had he cut thee a right diamond,
> Thou had'st been next in the dukedom's ring,
> When his worn self like Age's easy slave
> Had dropped out of the collet into the grave.
> What wrong can equal this?

> (I, ii, ll.144–152)

Thus Spurio's decision to commit incest emerges specifically as revenge against the Duke for his unfatherly neglect of his son: 'I'll be revenged for all: now hate begin, / I'll call incest but a venial sin' (I, ii, ll.168–169). Incest, unlike the Duke's abuse of patriarchal authority, emerges in Spurio's eyes as a venial sin, a pardonable offence. Spurio also perceives his adultery as a hereditarily transferred sin derived from the Duke himself who continues to live a sinful life: 'Duke on thy brow I'll draw my bastardy: / For indeed a bastard by nature should make cuckolds / Because he is the son of a cuckold maker' (I, ii, ll.200–202). Spurio thus implies that the Duke's abuse of his authority has created an endless cycle of abuses which will inevitably continue from generation to generation. The play itself implies as much through its depiction of the ducal family as exaggerated replicas of each other; Vindice, the arch revenger, similarly attributes the corruption of the times to a general decline in morals at court. In response to Lussurioso's question on whether he has been acquainted with 'strange lust', Vindice tops Lussurioso's intention to seduce Castiza by describing his general familiarity with an even more heinous crime, incest:

> Some father dreads not, gone to bed in wine,
> To slide from the mother and cling the daughter-in-law;
> Some uncles are adulterous with their nieces,
> Brothers with brothers' wives – Oh hour of incest!
> Any kin now next to the rim o' sister
> Is man's meat in these days . . .

(I, iii, ll.59–64)

He waxes so eloquent in describing the pervasiveness of incest and produces a paean to the midnight hour as the most appropriate time for incestuous liaisons that he provokes discomfort in Lussurioso who suggests changing the topic to the task at hand, namely seducing Castiza. Strikingly, in Vindice's description of incest, despite his general contempt for women and their vulnerability to folly, patriarchal figures (fathers, uncles, brothers) are ultimately to blame for the general degeneration of the times. Tourneur's play, like Middleton's and Ford's tragedies, blames abusive patriarchal figures for the degeneration of their families and society; Ford's violent yoking of sanctity and sin in 'Tis Pity thus carries theatre's deconsecration of patriarchy to its logical extreme by desanctifying it altogether.

The incestuous relationship between Hippolytus and Isabella in Women Beware Women similarly directs itself as an attack on tyrannical patriarchal authority. Isabella has been forced by the power of her father's instructions to consent to a match with the simple Ward; in explaining her initial decision to comply with her father's wishes, at first Isabella reaffirms the power of patriarchy to her aunt Livia: 'How can I [refuse to marry the Ward], being born with that obedience / That must submit unto a father's will? / If he command, I must of force consent' (II, i, ll. 86–88). Livia immediately perceives in her niece's sense of filial duty the means by which she might bring about an incestuous liaison between Hippolytus and Isabella; she proceeds to demonstrate that 'That which you call your father's command's nothing' (II, i, l.119), and spins a fantastic tale describing Isabella's mother's death-bed confession acknowledging a famous Spaniard as Isabella's real father. She concludes by emphatically deconsecrating Fabritio's authority over his daughter: 'How weak his commands now whom you call father! / How vain all his enforcements, your obedience! / And what a largeness in your will and liberty, / To take, or to reject, or to do both!' (II, i, ll. 158–161).

Interestingly, Livia and Isabella posit a literal definition of patriarchal authority (and by extension of incest) as a result of being related by blood; this is radically different from earlier plays such as The Revenger's Tragedy where Tourneur presents the Duchess's relationship to Spurio, her husband's bastard, as a clear instance of incest despite the fact that they are related by law and not by blood. Despite this shift in the later play's definition of incest, Middleton, like Tourneur, presents incest as a direct result of abuses in the exercise of patriarchal authority. Fabritio, voiceless and stunned by the revelations of the last scene in Middleton's tragedy, emerges as a pitiable but culpable figure, sharing responsibility for the play's abuses with his political counterpart, the Duke in Tourneur's tragedy, who has similarly abused his authority throughout. Fabritio's long silence in the last scene after Isabella's death presents a dramatic gesture of considerable import; as Keith Thomas has shown, 'The body can also transmit messages without any movement at all. To refrain from gesture, for example, . . . could be as demonstrative an act as bursting into tears' (Thomas 1992 p.1). Fabritio's awkward silence through more than two hundred lines at the conclusion of the play dramatically reiterates his culpability for the violations that have occurred within his family. Middleton's tragedy, like Ford's later one, stages incest as a direct result of patriarchal failings; though he does not sacralize incest as Ford does, Middleton nevertheless secularizes the institution of patriarchy, representing it as fallible and weak, indeed as directly responsible for moral transgressions by others.

Even plays that do not stage incest directly as a result of the patriarch's abuse of power nevertheless juxtapose these themes to suggests the inevitable link between them. Thus, for example, Edmund's adulterous and incestuous liaisons with Goneril and Regan in Shakespeare's *King Lear* emerge as a desire to be loved and wanted, a direct result of his father's preference for his legitimate older son Edgar, and consequent neglect of the younger. Not surprisingly, Edmund's villainies, which may be seen as attempts to gain legitimacy and usurp his father's authority, include attempted parricide and incest. A similar juxtaposition emerges in Massinger's *The Unnatural Combat*, a tragedy which also presents an interesting case of blurring generic boundaries.

Of all the Renaissance plays which stage incest as a result of the patriarch's abuse of authority and as a consequent filial assault on patriarchy, Massinger's tragedy *The Unnatural Combat* is most interesting in its simultaneous experimentation with genre. As Ira Clark argues, Massinger catered to the sophisticated audiences of the private theatres and his plays reveal a constant experimentation with dramatic form: 'The privileged Carolines who provided the primary support for the professional playwrights understood drama: they could appreciate expert displays of their rhetorical professions, they had backgrounds in drama and many of them had theatrical experience' (I. Clark 1992 p.10). Clark concentrates her study on Massinger's experiments in tragicomedy, a form for which she argues a superior theatrical status than has been conventionally assigned; *The Unnatural Combat* though a tragedy, experiments with form beyond the scope of tragicomedy.

The play opens with its central patriarchal figure, Malefort Senior, being questioned by authorities on suspicion of collusion with his son who has turned traitor against the state. Malefort Junior, who has gathered on the shores of Marseilles with a large army, sends a messenger promising to refrain from attacking the city if his father will fight him to the death in single combat. His ambiguous charges against his father, that he is 'a murderer, an atheist', causes surprise but does not provoke any questions from the authorities; the reason for these charges are explained only later in the play. Massinger provokes considerable curiosity in the reader through Malefort Junior's insistence that none ask him for his reasons: 'May the cause / That forces mee to this unnaturall act, / Be buried in everlasting silence' (II, i, ll.48–50), he tells the Captain. The authorities, convinced of Malefort Senior's loyalty, permit the duel between father and son which proceeds as planned. As the two face each other, Malefort Junior expresses his horror at what seems to have been a major violation of patriarchal responsibility by his father:

> As you are my father,
> I bend my knee, and uncompell'd professe
> My life, and all thats mine, to be your gift;
> . . .
> Why have you done that which I dare not speake?
> And in the action chang'd the humble shape
> Of my obedience, to rebellious rage
> And insolent pride?
>
> (II, i, ll.121–134)

In response to this charge, Malefort Senior insists on his rights as a patriarch to do what he wishes and yet command obedience from his son as his due. Against all odds, the father slays the son in combat; Malefort Senior's response to this triumph suggests that he does indeed have much to hide: 'That I have power to be unnaturall, / Is my securitie. Die all my feares, / And waking jealousies, which have so long / Been my tormentors, theres now no suspition' (II, i, ll.208–211). In the scene that follows Theocrine, Malefort Senior's daughter, is betrothed to Beaufort Junior but Malefort's obsessive fascination with his daughter's beauty, embarrassing to those who hear him and to Theocrine herself, prepares us for the tragedy that follows. Theocrine, Malefort Senior tells the court, reminds him of his dead second wife and the pleasures of his own marriage bed:

> Nor let it in your excellence beget wonder,
> Or any here, that looking on the daughter,
> I feast my selfe in imagination
> Of those sweet pleasures, and allowed delights,
> I tasted from the mother (who still lives
> In this perfect model) . . .
>
> (II, iii, ll.91–96)

His obsession prompts considerable suspicion from the onlookers and as Montrevile, his supposed friend, recognizes, 'There is something more / Than fatherly love in this' (III, iii, l.161). Malefort Senior himself only fully acknowledges his incestuous passion after being moved to jealousy by the love between Beaufort Junior and Theocrine. Finally admitting his unlawful passion to Montrevile, he entrusts Theocrine to his friend so that he might keep her safe in his fort. The scene now moves to the fort where Montrevile, who has simply been awaiting an opportunity to revenge the loss of his beloved several years earlier to Malefort Senior, threatens to rape Theocrine himself. It is in these brisk scenes of gathering disaster that Massinger experiments most with the generic form of the play. We move from the scene of Montrevile's threat to one where Malefort, feeling new misgivings about the trustworthiness of his friend, determines to get his daughter back. His arguments in favour of incest as natural and sanctioned by natural law anticipate the logic of figures such as Giovanni:

> say I had
> Injoyd what I desir'd, what had it beene
> But incest? . . . neither had the crime
> Wanted a praesident. . . . Universall nature,
> As every day tis evident, allowes it
> To creatures of all kinds. . . .
> . . . Why should envious man then
> Brand that close act which adds proximity
> To whats most neere him, with the abhorred title
> Of incest? or our later lawes forbid
> What by the first was granted?
>
> (V, ii, ll.14–36)

In the last lines quoted, Maleforte seems to allude specifically to such instances as the marriages of Cain, Abel and Abraham mentioned earlier. Though Massinger does not invoke the metaphors of divine love as Ford does in his tragedy, he allows Maleforte to cite natural law to justify his aberrant desire as Giovanni does in *'Tis Pity*.

Theatrically Massinger sandwiches this scene where Maleforte decides to bring his daughter back to live with him in an incestuous relationship between the scenes of Montreville's threatened and actual rapes of Theocrine. The playwright thus toys with the notion of two different endings to his play: one in which Montreville will enact his rape of Theocrine and prevent Maleforte from taking his daughter back and another whereby Maleforte will arrive in time to save Theocrine from Montreville's lust. Such dual possibilities had been, in fact, an aspect of Renaissance treatments of incest on the stage. In *A King and No King*, Beaumont and Fletcher poise the action at imminent disaster as Arbaces decides to act on his incestuous love for his sister; the last scene of the play averts incest through Gobrius's opportune revelations which establish that Arbaces is not related to Panthea after all. In this last scene the play, which had moved towards imminent tragedy, transforms into a tragicomedy. In *'Tis Pity* Ford invokes the model set up by Beaumont and Fletcher, though his own text moves relentlessly towards tragedy in its last scenes.

Massinger's play, however, presents more disturbing options than any other play that treats the subject of incest on the Renaissance stage. Though the play ends in multiple deaths, a convention of tragedy, with Theocrine dead from grief, Maleforte struck dead by lightning, and Montreville awaiting death, Massinger poses the possibility of these deaths being averted. This would constitute a conventional format for tragicomedy in which we move inevitably towards tragedy until the last scenes where opportune revelations and/or conversions by evil characters transform the action into tragicomedy. However, Massinger actually presents us with two options which are both tragic; in the alternate version that is tantalizingly presented to the audience as a real possibility, multiple deaths might be averted but the audience has to accept the imminent realization of incestuous desire between Maleforte and Theocrine. In short Massinger actually poses the scenario for a tragedy that would avoid death altogether, a bold theatrical suggestion in a period where tragedies always ended with multiple dead bodies on stage and comedies invariably concluded on the threshold of sexual gratification. Massinger's tragedy divorces both possible conclusions from their conventional generic associations.

As in many Renaissance depictions, Massinger's play also registers incest as a direct result of the abuse of power by patriarchal figures. Even Montreville's lustful desire for Theocrine presents itself as tainted by incestuous passion, for he sees her as a substitute for her mother to whom he had been betrothed before Maleforte stole her from him. His lust thus duplicates Maleforte's and results directly from Maleforte's earlier crimes, his wooing of another's beloved when he was already married and his subsequent murder of his wife so that he might marry again. While one might quarrel with the passive representation of women in all these events, the tragedy clearly assaults abusive patriarchy as the source of its horrors and represents female characters as unwitting victims of the lustful desires of men in positions of power. Massinger's play thus shares with numerous others which treat the subject of incest as an insistent association of sexual transgression with abusive patriarchal authority. Ira Clark's point about Massinger as 'a playwright of importance who constantly experiments with form to accommodate sociopolitical compromises' is most vividly apparent in *The Unnatural Combat* (I. Clark 1992 p.15).

As all the above plays demonstrate, Renaissance drama's deconsecration of patriarchy is inextricably linked with the staging of sexual and familial violations such as adultery and incest. And as I suggested previously, to read later tragedies such as *The Revenger's Tragedy, The Unnatural Combat, The Change-ling, Women Beware Women* and *'Tis Pity She's a Whore* primarily as attacks on patriarchy is to read at odds with critics such as Tennenhouse who sees later drama as staging repeated assaults on the female aristocratic body in order to consolidate 'the new image of the body politic as male' which emerged after Elizabeth's death:

> Under Elizabeth, the highest position that of the patron of patrons, was occupied by a woman, and so we may speculate that it made perfect sense to represent the aristocratic body as female. Indeed, . . . Elizabeth insisted upon it. Under James, however, this gender theme was revised and incorporated in a new image of the body politic. On the one hand, we find romances and tragi-comedies that celebrate the reunion of an originary family under a chastened monarch or father. . . . Tragedies . . . approached the same problem of revision from an entirely different angle. . . . Thus, on the Jacobean stage we see aristocratic women punished for possessing the very features that empowered such characters in Elizabethan romantic comedy. The ritual purification of these bodies . . . revised the political iconography identified with an earlier monarchy. . . . Only this, I believe, could have made an assault on the Elizabethan style of female so pervasive.
>
> (Tennenhouse 1989 p.79)

To make such a radical claim Tennenhouse executes some creative mental gymnastics, for the basis of his contention springs illogically from his comparison of Elizabethan comedies with Jacobean tragedies. Quite naturally those character-istics that empowered women in Elizabethan comedies would be punished in Jacobean tragedies; to argue that this change constitutes a political re-reading is to ignore generic differences that surely merit consideration.

But Tennenhouse's recognition that a radical re-examination occurred during the later Renaissance of the political metaphors that dominated Elizabeth's rule may be worth some attention. Certainly as James reinvented and reiterated the patriarchal basis of monarchy as Elizabeth could never have done, Jacobean dramatists such as Tourneur and Middleton and Rowley seem to have taken considerable license in exposing the fragility of the political equation between patriarchy and monarchy. And while Charles I continued to rely on the metaphors that dominated James's political discourse, the Caroline court, unlike the Jaco-bean, presented a more fragile front in this regard. Not the least of its problems was the Catholic queen Henrietta Maria. As Sophie Tomlinson has demonstrated, the presence of the French queen and her more active role at court prompted much discussion; Henrietta exposed to an even greater degree the fragility of the patriarch/monarch analogies (Tomlinson 1992). It might be argued that in the context of these shifts in the sociopolitical environment of early Stuart England, the idealized familial metaphors that had been central to devotional literature and political theory during the sixteenth century also underwent radical revaluation during the mid-seventeenth century. Recontextualized and literalized within secular contexts, the metaphors became potent weapons for undermining rather than reiterating existing systems of order.[11]

Ultimately such dramatic subversion played into the hands of Puritan opponents of the King and theatre in general; Milton, for example, could expertly convert associations between incest and tyrannical or weak patriarchy to political purpose. In *Paradise Lost*, when he depicts the relationship between Satan, Sin and Death as an incestuous parody of the heavenly trinity, he similarly collapses the sacred and the transgressive, though he clearly re-designates such a collapse as an unnatural and unholy deviance. Implicitly Milton thus aligns corrupt earthly monarchy and tyrannical patriarchy with transgressive misapplication of divine relationships.[12] It is precisely such a misapplication that playwrights such as Middleton and Ford render fascinating rather than execrable.

Notes

1. Richard McCabe similarly traces the complexities of its depiction in Elizabethan and early Stuart drama (McCabe 1993); for an earlier treatment of the subject of incest, see Mark Taylor's study of Shakespeare's plays (Taylor 1982).
2. For a discussion of drama's involvement with the political issues of the years immedi-ately preceding the conflict of the mid-century, see Martin Butler (1984); for a historical examination of political conflicts in early Stuart England, see R. Cust and A. Hughes (1989).
3. In his introduction to the play Bernard Beckerman typifies a response that always

persisted in Ford criticism, when he categorizes the work as a 'strange and disturbing tragedy' (Beckerman 1983 p.447).

4. For a detailed examination of the cult of Elizabeth as it developed during and after her reign, see Roy C. Strong (1977) and Malcolm Smuts (1987).

5. Shell goes so far as to suggest that Teresa, a contemporary of Elizabeth's, verges in her *Life* on confessing to spiritual incest and that 'a biographer, pressing too hard, might conclude that she had made love to a Dominican Brother' (Shell 1993 p.39).

6. Franco Moretti was perhaps the first to insist on Renaissance drama's sustained deconsecration of monarchy; in a claim that is perhaps more radical than what I mean to suggest here, he argues that Renaissance drama deconsecrates the king in order that society might decapitate him (Moretti 1983 pp.42–82).

   In these pages, I extend an earlier treatment of *The Changeling* and *'Tis Pity* as staging assaults on patriarchy (Smith 1991 pp.84–89).

7. My reading of the play's conclusion as decidedly tragic for the patriarch on stage who can never recoup his losses differs considerably from standard reactions to the play's concluding actions. See, for example, N. W. Bawcutt who argues that the play's tragic events merely caused a temporary disruption from everyday living to which characters return at the end (Bawcutt 1958 p.lxviii). More recently, Arthur L. Little has argued that the play returns to normalcy after a brief 'disruption of patriarchal normality' in its central scenes (Little 1993 p.36).

8. This scene has received considerable critical attention. For a reading of this scene and the play as an example of the 'baroque' style that dominated later Renaissance drama, see Ronald Huebert's study (1977).

9. For the nature of audiences at private theatres, see Andrew Gurr (1987).

10. For readings of Ford's tragedy within the context of early Stuart sociopolitical concerns but along different lines than I suggest here, see books by Dorothy Farr (1979), Ira Clark (1992) and Lisa Hopkins (1994) and edited volumes of essays by Donald K. Anderson (1986) and Michael Neill (1988).

11. For a reading that recognizes the positive depictions of Giovanni and Annabella but nevertheless sees their plight as the reassertion of social and moral order, see Mark Stavig's study of Ford (Stavig 1968 pp.95–121). My reading also differs radically from Ira Clark's evaluation of Ford; she insists that 'the absolute dominion of monarchs over subjects, of husbands over wives, of fathers or guardians over daughters and sons . . . remains unquestioned in his [Ford's] works' (Clark 1992 p.84). For a considerably more complex analysis of Ford's relationship to the sociopolitical environment of the 1630s, see Martin Butler's study (1984).

12. For an analysis of the deconsecration of monarchy in seventeenth-century literature, see Richard F. Hardin's study of Spenser, Shakespeare and Milton (Hardin 1992).

6

Theatre and the scaffold: social drama and public spectacle in 1649

The *Anarchia Anglicana* (1649) includes an incident remarkable for its subversion of ritual by the invocation of ritual itself. A Parliamentary soldier entered a village church in Surrey at the close of evening services and insisted that he had a message from God for the congregation. Having been denied the pulpit, he proceeded to provide God's message in the churchyard. Holding a lantern in one hand and four candles in the other, he elaborately and ceremoniously enacted what he described as an injunction from God to reject five points of conventional ecclesiastical behaviour: Sabbath, tithes, ministers, magistrates and the Bible itself. The four candles which were first lit from the lantern represented four of the five points to be eradicated; each candle was then symbolically extinguished and the speaker proceeded to declare that God's injunctions had thus been successfully carried out. The Bible itself was then ceremoniously burnt as an illustration of the destruction of the fifth point (Simpson 1955 pp.44–45).

Steven Mullaney explains the apparent contradiction within this highly ceremonious dismissal of ceremony:

> What he performed was a working through of Church ceremony, a last rite for Christian ritual. That he employed ceremony to extinguish ceremony was a contradiction, but just such a contradiction was fundamental to the recreation of early modern culture: a process that begins in the adoption of the strange and that ends with a full entrance into and recreation of alien or residual cultures, consummately rehearsed and thus consummately foreclosed.
>
> (Mullaney 1988 p.87)

The event presents a strategy of denunciation that typified the Renaissance. As Levine points out, attacks on the theatre frequently took the form of theatre itself; Stephen Gosson's complaints, for example, emerged under the revealing title *Plays Confuted in Five Actions* (Levine 1994 p.2). A similar impulse underlies another equally fascinating performance of the mid-century, Charles I's public trial and execution.

Charles I was executed on 30 January 1649 outside his own Banqueting house completed by Inigo Jones only twenty years earlier. The crowds who faced Charles, even the soldiers who had called so loudly and insistently for justice during the king's trial, remained remarkably subdued. The executioner and his assistant, apparently fearing the wrath of the people, were obviously and heavily disguised. When the axe struck, a huge groan rose from the crowd, who also dispersed quickly and quietly immediately after. The event provoked neither the jubilant celebration that followed the Earl of Strafford's or Archbishop Laud's execution nor the intense show of sympathy that sometimes characterized such occasions.[1] Contemporary drawings capture the stunned response of onlookers as they witnessed this most extraordinary social drama, surely an unimaginable act before 1649.

Commenting on attempts by historians through the years to comprehend these political events, Jerome Friedman questions the possibility of ever acquiring a logical and coherent understanding:

> Could it be that a major seventeenth-century event such as the English Revolution remains best conceived in wondrous terms as a conflict involving rival powers of enchantment? If such unsophisticated ideas explain seemingly complex conflicts, the cause and effect logic of modern rationalism and scholarship loses some of its meaning. Or, perhaps history loses the order and reason that university scholars wish it had.
>
> (Friedman 1992 pp.441–442)

I offer an alternative reading of this dramatic event of the mid-century, a cultural text remarkable for its complete dissolution of boundaries between theatre, carnival and public punishment. The event may be read as an elaborate example of what the Parliamentary soldier sought to achieve in the church in Surrey; Charles's execution constituted a recreation of early modern culture along new lines but a complete break with England's cultural past also involved a consummate rehearsal of the systems of theatre and festival that authorities wished to displace. This 'social drama', a term I borrow from Victor Turner, detheatricalized the world by enacting the supreme theatrical spectacle, decarnivalized community by appropriating and redefining the very essence of carnival festivity.[2] Thus supporters of the event who often retained deep reservations about theatre and playing in general, could nevertheless argue, as J. Spittlehouse did in 1653, that God was 'using our nation as a theatre to act as a precedent of what he intends to do in all nations under the scope of heaven' (quoted in Capp 1984 p.179).

Turner describes social dramas as 'units of aharmonic or disharmonic process, arising in conflict situations' (Turner 1974 p.37). He outlines four typical stages in social dramas: the breach of regular, norm-governed social relations between persons or groups, a phase of mounting crisis, redressive action and reintegration. Historians of Stuart England have with varying emphases described the crisis of the civil war and its aftermath in terms that could fit such a pattern.[3] The redressive phase might best describe historical events at the centre of the seventeenth century, namely, Charles's public execution and trial. Turner describes the redressive phase as that in which 'both pragmatic techniques and symbolic action reach their fullest expression'. The social unit is at its most 'self-conscious' during this phase (Turner 1974 pp.37–41). In Charles's public trial and execution, which were calculated to end the social crisis, we witness just such a coalescence of the pragmatic and the symbolic.

In pragmatic terms Charles's trial and execution functioned to end the political crisis, but symbolically by dissolving boundaries between theatre, festivity and public punishment, the event may have served as a visual reinforcement of two other official positions of the mid-century: to close theatres and to ban festivities. An ordinance of June 1647, for example, abolished Christmas, Easter and Whit-suntide and banned the Book of Common Prayer. And in 1655 when direct military rule was established over England and Wales, major-generals from the army who were charged with governing the regions were entrusted the task of moral reform; it was their duty to see that 'no horse races, cock-fighting, bear-baiting, stage plays, or any unlawful assemblies' occurred in the local counties (D. Smith 1992 p.24). The 'social drama' of the mid-century which intended to modify public attitudes towards monarchy and government implicitly modified attitudes towards popular cultural activities as well, and this modification involved a simultaneous appropriation and negation of the metaphors of theatre and festivity.

The dramatic metaphor used to profusion by Nashe in his fictional description of Cutwolf's death and by Chamberlain in his narrative account of the executions of Cobham, Markham and Gray discussed earlier, also emerges in contemporary accounts of Charles I's execution. Contemporaries focused on these events of the mid-century as theatre; as Friedman points out, 'rather than argue the legal, theological, or political merits of Parliament's cause or that of Charles I, popular authors perceived the conflict through the enchanted eyes of wonder and fear' (Friedman 1992 p.425). Even in modern narratives, Charles's life invariably invokes dramatic comparisons.[4] Speaking about the two Charles Stuarts, Richard Ollard in his comparative biography writes:

> Perhaps it was their nature, like Prospero's to cast spells rather than to formulate political philosophies. From first to last how they defy sobriety and probability. Through the half-shut eyes of imprecise historical recollection what a stir of colour and movement, what drama, what pathos, what inexorability . . . This no doubt goes a long way to explain why Charles I and II are more vividly present to the popular historical consciousness than monarchs whose achievements were more lasting or whose personal qualities were more remarkable.
>
> (Ollard 1979 p.24)

Theatrical metaphor and dramatic irony seem especially apt to the life and career of Charles I, a monarch who ascended a monetarily depleted throne and could not afford the spectacular 'entry' which had become so fashionable throughout Europe at this time (which both Elizabeth and James before him had afforded), but who enacted the most spectacular exit ever recorded in English history, one still likely to provoke vigorous controversy. 'Despite his defeat by Parliament and subsequent execution,' Friedman argues, 'Charles remained a magical figure and pamphlets continued to describe him in miraculous terms' (Friedman 1992 p.429).

The sense of theatre invoked by the format of Charles's trial and execution emerges most clearly in contemporary pictorial and descriptive accounts of the event. Significantly, almost all the popular prints provide inaccurate accounts of the events, the inaccuracies resulting from the artists' desire to sacrifice veracity for theatricality; the only print which provides a somewhat more accurate description was made by a foreign visitor who we can presume was less committed to the politics of the situation and the cultural mode of Stuart England. One especially popular drawing captures vividly the sense of drama inherent in the event; the raised platform, the shuffling crowds in a semi-circle around the stage and the upper classes watching from the windows and terrace of the building behind as the King knelt to suffer the blow, recall the theatres of Elizabethan and Stuart England. One print in circulation was revealingly titled 'The Direfull Tragedy of King Charles I' and the most famous literary account of the execution, Andrew Marvell's 'An Horatian Ode Upon Cromwell's Return from Ireland', cannot resist the theatrical metaphor which it uses brilliantly and abundantly. Marvell describes Cromwell's industry and ambition to 'cast the kingdoms old / Into another mould' and his foresight in weaving 'a net of such a scope'

> That Charles himself might chase
> To Carisbrooke's narrow case:
> That thence the royal actor born
> The tragic scaffold might adorn:
> While round the armed bands
> Did clap their bloody hands.
> *He* nothing common did or mean
> Upon that memorable scene:
> But with his keener eye
> The axe's edge did try:
> Nor called the gods with vulgar spite
> To vindicate his helpless right,
> But bowed his comely head,
> Down, as upon a bed.

(Marvell 1963 11.51–64)

The author of the royalist *Mercurius Brittanicus* issued on the morning of 30 January 1649, similarly adopts the theatrical metaphor, though perhaps with less literary acumen than Marvell: 'the Trayterous Tragedians are upon their Exit, and poor King Charles at the Brink of the Pitt; the Prologue is past, the Proclamation made, His Sentence is given, and we daily expect the sad Catastrophie; and then behold! The Sceane is chang'd; . . . The Play thus done, or rather the Worke Finish'd; the Epilogue remains, to wit the Epitaph of a slaughter'd King' (Raymond 1993 p.243).

Of course the ellipsis of boundaries between theatre and punitive practice demonstrated in the 'social drama' of Charles's execution depended, as did invocations of public punishment on the Renaissance stage, on a general recognition that these activities, while they shared certain strategies, remained discrete areas of social behaviour. The concept of distance and the difference between play activities such as theatre and non-play activities such as executions enumerated in my opening chapter might also be theoretically understood, as I mentioned earlier, through the metaphor of the frame; all play activities remain framed by participants' perception of events as temporally and spatially limited. Thus participants in a carnival or skimmington recognize the temporary nature of their 'play'. The establishing of distance in theatre and the invocation of a frame in festivity perform similar functions and the relationship between these entities might be understood in terms of Bateson's claims about play activities in general enumerated earlier. As we have seen, many Renaissance plays are constructed not on the premise 'This is play' but rather on the question 'Is this play?' In the political events of the mid-century, which invoked the format of theatre thus positing that the events constituted play but also simultaneously obliterated the distinction between play and non-play, we encounter an even more paradoxical aspect of metacommunication than that denoted by the question 'Is this play?' The situation approximates more closely to the following: 'These actions in which we now engage invoke play but constitute a categorical denial of play'. The actualized theatre of Charles's trial and execution thus culminates a period of intense experimentation with notions of 'theatre', 'play' and 'distance' in the Renaissance.

In fact, in the events of the mid-century we encounter a less self-conscious counterpart to modern radical attempts at manipulating distance. At the one extreme Bertolt Brecht wished to heighten and emphasize distance between actor/ event and viewer; at the other extreme theorists such as Antonin Artaud wished to obliterate any emotional and psychological distance between theatrical spectacle and reality, between theatrical participant and viewer. The political events that concluded the early Stuart era, it would appear, achieved the collapse that Artaud desired. The political violence of the mid-seventeenth century might be seen as the supreme realization of Artaud's 'Theatre of Cruelty' which enacted a surgery of the mind on its audience. Roger Copeland's critique of Artaud's expectations, which points to the impossibility of his vision, describes an attitude implicitly invoked in the highly theatrical decapitation scene which concluded the early Stuart era; Copeland argues that 'Artaud's project consists of nothing less than an all-out assault on the very idea of theatre', a destruction of 'the very concept of the theatre as *theatron*, or the seeing place' (Copeland 1978 p.46). A similar recognition informs the political violence of the mid-century in Stuart England; by merging cultural and legal activities, the momentous political drama dissolved long-established boundaries that had separated these activities. And by representing events as the culmination of a communal desire felt by the nation, the drama negated the sense of distance that separates spectator from spectacle, a criterion absolutely essential for the successful enactment of both theatre and festivity. The social drama thus enacted a destruction of theatre itself.

A similar appropriation and subversion of format occurred with regard to festivity as well. As I suggested earlier, within the arena of festivity the principle of distance might be more appropriately characterized as the framing or the invocation of bounds. Festival was framed by the authorities who sanctioned its licence; as in the case of distance in the theatre, framing may also be linked directly to the regulation of the interventionist impulse. Traditionally, official

recognition of the temporal nature of festivity prevented authorities from inter-
fering to regulate even the most blatant abuses or subversions of authority that
occurred within the frame. In fact the metaphor of the frame has been used by
anthropologists such as Turner to distinguish theatre and carnival (both being
forms of 'play') from actual events. Turner perceives framing as a device that
permits 'plural reflexivity' or communal reassessment of shared systems (Turner
1984 p.23). Framing also results from the naturally subjunctive mood of many
cultural activities such as theatre and carnival:

> Most cultural performances belong to a culture's 'subjunctive' mood. 'Subjunctive' is
> defined by Webster as 'that mood of a verb used to express supposition, desire,
> hypothesis, possibility, etc., rather than to state an actual fact. . . .' Ritual, carnival,
> festival, theatre, film and similar performative genres clearly possess many of these
> attributes. The indicative mood of culture . . . controls the daily arenas of economic
> activity, much of law and politics and a good deal of domestic life.
>
> (V. Turner 1984 pp.20–21)

Though the staging of performative genres such as festival and theatre can often
be problematic, 'the venue and occasion for the most radical scepticism', the
condition of the frame remains essential for their enactment (Turner 1984 p.22).
Framing thus performs a necessary function within the festive mode even as
distance does in the theatre.

The format of Charles's trial and execution suggests one form of festivity
specifically, carnival celebrations. As social historians have shown, carnival was
an especially popular form of activity in early modern Europe, its festivities
beginning in late December and increasing in intensity as Lent approached. Peter
Burke describes vividly the inherent theatricality of the carnival world: 'The
place of carnival was the open air in the city center. . . . Carnival may be seen as
a huge play in which the main streets and squares became stages, the city
became a theatre without walls and the inhabitants, the actors and the spectators,
observing the scene from the balconies' (Burke 1978 p.182). Burke goes on to
discuss the central theatrical spectacle within carnival, namely the decapitation
of the Carnival King by the common people. The event was preceded by a
procession and a mock trial resulting in a mock confession. The image of the
world-upside-down which dominated carnival festivities thus received its fullest
expression in this theatrical enactment of the decapitation of the king by the
common people.

The political events of 1649 implicitly invoke this central spectacle of carnival
celebrations. Charles's trial and execution took place in January, well within the
traditional carnival season. Colonel Pride's infamous purge of Parliament in
December 1648 and the convenient disappearance of the Peers into the country
left events in the hands of a partial House of Commons. Charles's trial thus
represents a remarkably literal world-upside-down; the King himself repeatedly
insisted on the illegality of the proceedings by questioning the rights of a partial
Lower House to try an anointed King.[5] On 30 January when he was taken from
the palace at two in the afternoon, despite the delay in schedule, the crowds

who had gathered earlier remained to witness the events. The public procession, the trial by the summarily created High Court of Justice and the public execution, all of which took place in January during the regular carnival season outside the Banqueting house, emphasize the iconoclastic significance of the proceedings. Burke suggests that in general public execution rituals would have reminded crowds of carnival executions; Charles's case, unprecedented in scope and bold- · ness, must certainly have provided spectators with a vivid reminder of its festive counterpart (Burke 1978 p.197). As in the case of theatre, the format of carnival was implicitly invoked and then undermined in the events of 1649.

In this context Michael André Bernstein's modifications of Bakhtin's theories on carnival may prove especially useful. Bernstein argues that even as actual carnival functions within the bounds licensed by authority, the textualized literary carnival invokes the reader as authority. According to Bernstein, the ritual liberation that Bakhtin celebrates in Rabelais as actual proves to be temporary precisely because of the authority exercised by the reader. He insists that only 'when the laughter turns bitter' does 'Bakhtin's paradigm of all-inclusive ritual come closest to realization' (Bernstein 1983 p.299). In carnival 'turned bitter' the reader or spectator is unable to function as authority; 'carnival turned bitter' creates a real ambivalence quite unlike the temporary ambivalence invoked by the licensed and bounded carnival. Charles I's trial and death may be regarded as 'carnival turned bitter', for Charles's death was officially presented as the outcome of a communal desire for change. The spectator who could validate the relevance of the occasion as temporary and wholly metaphoric was effectively silenced by the implicit invocation of festival and theatre but outside the subjunctive mood characteristic of these events until then.

In this regard, in negating the boundaries that separated spectator from spectacle, the political drama of January 1649 may be seen as doubling the iconoclastic frenzy that also seized the nation during the mid-century. As Barry Reay points out, the period between 1640 and 1660 'witnessed the most complete revolution that the Church of England has ever undergone, . . . the removal of altar rails, destruction of crosses, crucifixes and images of the Trinity, the Virgin · Mary, angels and saints' (Reay 1984 p.8). The removal of altar rails, the divider between spectator and spectacle, was effected metaphorically during Charles's execution by conveying the general impression that the political events represented a communal desire acceded to by the majority of people. As historians have shown, this was far from the reality and the Interregnum was created not by popular consent but by 'acts of violence' and the regime was 'sustained only by shows of force' (Morrill 1992 p.12).

By actualizing theatre and by presenting this actualization as the fulfilment of a communal desire, by appropriating the format of the theatrical spectacle but violating its fundamental principle of distance, Charles's trial and execution thus redefined and created new iconic associations for this popular cultural activity. The political violence thus metaphorically reinforced official decisions made during the same period, to close public theatres and to ban various forms of communal festivities. Most importantly, such appropriation appears to have been a natural culmination of the earlier close alliance between two other centres of spectacle power, centres that were to be displaced and whose powers were to be appropriated and reapportioned, namely, the monarchy and the theatre. As Roy Strong describes it, 'Before the invention of the mechanical mass media of today, the creation of monarchs as an "image" to draw people's allegiance was the task of humanists, poets, writers and artists' (Strong 1973 p.19). In seeking to suspend such allegiance, who better to invoke than the dramatist, the artist most communally engaged during earlier years in the enlisting of allegiance? As events loaded with significance, the trial and execution thus functioned as metaphoric iconoclasm. Margaret Aston's characterization of the literal iconoclasts of the sixteenth century might apply even more potently to Puritan opponents of the king in the seventeenth: 'They saw, as none of their predecessors had seen so clearly, the possibilities of controlling minds through imagery or destruction of imagery, loading or unloading mental processes with visual effects' (Aston 1988 p.5).

In other words, the events of the mid-century may be viewed as theatre and carnival turned real, as metaphoric destructions of the spirit of these popular activities whose success had always depended on tacit communal acknowledgement of their artificial and temporary nature. By transposing and actualizing carnival and theatre, Charles's trial and execution redefined and thereby created new iconic associations for these popular cultural worlds. To return to Turner's terms, the political events violated the fundamental element of play; the subjunctive mood of theatre and communal celebration was simultaneously invoked and then transformed into the indicative. 'The Regicide' which was, as Scott argues, 'a declaration of war upon English political history', was equally a war upon English social and cultural history (J. Scott 1992 p.35).

Such actualization of festivity and theatre with its accompanying violation of distance and framing may even have evolved metatheatrically within Renaissance theatre. I do not mean to suggest that Puritan opposition to the king owed its format to theatre but Renaissance drama had revealed a similar tendency increasingly to blur and renegotiate boundaries between cultural practices. In this sense Raymond's optimistic assessment of the power of newsbooks in shaping society may apply equally to its predecessor, the theatre: 'In these days, when we are saturated by the media, we paradoxically believe that literary texts are necessarily passive documents. Newsbooks are a reminder that . . . writing was a way of inventing the future' (Raymond 1993 p.25). Of course, supporters of the monarchy viewed events as a carnival world-turned-upside-down, but the vivid reality of the proceedings must have undermined such a perception. Indeed descriptions of the event as carnivalesque occurred during the trial but this view seems to have reached its highest pitch only in 1660 at Charles II's instatement, when original events had been decidedly and effectively reversed, when the possibility of reinstating the frames that had been broken earlier appeared certain. In the texts of the mid-century, the representation of topsy-turviness is accompanied by a sense of ambivalence and discomfort. Political and literary texts, irrespective of their political allegiances, capture this sense of ambivalence and paradox most vividly. A real sense of ambivalence is evident, for example, in John Howell's description of Parliament in a letter to the Earl of Pembroke as 'this makeshift assembly' which was 'no more Parliament than a pie-powder court at Bartholomew Fair, there being all the essential parts of a true Parliament wanting in this, as fairness of elections, freedom of speech, fullness of Members, nor have they any head at all' (Ashton 1983 p.187). Parliament sans King was a headless carnival-grotesque belonging conventionally only within the festive world of the marketplace and the fairs. Clement Walker in a description that recalls Howell's, wonders 'whether our Lawes, Liberties and properties are not now as liable to an invasion from the Legislative power as formerly from the Prerogative', for now Parliament's 'little finger is heavier than the loins of the King' (Ashton 1983 p.205). The investiture of phallic power to Parliament and the depletion of power from the 'loins' of the King captures vividly the carnival-grotesque world of things gone awry.

In a similar discussion of the High Court of Justice, Walker condemns the institution as a 'formidable monster'; he goes on to describe the Court's effects on England as also transformative, for England has become a monster with teeth in its head, snapping at its 'Neighbours before it be out of its Swaddling clouts' (Walker 1651 p.27). The author of a premature elegy in *Mercurius Elencticus in April 1648* uses similar vocabulary to describe the political situation:

> Here lyes the Ruines (who can but Lament)
> Of England's Mad and Bloody Parliament.
> Here lies Rebellion, Murder, Sacriledge,
> Here are the Achans stole the Golden wedge:
> Here lye the Grand Imposters of our Nation,
> Who surfeited with too much Revelation.
> . . .
> Reader behold these Monsters! Then relate
> The fate, the ruine, of a rotten State.
>
> (Raymond 1993 p.114)

Surfeiting on its own gluttonous diet of 'revelations', Parliament presents a carnivalesque figure of excess and decay soon to die an inglorious death. And yet, unlike in conventional carnivalesque inversions of the sixteenth and seventeenth-centuries, these contemporary descriptions encode a deep and genuine ambivalence; the political situation clearly posed a threat to royalist supporters, for it could hardly be dismissed as a temporary and correctable inversion sanctioned to re-emphasize the very norms that it violated.[6]

In the orchestration of this 'social drama', as in rituals of punishment in general, there were three elements that proved elusively beyond control: Charles's equal determination to outperform them by staging a martyrdom, pro-royalist ability to convert the metaphor of theatre to their own purpose through its effective reproduction in newsbooks and pamphlets, and the power that the institution of monarchy itself exercised over the minds of the English people. Monarchy could be abolished by beheading the king and by acts of Parliament, but as Jonathan Scott questions, 'how was the *idea* of monarchy to be abolished from the English public mind? There it sat enthroned, not only by all the social and political structures of the time but by the record of time itself' (J. Scott 1992 p.35).

Indeed Charles remained acutely aware of his role in the larger social drama and attempted at every stage to subvert the event. Conscious of the dramatic nature of his performance, he put on two shirts before he mounted the scaffold so that he might not appear to shiver on that frosty morning. His request for a higher block so that he might kneel rather than lie down in undignified fashion seems to have been similarly motivated by the desire to create an apt visual effect on the watching crowds. His final remarks were addressed to the figures on the scaffold because the presence of troops between him and the crowds made any address to them useless but, despite his distance from the crowd, the figure of the king on the scaffold exercised so great a power on the nation that all copies of the *Eikon Basilike*, supposedly a record of the king's last days, sold out when it was released.[7] Like the Duchess of Malfi and Dorothea in *The Virgin Martyr*, Charles converted the moment of his ignominy into one of unprecedented triumph and martyrdom. The monarch's words seemed to acquire even greater authority from beyond the scaffold and, as Raymond notes, 'so powerful was the impact of this work that not even John Milton's exact repudiation of it . . . could reverse its impact on the people' (Raymond 1993 p.208). And supporters of the king continued to market this power in pamphlets and broadsides; 'A Miracle of Miracles', for example, recorded that a maid who had a horrible skin problem was cured by the kingly touch when a handkerchief 'which had been dipped in the King's blood on the day that he was beheaded' was applied to her sores (Friedman 1992 pp.229–230). Charles had become a martyr, a version of Christ and newsbooks contributed greatly to this image of the king. As Michael Walzer describes it, speaking of the executions of Charles I and Louis XVI more than a century later, 'The public stage could not . . . be denied the public person: all France and all Europe knew that a king was on trial. . . . the king defeated and brought low remained somehow a royal figure' (Walzer 1973 p.4). Maurice Ashley even suggests that Charles's expert performance may have saved the monarchy and ensured its return (Ashley 1987 p.216).

Naturally, the reinstation of frames in 1660 at the Restoration of Charles II involved a conscious reappropriation of those very items that had in 1649 been expertly displaced from one cultural mode to another: the return of monarchy was accompanied everywhere by images of the world turned right side up again. At Sherborne, street theatre re-enacted the earlier inversion through a trial of the revolutionaries by a mock High Court of Justice. The author of the *Mercurius Publicus* describes the parodic trial in detail:

> In the close of the day, some of the witty wags of the Town, did very formally represent an High Court of Justice. . . . John Bradshaw and Oliver Cromwells, whose effigies were artificially prepared and brought thither by a guard of Soldiers, were indited of High Treason and murdering of the King . . . They were asked whether they did own the authority of the Court, at which, being silent the whole multitude present cryed out, Justice! Justice! my Lord, Justice for these bloody Traitors and murderers. They

were asked again, whether they owned the authority of the Court, and upon refusal, sentence was passed upon them to be dragged to the place of Execution, to be there hanged upon two Gibbets of forty foot high . . . As they hung upon the Gibbets, they were so hacked and hewed, so gored and shot throw, that in a short time but little remained.

(Raymond 1993 pp.461–462)

The mock enactment, so closely modelled on Charles's trial by the High Court of Justice, preceded the real trials and punishments that followed shortly after. On 4 December 1660, a resolution passed in the House of Commons and ratified by the Upper House completed the course of monarchical reappointment; the resolution read: 'Resolved, by the Lords and Commons assembled in Parliament, that the carcasses of Oliver Cromwell, Henry Ireton, John Bradshaw, Thomas Pride, whether buried in Westminster Abbey or elsewhere, be with all expedition, taken up and drawn upon a hurdle to Tyburn, and there hanged in their coffins for some time' (Marks 1908 p.191). The bodies were dug up on 30 January 1661, the twelfth anniversary of Charles's death, and as the *Mercurius Publicus* records, 'Today they were drawn upon sledges to Tiburn, all the way . . . the universal outcry of the people went along with them. When their carcasses were at Tyburn, they were pull'd out of their Coffines and hang'd at the several angles of that Triple Tree, where they hung till the Sun was set; after which they were taken down, their heads cut off and their loathsome Trunks thrown into a deep hole under the Gallowes' (Raymond 1993 p.473). The next issue of *Mercurius Publicus* announced that 'The Heads of those three notorious Regicides, Oliver Cromwell, John Bradshaw and Henry Ireton, are set upon Poles on the top of Westminster-hall by the common Hangman' (Raymond 1993 p.473). The punishment meted to the regicides was certainly not unusual in its extremity; in August, 1650, the pro-parliamentary *Mercurius Politicus* had recorded a similar posthumous punishment of those who supported the King's cause: 'The Ringleader was convicted in prison, who afterwards laid violent hands on himself: Nevertheless, his corps were exposed upon the Gallows, his estate confiscated, his children degraded, and banish't forever' (Raymond 1993 p.307). The punishments at the Restoration simply rehearsed and reversed the trends of the previous decade.

Despite the reversals of the 1660s, the 'social drama' of the mid-century was not entirely without effect; several age-old traditions either faded or were watered down after the mid-century and the Puritan official position about festivity, as in the case of monarchy, achieved at least partial success. The same might be argued for the theatrical mode which never quite regained its earlier communal relevance after the Restoration. As Raymond argues, after the Parliamentary ordinance of 1642 closed the theatres, 'once and for all another medium supplanted the public stage . . . journalism, and the newsbook became a dominant literary form' (Raymond 1993 pp.1–20). The 'social drama' of the mid-century, by eliding boundaries between theatre, carnival and punitive practice, may have contributed much to this transformation of the English social and cultural landscape.

Notes

1. Peter Burke records that crowds sometimes showered flowers on the victim and condemned the executioner, and that often 'official rituals had to coexist with popular rituals which presented the hangman as the villain and the criminal as the hero' (P. Burke 1978 p.198). This was the case in 1603 when Markham, Grey and Cobham narrowly escaped being hanged; Carleton records that their pardon was greeted by the crowds with hues and cries of celebration, a marked contrast to Brooke's successful execution earlier when, decidedly displeased, the crowds refused to second the executioner's customary cry of 'God save the King' thus showing their sympathy for the unfortunate victim (Birch 1849 pp.31–32).
2. Viewed in this light, John Morrill's claim that Puritan desire to abolish various forms of popular festivity may have contributed to the ultimate failure of their cause appears to be very much to the point; as he suggests, 'further studies may show that the more the Puritans tried to abolish Christmas, the more certain their downfall became' (Morrill 1982 p.114). In the early years of the mid-century, attempts at destroying established systems were carefully orchestrated to include the appropriation of these systems but few attempts were made in the later years to sustain this mode of appropriation. Thus, though Christmas and Whitsuntide were abolished, no substitutes for communal celebration such as the day of Cromwell's accession were provided.
3. For studies of the mid-century crisis, see books by Roger Lockyer (1959), Richard Ollard (1979), Pauline Gregg (1984), Christopher Hill (1986), Maurice Ashley (1987), Noel Mayfield (1988) and David Lagomarsino and Charles Wood (1989).
4. The extremely popular accounts by Veronica Wedgwood may be cited as another example (Wedgwood 1964); Michael Walzer captures the same dramatic intensity in his account of the executions of Louis XVI and Charles I (Walzer 1973).
5. In this context, it may be significant that Charles I was tried and sentenced as king, a contrast to the execution of Louis XVI; Louis was first stripped of his kingship and tried and beheaded as the citizen, Louis Capet.
6. In the later years of the Interregnum, even Cromwell's language of despair registers a mood of ambivalence and inevitability; 'We have an appetite to variety,' he noted wryly, 'to be not only making wounds, but widening those already made. As if you should see one making wounds in a man's side and eager only to be groping and grovelling with his fingers in those wounds' (quoted in Morrill 1992 p.12).
7. Thirty-five editions appeared by the end of 1649 and the work was translated into Latin and several European languages (Knott 1993 p.160).

Conclusion

Thus the period between 1585 and 1649 may be seen as one of intense experimentation with boundaries. The elision of boundaries evident in early works such as Kyd's *The Spanish Tragedy* and Shakespeare's *Titus Andronicus* inaugurates a trend that culminates in radical realignments in Massinger, Middleton and Ford and in the complete dissolution of boundaries between theatre, punitive practice and carnival play in the 'social drama' of 1649. Of course elision of boundaries remains one lens through which one might view this period of intense theatrical activity and simultaneous opposition to theatre, but the concept of boundaries and their violation remains a particularly apt image for a period in which theatrical spectacle emerged as a viable and alternative form of popular cultural entertainment to activities such as punitive practices and carnival festivity.[1] The iconoclastic frenzy of the mid-century which saw the destruction of altar rails, the divider between those who enacted ritual and those who witnessed it, literalized a tendency implicitly evident throughout the late sixteenth and early seventeenth centuries in drama's invocation of violence and punishment's invocation of theatre and carnival licence. In this sense, Kenneth Burke's claim about artistic works applies particularly to the drama of Shakespeare and his contemporaries and equally to the 'social drama' which concluded the Renaissance: 'Critical and imaginative works are answers to questions posed by the situation in which they arose. They are not merely answers, they are *strategic* answers, *stylized* answers' (Burke 1974 p.230).

In my opening chapter, I also suggested that the stark break between Elizabethan high drama and Jacobean decadence continues to retain its hold on critics, even revisionist new historicist ones. My work argues for a greater continuum in our perception of these periods; the merging of theatre, festive topsy-turviness and punishment in the mid-seventeenth century may owe much to the deconsecration of authority in the drama that preceded it, but the drama of the early seventeenth century owes as much to the highly experimental and bold invocation of spectacles of death in the 1580s and 1590s in the drama of Kyd and Shakespeare. In this sense, my focus on breaking boundaries concerns itself with the dissolution of boundaries between cultural practices; I discount the erection of difference between Elizabethan and early Stuart drama and insist on a dissolution of boundaries between cultural practices such as theatre, festival and public punishments throughout the late sixteenth and seventeenth centuries.

Notes

1. For a similar focus on blurring boundaries but through a consideration of paradox, see Bryan Crockett's exploration of relationships between the stage and the pulpit in the Renaissance (Crockett 1995).

Bibliography

Anon. (1676), 'Great Newes from the Barbadoes or a True and Faithful Account of the Grand Conspiracy of the Negroes against the English', London: Printed for L. Curtis in Groat-Court upon Ludgate Hill.

Anon. (1962), *The Bloody Banquet*, Shoenbaum, Samuel (ed.), Oxford: Oxford University Press, Malone Society Reprints.

Adelman, Janet (1992), *Suffocating Mothers: Fantasies of Maternal Origin in Shakespeare's Plays, Hamlet to the Tempest*, New York and London: Routledge.

Anderson, Donald K. (ed.) (1986), *'Concord in Discord': The Plays of John Ford, 1586–1986*, New York: AMS Press.

Andrews, Michael Cameron (1989), *This Action of Our Death: The Performance of Death in English Renaissance Drama*, Newark, Delaware: University of Delaware Press.

Andrews, William (1899), *Bygone Punishments*, London: William Andrews and Co., the Hull Press.

Ardolino, Frank (1990), ' "In Paris? Mass, and Well Remembered!": Kyd's *The Spanish Tragedy* and the English Reaction to the St. Batholomew's Day Massacre', *The Sixteenth Century Journal*, **21** (3), Fall, 401–409.

Armstrong, Nancy and Tennenhouse, Leonard (ed) (1989), *The Violence of Representation: Literature and the History of Violence*, London and New York: Routledge.

Ashley, Maurice (1987), *Charles I and Oliver Cromwell: A Study in Contrasts and Comparisons*, London: Methuen.

Ashmole, Elias (ed.) (1967), *Theatrum Chemicum Britannicum*, New York and London: Johnson Reprint Corporation.

Ashton, Robert (1982), 'From Cavalier to Roundhead Tyranny' in Morrill, John (ed.), *Reactions to the English Civil War: 1642–49*, New York: St Martin's Press, pp.185–207.

———— (1983), 'Popular Culture in Seventeenth-century London', *London Journal*, **9**, 3–19.

Assheton, Edmund (1580), 'Letter to William Ffarington (1580)' in *Remains Historical and Literary Connected with the Palatine Counties of Lancaster and Chester*, **Vol. XXXIX**, Manchester: Chetham Society, 1856.

Aston, Margaret (1988), *England's Iconoclasts*, **Vol 1**, Oxford: Oxford University Press.

Ayres, Philip J. (1987), 'The Nature of Jonson's Roman History' in Kinney, Arthur F. and Collins, Dan S. (eds), *Renaissance Historicism: Selections from English Literary Renaissance*, Amherst, Massachusetts: University of Massachusetts Press, pp.207–222.

Bakhtin Mikhail (1965), *Rabelais and His World*, Iswolsky, Helene (trans.), Cambridge, Massachusetts: MIT Press.

—— (1984), *Problems of Dostoevsky's Politics*, Emerson, Caryl and Booth, Wayne C. (eds and trans.), Minneapolis, Minnesota: University of Minnesota Press.

—— (1986), *Speech Genres and other Late Essays*, Emerson, Caryl and Holquist, Michael (eds), McGee, Vern W. (trans.), Austin, Texas: University of Texas Press.

Baldwin, T. W. (1931), *William Shakespeare Adapts a Hanging*, Princeton, New Jersey: Princeton University Press.

Bale, John (1993), 'Conclusion' in Shell, Marc (ed.), *Elizabeth's Glass of the Sinful Soul*, Lincoln, Nebraska: University of Nebraska Press, pp.93–102.

Barker, Francis (1993), *The Culture of Violence: Tragedy and History*, Manchester: Manchester University Press.

Bartels, Emily (1990), 'Making the Moor: Aaron, Othello, and Renaissance Refashioning of Race', *Shakespeare Quarterly*, **40** (4), 433–454.

—— (1993), *Spectacles of Strangeness: Imperialism, Alienation, and Marlowe*, Philadelphia, Pennsylvania: University of Pennsylvania Press.

Barthelemy, Anthony Gerard (1987), *Black Face, Maligned Race: The Representations of Blacks in English Renaissance Drama from Shakespeare to Southerne*, Baton Rouge, Louisiana: Louisiana State University Press.

Bate, Jonathan (1996), 'The Elizabethans in Italy' in Maquerlot, Jean-Pierre and Willems, Michele (eds), *Travel and Drama in Shakespeare's Time*, Cambridge: Cambridge University Press, pp.55–74.

Bateson, Gregory (1985), 'A Theory of Play and Fantasy' in Innis, Robert E. (ed.), *Semiotics: An Introductory Anthology*. Bloomington, Indiana: Indiana University Press, pp.129–144.

Bawcutt, N. W. (1958), 'Introduction' in *The Changeling*, London: Methuen and Company, pp.xv–lxviii.

Bean, John C. (1980), 'Comic Structure and the Humanizing of Kate in *The Taming of the Shrew*' in Lenz, Carolyn R. S., Green, Gayle and Neely, Carol Thomas (eds), *The Woman's Part: Feminist Criticism of Shakespeare*, Urbana, Illinois: University of Illinois Press, pp.65–78.

Beaumont, Francis and Fletcher, John Fletcher (1963), *A King and No King*, Turner, Robert K. Jr. (ed.), Lincoln, Nebraska: University of Nebraska Press.

—— (1968), *The Maid's Tragedy*, Norland, Howard B. (ed.), Lincoln, Nebraska and London: University of Nebraska Press.

Beck, William (1980), 'Popular Culture and Elite Expression in Early Modern Europe', *Journal of Interdisciplinary History*, **II** (1), 97–103.

Beckerman, Bernard (1983), 'Introduction' in *Five Renaissance Plays*, New York and London: Penguin Books, pp.ix–xxiii.

Bellamy, John (1979), *The Tudor Law of Treason: An Introduction*, London: Routledge and Kegan Paul.

Berce, Yves-Marie (1987), *Revolt and Revolution in Early Modern Europe*, Manchester: Manchester University Press.

Berek, Peter (1988), 'Text, Gender, and Genre in *The Taming of the Shrew*' in Charney, Maurice (ed.), *'Bad' Shakespeare: Revaluations of the Shakespeare Canon*, London and Toronto: Associated University Presses, pp.91–104.

Bergeron, David M. (1986), 'Brother–Sister Relationships in Ford's 1633 Plays' in Anderson, Donald K. (ed.), *'Concord in Discord': The Plays of John Ford, 1586–1986*, New York: AMS Press, pp.195–219.

———— (1991), '*Richard II* and Carnival Politics', *Shakespeare Quarterly*, **42** (1), Spring, 33–43.

Bernstein, Michael Andre (1983), 'When the Carnival Turns Bitter: Preliminary Reflections on the Abject Hero', *Critical Inquiry*, **10**, December, 283–305.

Berry, Herbert (1989), 'The First Public Playhouses, especially the Red Lion', *Shakespeare Quarterly*, **40** (2), Summer, 133–148.

Birch, Thomas (1849), Williams, R. F. (ed.), *The Court and Times of James I*, 2 volumes, London: Henry Colburn.

Bland, James (1984), *The Common Hangman: English and Scottish Hangmen Before the Abolition of Public Executions*, Hornchurch, Essex: Ian Henry Publications Ltd.

Blau, Herbert (1986), 'The Absolved Riddle: Sovereign Pleasure and the Baroque Subject in the Tragicomedies of John Fletcher', *New Literary History: A Journal of Theory and Interpretation*, **17** (3), Spring, 539–554.

Bliss, Lee (1983), *The World's Perspective: John Webster and Jacobean Drama*, New Jersey: Rutgers University Press.

Boehrer, Bruce Thomas (1992), *Monarchy and Incest in Renaissance England: Literature, Culture, Kinship, and Kingship*, Philadelphia, Pennsylvania: University of Pennsylvania Press.

Boehrer, Bruce (1984), ' "Nice Philosophy": *'Tis Pity She's a Whore* and the Two Books of God', *Studies in English Literature*, **24** (2), Spring, 355–371.

Boling, Ronald J. (1991), 'Prayer, Mirrors, and Self-Deification in John Ford's *'Tis Pity She's a Whore*', *Publications of the Arkansas Philological Association*, **17** (1), Spring, 1–12.

Boose, Lynda (1991), 'Scolding Brides and Bridling Scolds: Taming the Woman's Unruly Member', *Shakespeare Quarterly*, **42** (2), Summer, 178–213.

Bowers, Fredson (1940), *Elizabethan Revenge Tragedy, 1587–1642*, Princeton, New Jersey: Princeton University Press.

Bradbrook, Muriel C. (1935), *Themes and Conventions of Elizabethan Tragedy*, Cambridge: Cambridge University Press.

Braden, Gordon (1985), Tragedy and the Senecan Tradition: Anger's Privilege, New Haven, Connecticut: Yale University Press.

Brauner, Sigrid (1989), 'Martin Luther on Witchcraft: A True Reformer?' in Brink, Jean R., Coudert Allison P. and Horowitz, Maryanne (eds), *The Politics of Gender in Early Modern Europe*, Kirksville, Missouri: Sixteenth Century Journal Publishers, pp.29–42.

Breight, Curt (1990), ' "Treason doth never prosper": *The Tempest* and the Discourse of Treason', *Shakespeare Quarterly*, **41** (1), Spring, 1–28.

Bremmer, Jan and Herman Roodenburg (ed) (1992), *A Cultural History of Gesture*, Ithaca, New York: Cornell University Press.

Bristol, Michael (1994), ' "Funeral bak'd meats": Carnival and the Carnivalesque in *Hamlet*' in Wofford, Suzanne (ed.), *Hamlet*, Boston and New York: Bedford Books of St Martin's Press, pp.348–367.

Bruce, Sir John (1840), 'Introduction' to *Annals of the First Four Years of the Reign of Queen Elizabeth*, London: John Bowyer Nichols and Son.

Bruster, Douglas (1992), *Drama and the Market in the Age of Shakespeare*, Cambridge and New York: Cambridge University Press.

Bulles, A. H. (1964), *A Collection of Old English Plays*, New York: B. Blom.

Burgin, Victor (1992), 'Perverse Space' in Colomina, Beatriz (ed.), *Sexuality and Space*, Princeton, New Jersey: Princeton University Press, pp.219–240.

Burke, Kenneth (1974), *The Philosophy of Literary Forms*, Berkeley, California: University of California Press.

Burke, Peter (1978), *Popular Culture in Early Modern Europe*, New York: New York University Press.

Burrow, Colin (1994), 'Is Shakespeare Still a Player?' *The Sunday Times: the Culture Magazine*, 24 July, 8–11.

Bushnell, Rebecca (1990), *Tragedies of Tyrants: Political Thought and Theater in the English Renaissance*, Ithaca, New York: Cornell University Press.

Butler, Martin (1984), *Theatre and Crisis, 1632–42*, Cambridge: Cambridge University Press.

Callaghan, Dympna (1989), *Woman and Gender in Renaissance Tragedy: A Study of King Lear, Othello, The Duchess of Malfi and The White Devil*, New York: Humanities Press International.

Capp, Bernard (1984), 'The Fifth Monarchists and Popular Millenarianism' in Reay, Barry (ed.), *Radical Religion in the English Revolution*, Oxford: Oxford University Press, pp.165–189.

Case, Sue Ellen and Reinelt, Janelle (eds) (1991), *The Performance of Power: Theatrical Discourse and Politics*, Iowa: University of Iowa Press.

Chaim, Daphna Ben (1984), *Distance in the Theatre: The Aesthetics of Audience Response*, Ann Arbor, Michigan: University of Michigan Press.

Charney, Maurice (ed.) (1988), *'Bad' Shakespeare: Revaluations of the Shakespeare Canon*, London: Associated University Presses.

Clark, Ira (1992), *Professional Playwrights: Massinger, Ford, Shirley, and Brome*, Lexington, Kentucky: University Press of Kentucky.

—— (1993), *The Moral Art of Philip Massinger*, Lewisburg, Pennsylvania: Bucknell University Press.

Clark, Sandra (1994), *The Plays of Beaumont and Fletcher: Sexual Themes and Dramatic Representation*, New York and London: Harvester Wheatsheaf.

Clerico, Terri (1992), 'The Politics of Blood: John Ford's *'Tis Pity She's a Whore'*, *English Literary Renaissance*, **22** (3), Fall, 405–434.

Coddon, Karin (1989), ' "Unreal Mockery": Unreason and the Problem of Spectacle in *Macbeth*', *English Literary History*, **56** (3), Fall, 485–501.

——— (1993), 'The Duchess of Malfi: Tyranny and Spectacle in Jacobean Drama' in Redmond, James (ed.), *Madness in Drama*, Cambridge: Cambridge University Press, pp.1–17.

——— (1994), ' "Suche strange desygns": Madness, Subjectivity, and Treason in *Hamlet*' in Wofford, Susanne (ed.), *Hamlet*, Boston and New York: Bedford Books of St Martin's Press, pp.380–402.

——— (1994), ' "For Show or Useless Property": Necrophilia and *The Revenger's Tragedy*', *English Literary History*, **61** (1), Spring, 71–88.

Cohen, Derek (1992), Shakespeare's Culture of Violence, New York: St. Martin's Press.

Cohen, Walter (1992), 'Prerevolutionary Drama' in McMullen, Gordon and Hope, Jonathan (eds), *The Politics of Tragicomedy*, London: Routledge, pp.122–150.

Copeland, Roger (1978), 'Brecht, Artaud, and the Hole in the Paper Sky', *Theatre*, Summer, 46–48.

Coudert, Allison P. (1989), 'The Myth of the Improved Status of Protestant Women: The Case of the Witchcraze' in Brink, Jean R., Coudert, Allison P., Horowitz, Maryanne (eds), *The Politics of Gender in Early Modern Europe*, Kirksville, Missouri: Sixteenth Century Journal Publishers, pp.61–90.

Cressy, David (1980), *Literacy and the Social Order: Reading and Writing in Tudor and Stuart England*, Cambridge: Cambridge University Press.

Crewe, Jonathan (1982), *Unredeemed Rhetoric: Thomas Nashe and the Scandal of Authorship*, Baltimore, Maryland: Johns Hopkins University Press.

Crockett, Bryan (1995), *The Play of Paradox: Stage and Sermon in Renaissance England*, Philadelphia, Pennsylvania: University of Pennsylvania Press.

Cunningham, Karen (1990), 'Renaissance Execution and Marlovian Elocution: the Drama of Death', *Publications of the Modern Language Association*, **105** (2), March, 209–222.

Cust, R. and Hughes A. (eds) (1989), *Conflict in Early Stuart England: Studies in Religion and Politics, 1603–42*, London: Longman.

Davis, Natalie Zemon (1975), *Society and Culture in Early Modern France*, Stanford, California: Stanford University Press.

Dawson, Anthony (1987), '*Women Beware Women* and the Economy of Rape', *Studies in English Literature*, **27** (2), Spring, 303–320.

De Certeau, Michel (1984), *The Practice of Everyday Life*, Randall, Steven (trans.), Berkeley and Los Angeles, California and London: University of California Press.

Desens, Marliss C. (1994), *The Bed-Trick in English Renaissance Drama: Explorations in Gender, Sexuality, and Power*, Newark, Delaware: University of Delaware Press.

Dickey, Stephen (1991), 'Shakespeare's Mastiff Comedy', *Shakespeare Quarterly*, **42** (3), 255–275.

Doebler, Betty Anne (1994), *'Rooted Sorrow': Dying in Early Modern England*, New Jersey: Fairleigh Dickinson University Press.

Dolan, Frances E. (1992), ' "Gentlemen, I have one thing more to say": Women on Scaffolds in England', *Modern Philology*, **92** (2), November, 157–178.

―――― (1994), *Dangerous Familiars: Representations of Domestic Crime in England, 1550–1700*, Ithaca, New York: Cornell University Press.

DuCann, C. G. L. (1964), *English Treason Trials*, London: Frederick Mullen.

Dutton, Richard (1991), *Mastering the Revels: The Regulation and Censorship of English Renaissance*, London: McMillan.

Elizabeth I, *The Glass of the Sinful Soul*, Shell, Marc (ed.) (1993), Lincoln, Nebraska: University of Nebraska Press.

Erickson, Peter, (1987), 'Rewriting the Renaissance, Rewriting Ourselves', *Shakespeare Quarterly*, **38** (3), Autumn, 327–337.

Farr, Dorothy (1979), *John Ford and Caroline Theatre*, London: McMillan.

Ferguson, Arthur B. (1993), *Utter Antiquity: Perceptions of Prehistory in Renaissance England*, Durham, North Carolina: Duke University Press.

Ferguson, George B. (1966), 'Introduction' to *The Woman's Prize or the Tamer Tamed*, The Hague, Netherlands: Mouton and Co., pp.11–35.

Finkelpearl, Philip J. (1990), *Court and Country Politics in the Plays of Beaumont and Fletcher*, Princeton, New Jersey: Princeton University Press.

Fletcher, John (1966), *The Woman's Prize or the Tamer Tamed*, Ferguson, George B. (ed.), London: Mouton and Co.

Ford, John (1966), *'Tis Pity She's a Whore*, Bawcutt, N. W. (ed.), Lincoln, Nebraska: University of Nebraska Press.

Forker, Charles (1986), *Skull Beneath the Skin: the Achievement of John Webster*, Carbondale, Illinois: Southern Illinois University Press.

Foster, Verna A. (1992), 'Sex Averted or Converted: Sexuality and Tragicomic Genre in the Plays of Fletcher', *Studies in English Literature*, **32** (2), Spring, 311–322.

Foucault, Michel (1979), *Discipline and Punish: The Birth of the Prison*, Sheridan, Alan (trans.), New York: Vintage Books.

―――― (1988–90), *History Of Sexuality*, 3 volumes, Hurley, Robert (trans.), New York: Vintage Books.

Frank, Joseph (1961), *The Beginnings of the English Newspaper 1620–1660*, Cambridge, Masachussetts: Harvard University Press.

Frazer, Lady Antonia (1971), *Mary Queen of Scots*, New York: Dell Publishing Company.

French, Tita Baumlin (1989), 'Petruchio the Sophist and Language as Creation in *The Taming of the Shrew*', *Studies in English Literature*, **29** (2), 237–257.

Friedenreich, Kenneth (ed.) (1983), *'Accompaninge the players': Essays Celebrating Thomas Middleton, 1580–1980*, New York: AMS Press.

Friedman, Jerome (1992), 'The Battle of the Frogs and Fairford's Flies: Miracles and Popular Journalism During the English Revolution', *Sixteenth Century Journal*, **xxiii** (3), 419–442.

Garner, Shirley (1988), '*The Taming of the Shrew*: Inside or Outside of the Joke?' in Charney, Maurice (ed.), *'Bad' Shakespeare: Revaluations of the Shakespeare Canon*, London and Toronto: Associated University Presses, pp.105–109.

Gasper, Julia (1990), *The Dragon and the Dove: The Plays of Thomas Dekker*, Oxford: Oxford University Press.

Gent, Lucy and Llewellyn, Nigel (eds) (1990), *Renaissance Bodies: The Human Figure in English Culture, 1540–1660*, London: Reaktion Books.

Gerard, John Fr (1898), *Contributions Towards the Life of Father Henry Garnet, S. J.*, Roehampton, England: J. Griffin.

Gibbons, Brian (1993), *Shakespeare and Multiplicity*, Cambridge: Cambridge University Press.

Goddard, Harold C. (1951), *The Meaning of Shakespeare*, Chicago, Illinois: Chicago University Press.

Goldberg, Dena (1987), *Between Worlds: A Study of the Plays of John Webster*, Waterloo, Ontario: Wilfrid Laurier University Press.

Gomez, Christine (1989), 'Profaning the Sacred: The Juxtaposition of Incest and Marriage in Ford, Ibsen and Osborne', *Aligarh Critical Miscellany*, **2** (1), 74–84.

Gorfain, Phyllis (1991), 'Toward a Theory of Play and the Carnivalesque in *Hamlet*', *Hamlet Studies*, **13** (i–ii), Winter, 25–49.

Gossett, Suzanne (1984), ' "Best Men Are Molded Out of Faults": Marrying the Rapist in Jacobean Drama', *English Literary Renaissance*, **14** (3), Autumn, 305–327.

Gosson, Stephen (1582), *Plays Confuted in Five Actions*, New York: Johnson Reprint Society, 1972.

Green, Douglas E. (1989), 'Interpreting "Her Martyred Signs": Gender and Tragedy in *Titus Andronicus*', *Shakespeare Quarterly*, **40** (3), Fall, 317–326.

Greenblatt, Stephen (1988), *Shakespearean Negotiations: The Circulation of Social Energy in Renaissance England*, Berkeley, California: University of California Press.

Gregg, Pauline (1984), *King Charles I*, Berkeley, California: University of California Press.

Gurr, Andrew (1987), *Playgoing in Shakespeare's England*, Cambridge: Cambridge University Press.

Hallett, Charles A. and Hallett, Elaine S. (1980), *The Revenger's Madness: A Study of Revenge Motifs*, Lincoln, Nebraska: University of Nebraska Press.

Hamilton, Donna B. (1992), *Shakespeare and the Politics of Protestant England*, New York and London: Harvester Wheatsheaf.

Hardin, Richard F. (1992), *Civil Idolatry: Decascralizing and Monarchy in Spenser, Shakespeare, and Milton*, Newark, Delaware: University of Delaware Press.

Harrison, William (1968), 'Of Sundry Kinds of Punishment Appointed for

Offenders' in Edelin, George (ed.), *The Description of England* (1587), Ithaca, New York: Cornell University Press, pp.187–188.

Hart, Jonathan (1992), *Theatre and the World: The Problematics of Shakespeare's History*, Boston, Massachusetts: Northeastern University Press.

Haselkorn, Anne M. (1990), 'Sin and the Politics of Penitence: Three Jacobean Adultresses' in Haselkorn, Ann M. and Travitsky, Betty S. (eds), *The Renaissance Englishwoman in Print: Counterbalancing the Canon*, Amherst, Massachusetts: University of Massachusetts Press, pp.119–136.

Hay, Douglas (1975), 'Property, Authority and the Criminal Law' in Hay, Douglas, Linebaugh, Peter, Rule, John G., Thompson, E. P. and Winslow, Cal (eds), *Albion's Fatal Tree: Crime and Society in Eighteenth-Century England*, New York: Pantheon Books, pp.17–63.

Hayward, John (1840), *Annals of Queen Elizabeth*, Bruce, Sir John (ed.), London: John Bowyer Nichols and Son.

Helms, Lorraine (1989), 'Roaring Girls and Silent Women: the Politics of Androgyny on the Jacobean Stage' in Redmond, James (ed.), *Women in Theatre*, Cambridge, Cambridge University Press, pp.59–73.

Heywood, Thomas (1941), *An Apology for Actors*, New York: Scolars Facsimilies and Reprints.

Heinemann, Margot (1980), *Puritanism and Theatre: Thomas Middleton and Opposition Drama Under the Early Stuarts*, Cambridge: Cambridge University Press.

Hill, Christopher (1982), *The World Turned Upside Down*, Harmondsworth: Penguin.

—— (1986), *Puritanism and Revolution: Studies in the Interpretation of the English Revolution of the Seventeenth Century*, Harmondsworth: Penguin.

Hillard, Stephen S. (1986), *The Singularity of Thomas Nashe*, Lincoln, Nebraska: University of Nebraska Press.

Hillman, Richard (1992), *Shakespearean Subversions: The Trickster and the Play Text*, London and New York: Routledge.

Holbrook, Peter (1993), *Literature and Degree in Renaissance England*, Newark, Delaware: University of Delaware Press.

Hope, Jonathan (1994), *The Authorship of Shakespeare's Plays: A Socio-Linguistic Study*, Cambridge: Cambridge University Press.

Hopkins, Lisa (1994), *John Ford's Political Theatre*, Manchester: Manchester University Press.

Houston, R. A. (1988), *Literacy in Early Modern Europe: 1500–1800*, London: Longman.

Howard, Jean (1988), 'Crossdressing, the Theatre, and Gender Struggle in Early Modern England', *Shakespeare Quarterly*, 39 (4), Winter, 418–440.

Howell, Thomas Bayley (1809) (ed.), *Cobbett's Complete Collection of State Trials and Proceedings for High treason and Other Crimes and Misdemeanors from the Earliest Period to the Present Time*, 12 volumes, London: R. Bagshaw.

Huebert, Ronald (1977), *John Ford: Baroque English Dramatist*, Montreal: McGill-Queen's University Press.

Hunt, Lynn (1989), 'Introduction: History, Culture, Text' in *The New Cultural History*, Berkeley and Los Angeles, California and London: University of California Press, pp.1–24.

Hunt, Maurice (1988), 'Webster and Jacobean Medicine: The Case of *The Duchess of Malfi*', *Essays in Literature*, 16 (1), Spring, 33–49.

——— (1988), 'Compelling art in *Titus Andronicus*', *Studies in English Literature*, 28 (2), Spring, 197–218.

Hutson, Lorna (1989), *Thomas Nashe in Context*, Oxford: Clarendon Press.

Ingram, Martin (1984), 'Ridings, Rough Music and Mocking Rhymes in Early Modern England', in Reay, Barry (ed.), *Popular Culture in Seventeenth-century England*, London: Croom Helm, pp.166–197.

James I (1984), *Letters of King James VI and I*, Akrigg, G. P. V. (ed.), Berkeley, California: University of California Press.

Jameson, Frederic (1990), *Signatures of the Visible*, New York and London: Routledge.

Jankowski, Theodora (1992), *Women in Power in Early Modern Drama*, Urbana-Champaign, Illinois: University of Illinois Press.

Jardine, Lisa (1983), *Still Harping on Daughters: Women and Drama in the age of Shakespeare*, Brighton: Harvester Press.

Jonson, Ben (1960), *Bartholomew Fair*, Horsman, E. A. (ed.), Cambridge, Massachusetts: Harvard University Press.

——— (1966), *Sejanus*, Boulton, W. F. (ed.), London: Ernest Benn Ltd.

——— (1979), *The Poetaster*, Parfitt, George (ed.), Nottingham: Nottingham Drama Texts.

Kahn, Coppelia (1977), '*The Taming of the Shrew*: Shakespeare's Mirror of Marriage' in Diamond, Arlyn and Edwards, Lee R. (eds), *The Authority of Experience: Essays in Feminist Criticism*, Amherst, Massachusetts: University of Massachusetts Press, pp.84–100.

——— (1991), 'Whores and Wives in Jacobean Drama' in Kehler, Dorothea and Baker, Susan (eds), *In Another Country: Feminist Perspectives on Renaissance Drama*, Metuchen, New Jersey: Scarecrow Press, pp.246–260.

Kastan, David Scott and Stallybrass, Peter (1991) (eds), *Staging the Renaissance: Representations of Renaissance Drama*, London and New York: Routledge.

Khare, R. S. (1992), 'The Other's Double – The Anthropologist's Bracketed Self: Notes on Cultural Representation and Privileged Discourse', *New Literary History*, 23 (1), Winter, 1–23.

Kendall, Gillian Murray (1989), ' "Lend me thy hand": Metaphor and Mayhem in *Titus Andronicus*', *Shakespeare Quarterly*, 40 (3), Fall, 299–316.

Kinney, Arthur F. and Collins, Dan Collins (1987) (eds), *Renaissance Historicism*, Amherst, Massachusetts: University of Massachusetts Press.

Knott, John R. (1993), *Discourses of Martyrdom in English Literature, 1563–1694*, Cambridge: University of Cambridge Press.

Kramer, Lloyd S. (1990), 'Literature, Criticism, and Historical Imagination: The Literary Challenge of Hayden White and Dominick LaCapra' in Hunt, Lynn (ed.), *The New Cultural History*, pp.97–130.

Kronik, John (1992), 'Editor's Column', *Publications of the Modern Language Association*, **107** (1), January, 9–12.

Kuhn, Annette (1985), *The Power of the Image: Essays on Representation and Sexuality*, London: Routledge.

Kyd, Thomas (1989), *The Spanish Tragedy*, Mulryne, J. R. (ed.), New York: W. W. Norton.

Lacan, Jaques (1977), *The Four Fundamental Concepts of Psychoanalysis*, London: Hogarth Press.

Lagomarsino, David and Wood, Charles T. (1989), *The Trial of Charles I: A Documentary History*, Hanover and London: University Press of New England.

Langbein, John (1977), *Torture and the Law of Proof: Europe and England in the Ancien Régime*, Chicago: University of Chicago Press.

Laslett, Peter (1977), *Family Love and Illicit Sex in Earlier Generations*, Cambridge: Cambridge University Press.

Laurence, John (1960), *A History of Capital Punishment*, New York: The Citadel Press.

Leech, Clifford (1957), *John Ford and the Drama of his Time*, London: Chatto and Windus.

Levine, Laura (1994), *Men in Women's Clothing: Anti-theatricality and Effeminization, 1579–1642*, Cambridge: Cambridge University Press.

Leyser, Henrietta (1995), *Medieval Women: A Social History of Women in England*, London: Wiedenfeld and Nicholson.

Linebaugh, Peter (1967), 'The Tyburn Riot against Surgeons' in Hay, Douglas *et al.* (eds), *Albion's Fatal Tree*, New York: Random House, pp.65–118.

Little, Arthur (1993), ' "Transhaped" Women: Virginity and Hysteria in *The Changeling*' in Redmond, James (ed.), *Madness in Drama*, Cambridge: Cambridge University Press, pp.19–42.

Lockyer, Roger (1959), *The Trial of Charles I*, London: Folio Society.

Loomba, Ania (1992), *Gender, Race, Renaissance Drama*, Oxford University Press.

Lotman, Yuri (1990), *Universe of the Mind: A Semiotic Theory of Culture*, Shukman, Ann (trans.), Bloomington and Indianapolis, Indiana: Indiana University Press.

Luckyj, Christina (1989), *A Winter's Snake: Dramatic Form in the Tragedies of John Webster*, Athens, Georgia: University of Georgia Press.

Macfarlane, Alan (1981), *The Justice and the Mare's Ale: Law and Disorder in Seventeenth-century England*, Cambridge: Cambridge University Press.

Manning, B. (1988), *Village Revolts: Social Protest and Popular Disturbances in England, 1509–1640*, Oxford: Oxford University Press.

Marcus, Leah (1986), *Politics of Mirth: Jonson, Herrick, Milton, Marvell, and the Defense of Old Holiday Pastimes*, Chicago, Illinois: University of Chicago Press.

Margolies, David (1992), *Monsters of the Deep: Social Dissolution in Shakespeare's Tragedies*, Manchester: Manchester University Press.

Marks, Alfred (1908), *The Tyburn Tree*, London: Brown and Co.

Marsh, Christopher (1994), *The Family of Love in English Society, 1550–1630*, Cambridge and New York: Cambridge University Press.

Marvell, Andrew (1963), 'An Horatian Ode Upon Cromwell's Return from Ireland' in Margoliouth, H. M. (ed.), *The Poems and Letters of Andrew Marvell*, 2 volumes, Oxford: Clarendon Press, pp.87–89.

Massinger, Philip (1860), *The Virgin Martyr* in Gifford, William (ed.), *Plays of Philip Massinger*, New York: H. B. Mahn, pp.3–31.

——— (1976), *The Roman Actor* in Edwards, Philip and Gibson, Colin (eds), *The Plays and Poems of Philip Massinger*, Oxford: Clarendon Press, Vol. III, pp.1–94.

——— (1976), *The Unnatural Combat* in Edwards, Philip and Gibson, Colin (eds), *The Plays and Poems of Philip Massinger*, Oxford: Clarendon Press, Vol. II, pp.181–272.

Maxwell, J. C. (ed.) (1968), 'Introduction' in *Titus Andronicus*, London and New York: Methuen, pp.xi–xl.

Mayfield, Noel (1988), *Puritans and Regicide: Presbyterian Independent Differences on the Trial and Execution of Charles (I) Stuart*, Laneham, Maryland: University Presses of America.

McCabe, Richard A. (1993), *Incest, Drama and Moral Law, 1550–1700*, Cambridge: Cambridge University Press.

McLuskie, Kathleen (1982), 'Feminist Deconstruction: The Example of Shakespeare's *The Taming of the Shrew*', *Red Letters*, **12**, 33–40.

——— (1992), ' "A maidenhead, Amintor, at my yeares": Chastity and Tragicomedy in the Fletcher Plays' in McMullen, Gordon and Hope, Jonathan (eds), *The Politics of Tragicomedy: Shakespeare and After*, London: Routledge, pp.92–121.

McMullen, Gordon and Hope, Jonathan (1992), 'The Politics of Tragicomedy' in *The Politics of Tragicomedy: Shakespeare and After*, London: Routledge, pp.1–20.

Medvedev, P. N. and Bakhtin, M. M. (1978), *The Formal Method in Literary Scholarship*, Wehrle, Albert J. (trans.), Baltimore, Maryland: Johns Hopkins Press.

Melinkoff, Ruth (1973), 'Riding Backwards', *Viator*, **4**, 153–176.

Middleton, Thomas (1958), *The Changeling*, Bawcutt, N. W. (ed.), London: Methuen and Company.

——— (1964), *The Family of Love*, Vol. 3 in Bullen, A. H. (ed.), *The Works of Thomas Middleton*, 8 volumes, New York: AMS Press.

——— (1964), *The Witch*, Vol. 5 in Bullen, A. H. (ed.), *The Works of Thomas Middleton*, New York: AMS Press, pp.351–453.

——— (1975), *Women Beware Women*, Mulryne, J. R. (ed.), Manchester: Manchester University Press.

Miles, Gary (1989), 'How Roman are Shakespeare's Romans?', *Shakespeare Quarterly*, **40** (3), Fall, 257–283.

Moretti, Franco (1983), *Signs Taken for Wonders: Essays on the Sociology of Literary Forms*, London: Verso Editions.

Morrill, John (ed.) (1982), 'The Church in England: 1642–49' in *Reactions to the English Civil War, 1642–49*, New York: St Martin's Press, pp.89–114.

—— (ed.), (1992) *Revolution and Restoration: England in the 1650s*, London: Collins and Brown.

Morris, Brian (1981), 'Introduction' to *The Taming of the Shrew*, New York and London: Methuen and Co., pp.1–149.

Mullaney, Steven (1988), *The Place of the Stage: License, Play, and Power in Renaissance England*, Chicago, Illinois: University of Chicago Press.

Mulvey, Laura (1989), *Visual and Other Pleasures*, Bloomington and Indianapolis: Indiana University Press.

Nashe, Thomas (1987), *The Unfortunate Traveller*, in Salzman, Paul (ed.), *An Anthology of Elizabethan Prose Fiction*, Oxford and New York: Oxford University Press.

Neill, Michael (1988), ' "What strange riddle's this?": Deciphering *'Tis Pity She's a Whore*' in *John Ford: Critical Re-Visions*, Cambridge: Cambridge University Press, 153–179.

Newman, Karen (1986), 'Renaissance Family Politics and Shakespeare's *The Taming of the Shrew*', *English Literary Renaissance*, **16**, Winter, 86–100.

—— (1991), *Fashioning Femininity and English Renaissance Drama*, Chicago, Illinois: University of Chicago Press.

Nichols, John (1828), *The Progresses, Processions, and Magnificent Festivities of King James the First, His Royal Consort, Family, and Court*, 4 volumes, London: J. B. Nichols.

Noling, Kim (1988), 'Grubbing up the Stock: Dramatizing Queens in *Henry VIII*', *Shakespeare Quarterly*, **39** (3), Fall, 291–306.

Ollard, Richard (1979), *The Image of the King: Charles I and Charles II*, London: Hodder and Stoughton.

Pacteau, Francette (1986), 'The Impossible Referent: Representations of the Androgyne' in Burgin, Victor, Donald, James and Kaplan, Cora, *Formations of Fantasy*, London and New York: Methuen and Co., pp.62–84.

Patterson, Annabel (1994), 'Framing the *Taming*' in Kishi, Tetsuo, Pringle, Roger and Wells, Stanley (eds), *Shakespeare and Cultural Traditions*, Newark, Delaware: University of Delaware Press, pp.304–313.

Pennington, D. H. and Thomas, Keith (eds) (1978), *Puritans and Revolutionaries*, Oxford: Oxford University Press.

Paster, Gail Kern (1992), *The Body Embarrassed: Drama and Discipline: Drama and the Discipline of Shame in Early Modern England*, New York: Cornell University Press.

Pechter, Edward (1995), *What Was Shakespeare?: Renaissance Plays and Changing Critical Practice*, Ithaca, New York: Cornell University Press.

Pentzell, Raymond J. (1986), '*The Changeling* and Notes on Mannerism in Dramatic Form' in Davidson, Clifford, Gianakaris, C. J. and Stroupe, John H., *Drama in the Renaissance: Comparative and Critical Essays*, New York: AMS Press, pp.274–299.

Platter, Thomas (1937), *Travels in England*, Williams, Claire (trans.), London: Jonathan Cape, Ltd.

Potter, Lois (1989), *Secret Rites and Secret Writing: Royalist Literature, 1641–1660*, New York: Cambridge University Press.

Purchas, Samuel (1905–07), *Hackluytus Posthumous, or Purchas His Pilgrims*, Glasgow: J. Maclehose and Sons.

Rait, Robert S. and Cameron, Annie I. (1927), *King James's Secret: Negotiations Between Elizabeth and James VI Relating to the Execution of Mary Queen of Scots, from the Warrendon Papers*, London: Nisbet and Co., Ltd.

Raymond, Joad (ed.) (1993), *Making the News: An Anthology of the Newsbooks in Revolutionary England: 1641–1660*, Gloucestershire: Windrush Press.

Rayner, Alice (1987), *Comic Persuasion: Moral Structure in British Comedy from Shakespeare to Stoppard*, Berkeley and Los Angeles, California and London: University of California Press.

Reay, Barry and J. F. McGregor (eds) (1984), *Radical Religion in the English Revolution*, Oxford: Oxford University Press.

Robin, Gerald (1964), 'The Executioner: His Place in Society', *British Journal of Sociology*, **XV**, 234–253.

Rose, Mary Beth (1988), *The Expense of Spirit: Love and Sexuality in English Renaissance Drama*, Ithaca, New York and London: Cornell University Press.

Rosen, Carol C. (1986), 'The Language of Cruelty in Ford's *'Tis Pity She's a Whore'* in Davidson, Clifford, Gianakaris, C. J. and Stroupe, John H. (eds), *Drama in the Renaissance: Comparative and Critical Essays*, New York: AMS Press, pp.315–327.

Salingar, L. G. (1982), *The Decline of Tragedy*, in Ford, Boris (ed.), *The New Pelican Guide to English Literature, Vol. 2: The Age of Shakespeare*, Harmondsworth: Penguin.

Salkeld, Duncan (1993), *Madness and Drama in the Age of Shakespeare*, Manchester: Manchester University Press.

Sasek, Lawrence A. (ed.) (1989), *Images of English Puritanism: A Collection of Contemporary Sources*, Baton Rouge, Louisiana: Louisiana University Press.

Scarry, Elaine (1985), *The Body in Pain: The Making and Unmaking of the World*, New York and Oxford: Oxford University Press.

Scott, George Ryley (1940), *The History of Torture Throughout the Ages*, London: Torchstream Books.

Scott, Jonathan (1992), 'The English Republican Imagination' in Morrill, John (ed.), *Revolution and Restoration*, pp.35–54.

Scott, Wilbur (1962), *Five Approaches to Literary Criticism: An Arrangement of Contemporary Critical Essays*, New York: McMillan.

Shakespeare, William (1961), *Richard II*, Ure, Peter (ed.), London and New York: Methuen.

———— (1968), *Henry VIII*, Foakes, R. A. (ed.), London and New York: Methuen.

———— (1972), *King Lear*, Muir, Kenneth (ed.), London and New York: Methuen.

———— (1981), *The Taming of the Shrew*, Morris, Brian (ed.), London and New York: Methuen.

———— (1982), *Hamlet*, Jenkins, Harold (ed.), London and New York: Methuen.

———— (1984), *Macbeth*, Muir, Kenneth (ed.), London and New York: Methuen.

———— (1985), *Titus Andronicus*, Maxwell, J. C. (ed.), London and New York: Methuen.

Shapiro, James (1991), ' "Tragedies Naturally Performed": Kyd's Representation of Violence in *The Spanish Tragedy*' in Kastan, David Scott and Stallybrass, Peter (eds), *Staging the Renaissance: Reinterpretations of Elizabethan and Jacobean Drama*, New York: Routledge, pp.99–113.

———— (1996), 'Recent Studies in Tudor and Stuart Drama' *Studies in English Literature*, **36** (2), Spring, 481–525.

Sharp, Andrew (1983), *Political Ideas of the English Civil Wars, 1641–1649*, London: Longman.

Sharpe, J. A. (1983), *Crime in Seventeenth-century England*, Cambridge: Cambridge University Press.

Shell, Marc (1993), 'Introduction' to *Elizabeth's Glass of the Sinful Soul*, Lincoln, Nebraska: University of Nebraska Press, pp.3–102.

Shepherd, Simon (1979), 'Introduction' to *The Family of Love*, Nottingham: Nottingham Drama Series, pp.i–vii.

Simpson, Alan (1955), *Puritanism in Old and New England*, Chicago: Chicago University Press.

Sinfield, Alan (1992), *Faultlines: Cultural Materialism and the Politics of Dissident Reading*, Oxford: Oxford University Press.

Smith, David (1992), 'The Struggle for New Constitutional and Institutional Forms' in Morrill, John (ed.), *Revolution and Restoration*, pp.15–34.

Smith, Molly (1991), *The Darker World Within: Evil in the Tragedies of Shakespeare and his Successors*, Newark, Delaware: University of Delaware Press.

Smuts, Malcolm (1987), *Court Culture and the Origins of the Royalist Tradition in Early Stuart England*, Philadelphia, Pennsylvania: University of Pennsylvania Press.

Spierenburg, Pieter (1984), *The Spectacle of Suffering: Executions and the Evolution of Repression*, Cambridge, Cambridge University Press.

———— (1991), *The Prison Experience: Disciplinary Institutions and their Inmates in Early Modern Europe*, New Brunswick, New Jersey: Rutgers University Press.

Stallybrass, Peter (1987), 'Reading the Body: *The Revenger's Tragedy* and the Jacobean Theater of Consumption', *Renaissance Drama*, **18**, 121–148.

———— (1989), 'Robin Hood, the Carnivalesque, and the Rhetoric of Violence' in Armstrong, Nancy and Tennenhouse, Leonard (eds), *The Violence of Representation*, London: London and New York: Routledge, pp.45–76.

Stavig, Mark (1968), *John Ford and the Traditional Moral Order*, Madison, Wisconsin: University of Wisconsin Press.

Steen, Sara Jayne (1993), *Ambrosia in an Earthen Vessel: Three Centuries of Audience and Reader Response to Middleton*, New York: AMS Press.

Stewart, Stanley (1991), 'Recent Studies in the English Renaissance', *Studies in English Literature*, **31** (1), Winter, 179–229.

Stone, Lawrence (1965), *The Crisis of the Aristocracy, 1558–1641*, Oxford: Oxford University Press.

Strong, Roy (1973), *Splendour at Court: Renaissance Spectacle and Illusion*, London: Weidenfeld and Nicholson.

—— (1977), *The Cult of Elizabeth: Elizabethan Portraiture and Pageantry*, London: Thames and Hudson.

Strout, Nathaniel (1990), 'The Tragedy of Annabella in *'Tis Pity She's a Whore*' in Allen, David G. and White, Robert A. (eds), *Traditions and Innovations: Essays on British Literature of the Middle Ages and the Renaissance*, Newark, Delaware: University of Delaware Press, pp.163–176.

Taylor, Mark (1982), *Shakespeare's Darker Purpose: A Question of Incest*, New York: AMS Press.

Tennenhouse, Leonard (1989), 'Violence done to Women on the Renaissance Stage' in Armstrong, Nancy and Tennenhouse, Leonard (eds), *The Violence of Representation*, London and New York: Routledge, pp.77–97.

Thomas, Keith (1992), 'Introduction' in Bremner, Jan and Roodenburg, Herman (eds), *A Cultural History of Gesture*, Ithaca, New York: Cornell University Press.

Tillyard, E. M. W. (1944), *Shakespeare's History Plays*, London: Chatto and Windus.

Tokson, Elliot H. (1982), *The Popular Image of the Black Man in Renaissance Drama, 1550–1688*, Boston, Massachusetts: G. K. Hall.

Tomlinson, Sophie (1992), 'Shee that Plays the King: Henrietta Maria and the Threat of the Actress in Caroline England' in McMullen, Gordon and Hope, Jonathan (eds), *The Politics of Tragicomedy: Shakespeare and After*, London and New York: Routledge, pp.189–207.

Tourneur, Cyril (1966), *The Revenger's Tragedy*, Ross, Lawrence J. (ed.), Lincoln, Nebraska: University of Nebraska Press.

Traub, Valerie (1992), *Desire and Anxiety: Circulations of Sexuality in Shakesperean Drama*, London: Routledge.

Turner, Victor (1974), *Dramas, Fields, and Metaphors: Symbolic Action in Human Society*, Ithaca, New York: Cornell University Press.

—— (1984), 'Liminality and the Performative Genres' in *Rite, Drama, Festival: Rehearsals Towards a Theory of Cultural Performance*, Philadelphia, Pennsylvania: Institute for the Study of Human Resources, pp.19–41.

Tyndale, William (1849), *The Practice of Prelates* (1538) in Walter, Rev. Henry (ed.), *Expositions and Notes on Sundry Positions of the Holy Scriptures*, Cambridge: Cambridge University Press, pp.237–344.

Underdown, David (1985), *Revel, Riot, and Rebellion: Popular Politics and Culture in England, 1603–1660*, Oxford: Clarendon Press.

Vickers, Brian (1993), *Appropriating Shakespeare: Contemporary Critical Quarrels*, New Haven, Connecticut: Yale University Press.

Veith, Ilza (1965), *Hysteria: The History of a Disease*, Chicago, Illinois: University of Chicago Press.

Wadsworth, Frank W. (1984), ' "Rough Music" in *The Duchess of Malfi*: Webster's Dance of Madmen and the Charivari Tradition' in MacAloon, John J. (ed.), *Rite, Drama, Festival, Spectacle: Rehearsals Towards a Theory of Cultural Performance*, Philadelphia, Pennsylvania: Institute for the Study of Human Issues, pp.58–78.

Waith, Eugene (ed.) (1984), *Titus Andronicus*, Oxford: Clarendon Press.

Walker, Clement (1651), *The High Court of Justice*, London.

––––––– (1815), 'The Mystery of the Two Juntoes, Presbyterian and Independent' (1648) in Maseres, F. (ed.), *Select Tracts Relating to the Civil War in England*, Vol. II, London, pp.348–349.

Walzer, Michael (1973), *Regicide and Revolution*, Cambridge: Cambridge University Press.

Wayne, Valerie (1985), 'Refashioning the Shrew', *Shakespeare Studies*, **17**, 159–187.

Webster, John (1993), *The Duchess of Malfi*, Brennan, Elizabeth (ed.), New York: W. W. Norton.

Wedgwood, C. V. (1964), *A Coffin for King Charles: The Trial and Execution of Charles I*, New York: Time Incorporated.

Whigham, Frank (1991), 'Incest and Idelogy: *The Duchess of Malfi*' in Kastan, David Scott (ed.), *Staging the Renaissance*, pp.263–274.

White, Hayden (1978), 'The Historical Text as Literary Artefact' in Canary R. H. and Kozicki, H. (eds), *The Writing of History*, Madison, Wisconsin: University of Wisconsin Press, pp.41–62.

White, Martin (1992), *Middleton and Turner*, Basingstoke: McMillan.

Williams, William Procter (1987), 'Not Hornpipes and Funerals: Fletcherian Tragicomedy' in Maguire, Nancy Klein (ed.), *Renaissance Tragicomedy: Explorations in Genre and Politics*, New York: AMS Press, pp.139–154.

Wilson, Richard (1993), *Will Power: Essays in Shakespearean Authority*, New York and London: Harvester Wheatsheaf.

Wilson, Richard and Dutton, Richard (eds) (1992), *New Historicism and Renaissance Drama*, London and New York: Longman.

Woodbridge, Linda and Berry, Edward (eds) (1992), *True Rites and Maimed Rites: Ritual and Anti-ritual in Shakespeare and his Age*, Urbana-Champaign, Illinois: University of Illinois Press.

Woolf, D. R. (1990), *The Idea of History in Early Stuart History*, Toronto and London: University of Toronto Press.

Zimmerman, Susan (1993), *Erotic Politics and Desire on the Renaissance Stage*, London and New York: Routledge.

Zwicker, Steven (1992), *Lines of Authority: Politics and English Literary Culture, 1649–1689*, Ithaca, New York: Cornell University Press.

Index